ALSO AVAILABLE FROM CQ PRESS:

Politics in Britain (2007)
Bruce F. Norton

Politics in Germany (forthcoming)
M. Donald Hancock
Henry Krisch

Politics in
France

POLITICS IN

FRANCE

Charles Hauss
George Mason University
Alliance for Peace Building

CQ PRESS

A Division of Congressional Quarterly Inc.
Washington, D.C.

CQ Press
1255 22nd Street, NW, Suite 400
Washington, DC 20037

Phone: 202-729-1900; toll-free, 1-866-4CQ-PRESS (1-866-427-7737)

Web: www.cqpress.com

Photo Credits:
AP Images: 34, 36, 40, 42, 66, 74, 78, 121, 144, 146, 188
The Granger Collection: 56
© Michel Philippot/Sygma/Corbis: 118

Cover design: Kimberly Glyder Design

[∞] The paper used in this publication exceeds the requirements of the American National Standard for Information Sciences—Permanence of Paper for Printed Library Materials, ANSI Z39.48-1992.

Printed and bound in the United States of America

11 10 09 08 07   1 2 3 4 5

Library of Congress Cataloging-in-Publication Data

Hauss, Charles.
    Politics in France / Charles Hauss.
        p. cm.
    Includes bibliographical references and index.
    ISBN 978-1-56802-670-1 (alk. paper)
    1. France—Politics and government—20th century. 2. France—Politics and government—21st century. I. Title.

    DC369.H317 2008
    944.083—dc22

                                                                2007037934

To
Amy Mazur

and the memory of
J. D. Lewis and Roy Pierce

Brief Contents

Contents

Tables, Figures, Map, and Boxes

Other Boxes

Preface

It has taken an embarrassingly long time—seven years, in fact—to write this book. I'd like to claim that the product you hold in your hands is the book world's equivalent to the "slow food" movement—where quality is paramount and measured by the time and attention paid to the process—but the truth of the matter is that, well, global conflict got in the way.

In spring 2000, Charisse Kiino of CQ Press asked me to meet with her to discuss a series of country studies on Western Europe that she and her team wanted to commission. Forgetting that there is never such a thing as a free lunch, I met with her shortly before I was to head to the West Bank to teach some young Palestinians about conflict resolution. Despite my fears about being overextended, Charisse talked me into writing this book. After I'd returned from the Middle East, I decided to make matters worse by joining the staff of Search for Common Ground, a conflict resolution organization, in order to become more than just a dilettante in the field. With that new commitment, for the next couple of years I was focused on countries that are significantly more turbulent than France. But things have a way of coming full circle. As the CQ Press list grew, Charisse handed me off to Elise Frasier, who not only is a Michigan football fan (as am I) but also has a husband who studied conflict resolution experts and actually interviewed me for his PhD thesis. Ultimately, this handoff brought me back to the study of France.

Despite the abnormal route this book took toward publication, the subject herein is anything but. In fact, that's the very theme of the book: a shift toward "normal" politics in France. From my point of view, French politics now has more in common with other Western democracies than ever. Like Britain, Canada, Germany, or the United States, France has had a stable and legitimate representative regime for some time now. But as you will see, that has not always been the case. More than anything else, viewing France as a stable democratic regime makes the study of its politics interesting and enjoyable. Nevertheless, readers will also find that, unlike most existing textbooks, which do not focus on controversial elements of French politics, this one takes some of the current controversies head on. Like it or not, we live at a time when French politics is controversial in most Anglophone countries if for no other reason than because of France's opposition to the American-led invasion and occupation of Iraq.

Whether discussing the normal or the controversial, this book is nonetheless organized the way most textbooks are. I start with an overview of

French society and history leading up to the present day and also talk about some of the methods and approaches this book will use along the way, paying special attention to some of the basic premises of systems theory. This is followed by analyses of French political culture, particularly with respect to recent changes in demographics, the new diversity, and the impact of globalization. Two historical chapters help readers put the current political system into context, and then subsequent chapters cover public participation in elections and beyond, look at the way the state functions, and examine its public policies at home and abroad. I also place special emphasis on the role the European Union plays in France's political life. As far as I know, no author has tried to do all of this in a reasonably short and readable book, one that contains at least a few funny stories about such things as French fries and French toast.

I've equipped this book with a series of boxes called "Comparative Perspectives," which feature information about other Western and non-Western countries in order to highlight substantive differences between France and the rest of the world. Most of those boxes have photographs, some of which reflect the whimsical side of French politics. Each chapter also contains bolded key terms (both conceptual in nature as well as of important people, entities, and events) that are then listed at the end of each chapter along with questions for discussion. At the back of the book are a copy of the French constitution, reference lists for suggested readings and suggested Web sites should you want to learn more about this fascinating and often frustrating country, and a glossary of terms.

Acknowledgments

Needless to say, over time I've accumulated a lot of intellectual debts.

The first is to the very patient staff at CQ Press. Charisse, Elise, and everyone else have been extremely supportive even when asking the embarrassing question, "When will it really be done?"

I also have a group of colleagues who started working on France when I did in graduate school. Many of us have broadened our interests, but David Cameron, Jim Hollifield, Anne Meyering, David Rayside, Rand Smith, and others too numerous to name have tried to convince me that this was a project worth doing. So too have Bill Safran and Marty Schain, who have written the leading books this one will compete against.

I'd like to thank my reviewers who took the time to assess my early proposal and then later manuscript chapters, including Paul Abramson, Michigan State University; Steven Majstorovic, University of Wisconsin–Eau Claire; and Mark Sachleben, Shippensburg University.

My colleagues in the conflict resolution field at Search for Common Ground and the Alliance for Peace Building have also helped me see things I might have missed as a conventional political scientist (that is, once they got over their shock that I was doing this book, at which point they typically tried out their French with their Burundian or Congolese accents). Thanks also have to go to my friends in and near the Department of Defense, most of whom despise France as much as I love it. In particular, Dick O'Neill of the Highlands Forum and a friend since nursery school days helped me think through the issues in the last three chapters.

The book is dedicated to three people who have shaped my thinking on France in ways I could never fully document.

Amy Mazur is my one former student who ignored my advice and became a student of French politics. She has taught me almost everything I know about feminism in France. We first worked together in the 1980s when she was a college senior; she and three of her classmates came with me to Caen to do a research project, some of which found its way into these pages. Amy is living proof that students and professors can later become colleagues and friends.

John (J. D.) Lewis taught the first course I took on European politics even though he was actually a specialist on American political thought. We truly got to know each other one day when I fell asleep in his class; I had been up for three days planning antiwar protests. In his odd combination of a Welsh and Wisconsin accent, he asked, "Mr. Hauss, was it you or was it me?" The next week we discovered that my off campus apartment was a few doors from his house. Since we both headed to the college at about six (I stupidly had agreed to be breakfast cook at my co-op), he started giving me rides. John came from a good left-wing family but had doubts about those of us who were majoring in ending the war in Vietnam. So he suggested I do a senior honors thesis on Christian Democracy in France and Italy to see a different side of the Left. Despite my arrogance in using French, Italian, and (who knows how) Russian sources, John passed me on the thesis and did not laugh too hard during my oral exam.

My academic stewardship was then passed on to Roy Pierce at the University of Michigan. Despite my incredibly boring senior thesis, I actually went to Michigan to do survey research and American politics. A week into the first semester, I realized I was too political to work on American issues in a department in which most members were obsessed with methodology. So I shifted to European politics and started working with Roy, first in his introductory seminar and then as a research assistant on the book he did with Phil Converse on elections and representation in France. Roy was even less of a fan of the 1960s Left than John, but when he learned that I needed to find a job to perform my alternative service as a conscientious objector, he hired me. Even though we argued a lot about politics, we discovered we shared a number of passions: baseball, Airedales (we each had several), and the novels about Inspector Maigret written by Georges Simenon, which also find their way into these pages.

Finally, I have to thank the two- and four-legged females I share my life with. Gretchen Sandles, also a Michigan PhD, was a longtime foreign policy analyst for the American government. We are now writing a book together on rethinking national security inspired by the bewildering events in the nearly twenty years since the Cold War ended. Jessie is our beloved half border collie and half who knows what. Border collies are among the world's smartest dogs (watch reruns of *One Man and His Dog* on BBC America). I use Jessie to help sort through a passage I can't quite get right. She thinks I'm taking her for a walk.

Charles Hauss
chiphauss@gmail.com
Falls Church, Virginia
September 2007

1

Toward Normal Politics

French voters went to the polls four times during the spring of 2002. First, two rounds of voting, on April 21 and May 5, led to the reelection of **Jacques Chirac** (1932–). Then, in June, another two rounds of voting were needed to choose a new **National Assembly**, the all-important lower house of parliament.[1]

The results of the elections shocked almost everyone. Despite all the pundits' predictions, the far right-wing (and some would say racist) **Jean-Marie Le Pen** (1928–) nosed out the incumbent Socialist prime minister, **Lionel Jospin** (1937–) for second place and a spot in the runoff against Chirac.

On June 9 and 16, legislative elections were held. The newly formed **Union for a Presidential Majority (UPM)** won a landslide victory of 357 out of 577 seats in the National Assembly, further demoralizing the Socialists and the rest of the Left that had been devastated by Jospin's third-place showing in the presidential election.

The elections had some peculiarly French features. Each, for instance, required two rounds of balloting before determining the winner. Sixteen candidates ran for the presidency. More than five thousand men and women vied for the 577 seats in the National Assembly. As often happens during French presidential campaigns, the president, Chirac, issued a blanket amnesty for all traffic offenses just before the election; traffic experts think the amnesty may have led to 100 more road deaths than in a normal year.

But in the end, the elections were not terribly different from those held in Britain or the United States. To be sure, the rhetoric was more heated than it usually is in the rest of Europe or North America. However, Chirac, Jospin, and most of the other candidates did not disagree all that much on key issues.

Table 1.1	Presidents of France, 1958–2007
President	Years in office
Charles de Gaulle	1958–1969
Georges Pompidou	1969–1974
Valéry Giscard d'Estaing	1974–1981
François Mitterrand	1981–1995
Jacques Chirac	1995–2007
Nicolas Sarkozy	2007–

In other words, the stakes of the election were not all that high, because the **Fifth Republic** was as secure as it had been at any time in its then forty-four-year history. Put simply, France's two elections, like its political life in general, were what one would expect from a smoothly functioning liberal democracy.

And that will be the theme of this book. Over the nearly fifty years since Charles de Gaulle and his colleagues created the Fifth Republic in 1958, French politics has become much like politics in other advanced democracies.

That had not been the case as recently as 1962, one of the few other years when the French voted both for the president and the Assembly. That August, an assassin fired more than 100 bullets into the limousine taking President **Charles de Gaulle** (1890–1970) to his country home. Somehow, the president's driver managed to escape the ambush even though all four tires of his car had been blown out. Somehow, too, the general was not hit. The attack was carried out by disgruntled former army officers who were furious with de Gaulle for granting Algeria independence and who were part of a wave of protest and violence that had swept the country for almost four years.

Within weeks de Gaulle announced that there would be a referendum to allow the direct election of the president. The one and only time the office had been filled, de Gaulle was chosen by an electoral college of about 81,000 national and local political leaders. Now, de Gaulle argued, France needed a popularly elected president, since his successor would not have the general's charisma or authority.

Critics argued (probably correctly) that the referendum was unconstitutional. They also claimed that directly electing the president was dangerous—a point returned to in Chapters 3 and 4 on French history.

As he often did with referenda, de Gaulle warned the people that if they did not vote "yes," he would resign. The referendum passed.

Then de Gaulle dissolved the National Assembly and called for new elections, something no president or prime minister had done since the late 1870s. That action further infuriated opposition politicians. Some, like **François Mitterrand** (1916–1996) and **Pierre Mendès-France** (1907–1982), called for de Gaulle's removal and the creation of a sixth republic. The

Gaullists and their allies won the election with a firm majority in the Assembly, the first time any such party or **coalition** had done so since the creation of the Third Republic in 1875.

In other words, French politics was anything but normal in 1962 and had not been for many years. Unlike the United States or the United Kingdom, which have been governed by the same **regime** for more than two hundred years, France has had three monarchies, five republics, two empires, and a neo-fascist regime in the years since its Revolution in 1789. It wasn't just that constitutions came and went, sometimes at breathtaking speed. France was deeply divided on just about every issue of the day and on the meaning of its own history. Historians debated the significance of the major turning points in its past. Some analysts claimed that the French were still debating the merits of the Revolution when they celebrated its bicentennial in 1989.

Those long-standing divisions colored everything from election campaigns to the curriculum of the school system.

Yet, as I try to show in the pages that follow, de Gaulle, the other leaders of the Fifth Republic, and the country's citizens have shifted the country toward a more "normal" politics since the tumultuous days that returned him to office.

We can get a glimpse at this turn toward normal politics by taking six snapshots of political life a decade apart from each other—1948, 1958, 1968, 1978, 1988, and 1998. I did not choose these dates at random. The four years in the middle of the string, in particular, include some of the most important political turning points in France since the end of World War II. Nonetheless, the general pattern would be the same whatever set of years I picked.

In 1948 the **Fourth Republic**'s first full year did not go well. General de Gaulle, who had led the **provisional government** from 1944 to 1946, was about to form his first political party, whose overriding goal was to get rid of this new republic that he detested. Moreover, just months into its existence, the country had reverted to the kind of "crisis and compromise" government in which the average cabinet, or governing coalition of ministers, lasted nine months and accomplished little, a system that many held responsible for France's shameful defeat in 1940, its occupation by Germany, and the Vichy government's collaboration with the Nazis. The Cold War had begun, which meant that the **Communist Party (PCF)** was no longer a potential member of a governing coalition, thus depriving France of its only possibility of forming a strong majority. The Communists were not considered viable candidates for holding office, because many worried that they would hand the country over to the Stalinist Soviet Union if they came to power. Finally, the country was still a long way from recovering from the physical and emotional devastation of World War II.

In 1958 de Gaulle succeeded and put the twelve-year-old Fourth Republic out of its misery. He had been taking verbal pot shots at it for more than a decade, but he had little chance of returning to power until a twin revolution broke out in Algeria. As was the case throughout the colonial world at the time, the native Algerian Arabs began demanding independence. Violence broke out in 1954. But Algeria also had about one million settlers of European origin. They chafed at the prospect of Algeria's gaining its independence, which would have jeopardized their economic and political standing. In April, when it appeared that a moderate would become prime minister and, perhaps, begin negotiations for Algerian independence, much of the army joined the settlers.

On the night of April 13, the military and settlers seized control of Algiers, the colony's capital city. Later, they landed in Corsica. Rumors spread that paratroopers would soon continue on to the mainland. Before the month was out, mainstream politicians realized that the only way to avoid a military coup was to bring de Gaulle back to power, even though many despised him and had doubts about his commitment to democracy. De Gaulle agreed but only if he were granted emergency powers for six months and could change the constitution. Reluctantly, the politicians agreed.

De Gaulle did not revise the constitution. He wrote a brand new one. As the year ended, the Fifth Republic was being created, and de Gaulle became its first president.

The **events of May 1968** brought yet another threat to another French republic. That spring saw student demonstrations against the war in Vietnam and other issues in almost all of the industrial democracies. Only in France did the protests spread to the working class and grow so big that the institutional order of the country was put in jeopardy.

After a minor demonstration, a group of students from the suburban campus at Nanterre was summoned to the Latin Quarter for a disciplinary hearing at the Sorbonne. Protests broke out that evening. Riot police attacked the students, who then started throwing rocks and building barricades. Millions of people were stunned by what they took to be police brutality. The trade unions and left-wing political parties came to the students' support. Within a week, protests and strikes had brought the country to a standstill. De Gaulle finally had to go to the army, which included many officers who had opposed him on Algeria, and ask for its support. The crisis ended when de Gaulle dissolved parliament and called for new elections. The Gaullists won, in large part because they played on fears of a Communist takeover, even though that was not in the cards. What did seem possible to many of us who were drawn to the events of May is that the far more radical New Left might grow by leaps and bounds and make profound changes in France and beyond.

We were wrong.

By 1978 the turn toward normal politics had begun. In 1972 the Communist and Socialist Parties agreed to a common program or platform they would enact were they to win the elections the next year. The agreement solidified the relationship between the two parties, which, as noted in Chapter 5, gave voters a choice between two teams of potential leaders until the late 1990s. The Left was defeated in the 1973 legislative and 1974 presidential elections, although it regained all the ground it had lost in 1968. The next legislative elections were scheduled for 1978, and the Left should have been able to win, given, among other things, the economic slump following the Organization of the Petroleum Exporting Countries (OPEC) oil embargo of 1973–1974. However, the left-wing parties had a hard time reestablishing their coalition, and the Gaullists and their allies won again, their ninth straight victory under the Fifth Republic.

What is important to note is that next to no one talked about the possible collapse of the Fifth Republic were the Left to win. Some people, of course, did object to its proposals, such as the one to nationalize France's leading industrial and commercial corporations. Nonetheless, it was clear that a government that included Communist cabinet ministers would no longer be a threat to democracy.

That was even more true in 1988. In 1981 the Left finally won the presidency on Mitterrand's third try. He immediately dissolved the National Assembly, and the Left won a landslide victory in the legislative elections that followed. The Socialist-led government, indeed, included Communist ministers and set out to make what Mitterrand exaggeratedly called a "break with capitalism."

Within two years, international economic conditions and public opinion at home forced Mitterrand to do a U-turn. The Left was then trounced in the 1986 legislative elections, ushering in the first period of **cohabitation,** in which the president came from one side of the political spectrum and the National Assembly was controlled by the other coalition of parties.

Mitterrand's first seven-year term ended in 1988. By that point, he and his leading opponent, the Gaullist prime minister Chirac, no longer disagreed on the most important issue facing the country—the reprivatization of the remaining companies the Socialists had nationalized in the early 1980s. In fact, the Socialists had abandoned almost all of their traditional left-wing goals. The Gaullists endorsed little of the promarket ideas that had swept the right wing in Britain and the United States. Perhaps most important of all, the Socialists and Gaullists seemed increasingly alike, both dominated by politicians who had been trained at the world-famous **ENA (National School of Administration)** and begun their careers as civil servants. Mitterrand easily won reelection, but no one expected dramatic change to occur in the aftermath of his triumph.

In 1998 there were no national elections. The Right had won the legislative elections in 1993, and Chirac had finally captured the presidency on his third try after Mitterrand's second term ended in 1995. However, the Left won the legislative elections held two years later, returning France to its unusual practice of cohabitation, which is discussed in more detail in Chapters 6 and 7.

Prime Minister Jospin's government did pass some intriguing legislation. A new **parity law** was enacted that required all parties to nominate an equal number of male and female candidates in most elections. The government lowered the legal workweek to thirty-five hours in an attempt to create new jobs. Jospin was given credit for helping to reinvigorate an economy that had been in the doldrums for many years, although he had a hard time getting the unemployment rate below 12 percent.

France did have at least one glaring problem. Le Pen's National Front (FN) Party continued to grow by appealing to French men and women who worried about the increasingly multicultural nature of French society and its growing integration into the European Union. Le Pen went so far as to argue that "real French citizens" should not support the country's national soccer team in that year's World Cup because only half of the players were really French (the rest were of Algerian, Armenian, Basque, Ghanaian, Polynesian Tunisian, and West Indian origin). Still, the threat posed by Le Pen was not widely viewed as serious, since he rarely won more than about 15 percent of the vote. And, when France won the Cup, the victory gave new support for France as a diverse and multiracial society.

This book was finished in mid-2007, so events in 2008 cannot be discussed. Nonetheless, three important events have occurred since 1998 that, at first glance, might undermine any notion that France has a political life that mirrors that of the other democracies. First was the confusing election of 2002 and its repercussions, which I used to begin the chapter. Second, France led the group of countries that opposed the United States–led invasion of Iraq in 2003, leading to an outburst of anti-French sentiment, primarily in the United States. Finally, in late 2005 and 2006 the country was wracked by demonstrations, first by angry Muslim youths who took to the streets burning, for example, hundreds of cars, and later by young people in general who opposed a proposed law that would strip workers under twenty-six of the job security protection that has long been a highlight of the French welfare state.

All of this is true. However, as I will begin to argue in the next section, none of these peculiarly French phenomena posed any significant danger to the Fifth Republic, something that could not have been said about events in 1958 or any of the years before it.

Why Normal Politics Matters

The shift toward "normal politics" is the key to understanding French politics today. Like any country, France has its distinctive issues and political figures. Le Pen's surprise showing in 2002 reminds us that racism is a very serious problem. The nation's political party system is more fragmented than the ones in any other major western European country. Paris is one of the few cities in the world with an openly gay mayor and the only one in which what to do about dog droppings has been a major political issue. Last but by no means least, France has had more than its share of juicy scandals, some of which have come close to implicating former president Chirac.

But by and large French politics is pretty much like American, British, Canadian, or German politics. Average citizens and politicians disagree about specific issues and often do so in heated terms. Protest movements hold demonstrations, some of which occasionally turn violent. There are even a handful of extremists like the neo-Nazis in Germany or the militias in the United States who would like to tear the system apart and start again from scratch.

However, there are clear limits to how far dissent will go or how disruptive it could be in the foreseeable future, because most people have drawn an invisible psychological line about their form of government that they will not cross. Political scientists often assess a country at three levels of analysis—the government in office at the time, the regime or constitutional order that persists from government to government, and the existence and acceptance of the country as a whole.

On the one hand, in any stable Western democracy there is plenty of opposition to whomever is in power at the moment. And few politicians or average citizens have any qualms about the legitimacy of stating one's point of view and organizing support for it on just about any concrete issue. Thus, plenty of Americans agreed that Bill Clinton should have been impeached and removed from the presidency. Many others disagreed with his successor's policies in Iraq, and there was even some limited discussion of impeaching George W. Bush.

On the other hand, it is only a handful of extremists that questions either the regime or the nation-state as a whole. The Fifth Republic, like the American, British, Canadian, or German regimes, enjoys widespread **legitimacy**. Its constitution has been amended, as was the case with the parity law. Still, virtually everyone takes the basic operations of the national institutions for granted. No one doubts that it is both legal and legitimate to advocate sweeping change, but next to no one thinks it is necessary to do so.

In sum, the main argument of this book is that the acceptance of this regime—indeed, of any regime—in France is new. And, it opens the door to the three main themes I stress in the pages that follow:

• How the transformation to normal politics occurred

• How this legitimate, stable, and reasonably effective political system operates

• How it is likely to evolve in a world in which France will be integrated ever more closely into European and global social, political, and economic networks

Alas, the transformation to normal politics means that French politics is much less exciting than it was thirty or fifty or one hundred years ago. That does not make it less important. Indeed, the speed and relative ease with which the Fifth Republic took root when no prior regime had done so in almost two centuries will go a long way toward helping us understand how democracies develop in general.

The same argument holds for the most controversial aspect of French politics, at least as viewed in the United States—its foreign policy. Many Americans strongly criticized France's opposition to the invasion of Iraq in 2003 and claimed it was typical of the country's foreign policy, which they think has always been disruptive and often anti-American. However, a closer look at the evidence in Chapters 9 and 10 shows a much more conventional and cooperative foreign policy today than in de Gaulle's day.

Thinking Systematically, Thinking Systemically

There are two broad ways to study French politics. The great nineteenth-century French (and other) historians wrote multivolume works on the Revolution and other key events that included just about every piece of available evidence.

My experience is that focusing on the evidence alone is never a good way to teach about any country, especially one like France, whose complicated political life can seem confusing. Even if students master the basic facts of French politics, they lack a platform to use what they have learned to draw comparisons with other countries or reach more general conclusions about the ways democracies work.

Therefore, it is important to use one of the many analytical frameworks that scholars of comparative politics have developed for organizing the evidence and seeing how the various aspects of politics and government in a given country affect each other. I find **systems theory** to be the most useful of these, although there are others that are almost as effective.

Systems theory has a long and complicated scientific history. In its current form, it was developed by engineers who designed weapons systems during World War II. It gained a foothold in political science during the 1960s but lost its popularity when many scholars decided (erroneously) that it had a conservative bias and (correctly) that it could not easily be used to structure empirical research.

It is useful here, however, because it focuses one's attention on the ways the components of the system, such as its political parties and institutions, interact with each other to produce change over an extended period of time. Those components fall into five main categories (see Figure 1.1).

The Environment

First, a system is "bounded." That is to say, there are interesting and important phenomena that lie outside it, which systems theorists call its **environment**.

To begin with, the environment includes a country's history. France may be unusual in that its history has been such a source of ideological division. However, any system's current situation is shaped by events that happened in the past, including some that occurred centuries ago.

Figure 1.1 A Systems Theory View

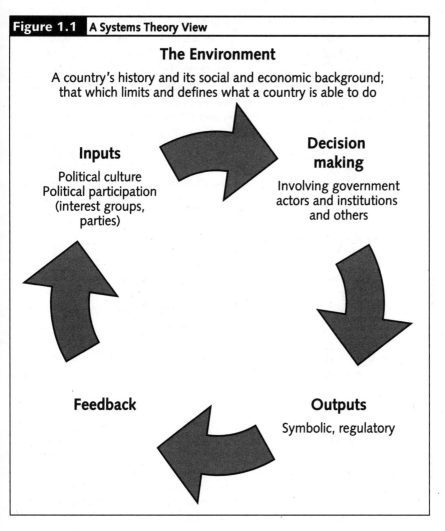

The Environment

A country's history and its social and economic background; that which limits and defines what a country is able to do

Inputs

Political culture
Political participation
(interest groups,
parties)

Decision making

Involving government
actors and institutions
and others

Feedback

Outputs

Symbolic, regulatory

Systems theorists also draw our attention to a country's social and economic backgrounds. These affect what a government can and cannot do. Thus, France's relative poverty between the two world wars was one of many reasons why it could not keep up with Germany after Hitler came to power and started to rearm. Its affluence in the 1990s meant that it was able to withstand an unemployment rate that was consistently over 10 percent without widespread protest. Similarly, its growing racial diversity since the 1960s helps explain why Jean-Marie Le Pen and his National Front have done well at the polls for more than a generation.

Politicians try to shape that social and economic environment. Indeed, much of French public policy since the late 1950s has been designed to promote and manage economic growth and immigration into the country.

The final element of the environment to be considered here covers the impact of forces arising outside France's borders. Until the end of World War II, the impact of international forces was most obvious in France's frequent wars with its neighbors, especially Germany. Since then, western Europe has become what Max Singer and Aaron Wildavsky call a "zone of peace," in which war between countries there has become all but impossible.[2]

That does not mean that international forces are unimportant, however. If anything, they are more powerful today as France is increasingly incorporated into a "globalizing" world. We will see that most prominently in the impact of the **European Union (EU)** and its ever more integrated economy and growing responsibility for other aspects of political life, including decision making on such issues as the rights of asylum seekers and some parts of foreign policy.

Inputs: The People and Politics

The second broad set of components—and the first within the system itself—includes what political scientists call **inputs**, or how people and the organizations they form help shape the way a country is run.

That begins with the country's **political culture**, which can be thought of in two ways. A culture, first, can be thought of as the impact of history on what people think about political life. Because of France's long tradition of centralization and its more recent history of effective economic policymaking, French citizens are more accepting of a strong state than are their American or British counterparts. A culture can also be thought of as the basic values and assumptions people bring to political life. In this sense, it is not so much what they think about President Chirac but what they feel about the presidency in general.

In both these senses, a culture amounts to what we might think of as our political second nature. We may not even be aware that we even have a political culture. Indeed, my students have a hard time defining what values make up the core of the American political culture. Nonetheless it plays a vital role, in essence, in setting the political "stage," determining what values, issues, and policies are likely to become popular and what are not.

Other than political culture, a system's inputs revolve around **political participation**, or what people do. Participation also includes what people do not do. Thus, political scientists were struck by the fact that abstention from voting hit an all-time high in the first round of the 2002 presidential election (28 percent) but that turnout rebounded to top 80 percent in Chirac's rout of Le Pen in the runoff ballot two weeks later.

People can participate as individuals. They can write letters to their representative in the National Assembly or to a newspaper. They can demonstrate their political views, as one young Socialist did by having a clothespin on his nose to show his displeasure when he went to cast his second ballot vote for Chirac.

Normally, however, people participate through one of two types of organizations. **Interest groups** deal with a relatively narrow set of issues and literally try to defend and promote the desires of people associated with them. In this book, I spend the most time with trade unions and business associations, but I also discuss the women's movement, environmentalists, groups supporting the rights of racial minorities, and more. **Political parties**, by contrast, pursue control of the national government either on their own or in a **coalition** with an ally or allies.

Decision Making: The State

Decision makers make up the third component of a system. They include the government but also other actors who help shape public policy. Political scientists call the whole cluster of them the **state**.

Because France has been so centralized for so long, almost all key decision makers live and work in Paris. That is the case even though local and regional authorities gained significant new powers as a result of decentralization laws enacted almost as soon as the Socialists first took power in 1981.

Our exploration of decision making will start with the formal institutions one finds in almost any democracy, many of which have already been mentioned. Thus, the people directly elect the president and the members of the National Assembly. When the same political party both occupies the Elysée Palace and has a majority in the Assembly, the president dominates for reasons that are made clear in Chapters 4 and 7. In other words, except during times of cohabitation, the prime minister and cabinet are less influential than their equivalents in most traditional parliamentary systems.

Just as important as these visible, elected institutions is the rest of the state, in particular France's remarkable senior civil service. The country has two tracks in its higher education system. The conventional university system is understaffed and underfunded, whereas the far more selective *grandes écoles*, such as the ENA and the **École polytechnique**, attract the lion's share of the country's most talented young men and women.

Students who pass the entrance exams and complete their course work enter the upper tier of the civil service and, typically, owe the state ten years' service to repay the cost of their education. Then, many of them engage in *pantouflage* (literally, putting on soft and comfortable slippers) to take top positions in industry or politics. Roughly half of the top executives in the leading firms in both the public and private sector are former civil servants. Most leading politicians, including Chirac and Jospin, are ENArques, as graduates of the school are known; many others went to one of the other prestigious grandes écoles. Some claim that this loose coalition of current civil servants and their former colleagues who have "migrated" into the worlds of politics and business are truly the elite that runs the country.

Public Policy

The fourth part of the system is its **output,** or the decisions made by these civil servants and other makers of **public policy.** These fall into three main categories for both domestic and foreign policy.

To begin with, there are **symbolic** decisions and policies. To cite the most visible examples, the French president is rarely seen without a flag nearby, and he (so far they have all been men) always flies on a French-made Airbus and is chauffeured in a French-made automobile. The European Union logo, as well as the French symbols, now adorn people's passports.

Other policies are **regulatory** and limit what people can and cannot do. Visitors to Paris, for instance, are often surprised to see signs on building walls saying that it is illegal to post political notices there or by the Metro's reserved seats for old people and mothers with large families. The EU now has extensive rules about such matters as university enrollment and immigration.

Finally, some policies alter the **distribution** of resources. France is well known for its *écoles maternelles,* which incorporate children from the age of two into the national educational system. Similarly, almost all health care and university tuition costs are paid by the state, not by patients or students. The government has also used tax incentives and subsidies to help transform the country's industrial base. The European Union has an important role here as well, ranging from the macroeconomic policies made by the new European Central Bank to the costly and wasteful Common Agricultural Policy.

Feedback

The fifth element of systems analysis makes it the best of the models for assessing change. **Feedback** is the process through which people learn about what the state has done and then use that information to shape how they will act (or not act, as the case may be) in the future.

Because of feedback, theorists argue that systems can change in three main ways. If, as has been the case since the late 1980s, there is little that deeply disrupts any part of the system, it is relatively stable or homeostatic. If, as was the case for much of the history of the Third and Fourth Republics, the state's inability to live up to popular expectations deepened distrust, division and alienation led to the system's deterioration in much the same way that a dysfunctional family faces mounting difficulties. By contrast, conservatives, at least, would argue that the state was so effective at stimulating economic growth during the first fifteen to twenty years of Gaullist rule that the system can be said to have grown or improved its performance.

France has long been known for its cadres of interest group and political party activists who, among other things, engage much of the population in regular political dialogue. Feedback thus occurs for many people on a face-to-face basis. Although that kind of activism has not disappeared, it is far less common and effective than it was thirty years ago. For example, in the early 1970s, I spent many weekend mornings with members of the Far Left political party I was studying as they talked politics with people at their neighborhood outdoor markets and Metro stops. But as in most advanced industrial democracies, most people now get most of their news from television and, to a lesser degree, radio and the press.

It should come as no surprise by now that France's media are more centralized than those in the United States. The influential newspapers are all Paris-based and distributed nationwide. There are a few respected regional newspapers, but opinion leaders typically focus on the roughly half-dozen high-quality newspapers published in Paris. Most newspapers have a clear political slant, and few people on the Left read conservative newspapers and vice versa.

During the early years of the Fifth Republic, the Gaullists tightly controlled radio and television news, because all stations were state owned. Indeed, the biased radio and television coverage during election campaigns was a common source of left-wing anger. All the stations also offered a single national feed through a network of regional retransmitters. In other words, France did not (and still really does not) have a tradition of independent local television stations as do Canada and the United States.

Since de Gaulle's departure, that situation has changed dramatically. First, Presidents Giscard d'Estaing and Mitterrand loosened government control (some would say censorship) of reporters and editors. Second, most of the state-owned stations were privatized. Mitterrand opened up the FM band so that there are now hundreds of local radio stations. Finally, the technological revolutions that introduced cable and satellite broadcasting have added dozens of new stations, including an all-news outlet that is roughly the equivalent of CNN in the United States or Sky News in Britain.

Using This Book

The book is divided into five parts that mirror the five components of a political system discussed above. Chapter 2 explores the environment, starting with France's social and economic structure today. Chapters 3 and 4 provide an overview of its long-term and recent history. Chapter 5 considers how French people think about and participate in political life, focusing on the changing nature of its political culture and party system. Chapter 7 focuses on the French state with roughly equal attention given to the formal institutions laid out in the Constitution and other laws and to the informal networks of the iron triangle. Chapter 8 analyzes what the French state does and how both Left and Right have converged on similar policies in the last two decades. Chapter 9 examines France's deep involvement in European integration; Chapter 10 does the same for the rest of its foreign policy. Chapter 11 explores the future of normal politics, speculating on France's future in the aftermath of Sarkozy's election.

Understanding French politics is not easy. Almost everything about it is more complicated than is the case with political life in the English-speaking democracies, where I assume most readers of this book live. For example, not only does France have more political parties than any of them, but they splinter and change their names so often that the French themselves have trouble keeping track of them.

Therefore, to help you focus on and make sense of the material in the rest of the book, each chapter will include:

- Comparative boxes that contrast France with the other leading industrial democracies.

- A list of key concepts and a list of key people, entities, and events, both at the end of the chapter. A glossary includes all of the terms at the end of the book.

- Discussion questions, also at the end of the chapter. These are designed to get you to think more deeply about the material. You can answer them on your own. However, my experience is that they are most useful when a group of students ponder them together, whether inside or outside of class.

There will also be short lists of books, articles, and Web sites for you to consult if you want to dig deeper into French politics. All of the printed works are in English. A few of the Web sites are only in French, but I have included them, since more and more French-only sites are adding English-language mirrors.

Learning about French politics can be just another part of a course you take on the way toward graduation. Or it can be fascinating in and of itself and can lead you to a deeper understanding of political life in general.

For the latter to happen, you will have to do more than read this book and highlight the key passages. You will have to do more than memorize class notes and readings and parrot them back on exams and papers.

Because France has been so different from most other industrial democracies and because it has changed so much since de Gaulle returned to power in 1958, it can be a powerful intellectual springboard for you to use to question your own political values and preconceptions. To do that, you have to keep asking why France is the way it is and whether trends there lead you to envision new alternatives for your own country that you hadn't considered before.

This is what we professors call active learning. The nineteenth-century French novelist Marcel Proust perhaps put it best in *Remembrance of Things Past*: "The voyage of discovery begins not with seeking new lands, but in seeing with new eyes."

Key Concepts

Key People, Entities, and Events

Questions for Discussion

1. Much has changed since this book was finished in mid-2007. Does the argument made here about normal politics still make sense? Why or why not?

2. France has had a more tumultuous history than any of the English-speaking democracies. Although we will return to these issues later, ask yourself why that has been the case?

3. Apply the ideas of systems theory to the country in which you live. In what ways does that analysis make France seem different from your own country? Why do you think that is the case?

2

"The Hexagon" France's Political and Social Geography

Logically, we probably should have moved on directly to the two chapters on French history that follow. However, readers who know little about France would have a hard time making sense of its history without first knowing more about what the country is like today. Therefore this chapter covers four overlapping topics:

- France's physical and geographic characteristics

- Its social structure

- Its economic conditions

- Its European and global contexts

The Hexagon

The French often refer to their country as "the hexagon," because its borders look a bit like that six-sided geometric figure.

France has almost 550,000 square kilometers of territory, which makes it about twice the size of Colorado. At that size, it is much larger than either Great Britain or Germany (Table 2.1 contrasts France with Germany, Great Britain, Italy, and the United States). That means it has more open space than either of them, since Britain has almost the same population as France, and Germany has over 10 million more people.

As the map shows, France borders Belgium, Germany, Italy, Luxembourg, Spain, and Switzerland. Just as important historically is the fact that France has about as long a coastline as it has on-land borders with those other countries.

Table 2.1	Basic Data on France and Similar Countries		
Country	Size (square kilometers)	Population (millions)	GNP per capita ($U.S. PPP)
France	547	63.7	31.1
Germany	357	82.4	31.9
Great Britain	245	60.8	31.8
Italy	301	58.1	30.2
United States	9,827	301.2	44.0

Source: CIA, The World Factbook, www.cia.gov/library/publications/the-world-factbook (accessed July 18, 2007).
Note: PPP = purchasing power parity.

France has had the same borders since the end of World War II. In fact, most of what is France today has been French territory for centuries. Alsace and Lorraine (the area surrounding Strasbourg) went back and forth between France and Germany, depending on who had won the most recent war. Similarly, the border between France and what became a unified Italy in the late nineteenth century also fluctuated with the political winds.

Even though Paris is almost as far north as the southern tip of Hudson Bay, it has a mild climate, in large part because the Gulf Stream passes nearby in the Atlantic. The southern coast along the Mediterranean Sea has extremely hot summers and includes some of Europe's leading seaside resorts.

France has Europe's two tallest mountain ranges—the Alps (along the Swiss and Italian borders) and the Pyrenees (on the Spanish frontier). There is also a large plateau (the *massif central*) in the middle of the country. Otherwise, the terrain is quite flat and the land is very fertile, which is one of the reasons France can produce some of the best wines, cheeses, meats, and vegetables in the world.

Unlike these features of French geography, the final one reflects human activity, not the forces of nature, and will be one of the most important themes raised in the rest of the book. For centuries, almost all of French life has been centered in Paris. It is the country's political, economic, cultural, and media capital. Just about every major business, government office, newspaper, and media enterprise is headquartered there. The country's rail and, later, its road network had Paris as its hub, which often meant that the quickest way to get between two major cities was to go by way of Paris. Parisians disparagingly refer to the rest of the country as "the provinces." So-called "turboprofs," who would never dream of living in Bordeaux or Grenoble, take the high-speed train from their Parisian homes and teach in provincial university towns for a day or two a week, where they keep either a *pied-à-terre* or rent a hotel room.

That **centralization** has been a key theme in French political history at least since Louis XIV reigned from 1661 to 1715. It was reinforced by the

winners of the Revolution of 1789, who sought to centralize and standardize everything. That included the creation of the metric system. That was, in many ways, a good idea, since the French used more than 700 units of weights and measures at the time. (A meter, by the way, was defined as one ten-millionth of the distance between the North Pole and the Equator.)

One of the key characteristics of centralization has been what the French call *dirigisme*, or a central role for the government in "directing" the economy. France always has had a basically capitalist economy, because the government has never owned more than about 20 percent of it. Nonetheless, for generations and perhaps for centuries the state has used its influence to help shape the decisions business executives in the private sector have made.

From the middle of the nineteenth century until the end of World War II, dirigisme was a brake on economic change. One of de Gaulle's first major accomplishments was to create the ENA, whose graduates have played a major role in modernizing French industry in the public and private sector alike.

Even under the five republics, the Parisian authorities had all but total control over what local governments did and what public schools taught. Much of Paris's institutional control has been diminished in recent years, especially with the passage of decentralization laws beginning in 1981. However, centuries-old habits and values give way slowly, and France remains as centralized as any major country in Europe.

From Diversity to Homogeneity to Diversity

In July 2006 the U.S. Central Intelligence Agency (CIA) estimated that the French population stood at a bit over 59.5 million people. The birth rate is low enough (0.37 percent population growth per year) that it will probably be some time late in this decade before it hits the 60 million mark. Still, France is Europe's second most populous country, trailing only Germany, at least if you exclude Russia and Turkey.

Like most wealthy countries, France has an aging population. Sixteen percent of the population is over sixty-five, and that number will continue to grow. Women over sixty-five outnumber men by about three to two, reflecting both the fact that women generally outlive men and the effect of France's losses in World War II.

Some people think that a centralized country is a homogeneous one as well. In the 1950s, that was pretty much the case. Just about everyone spoke standard French, although a few older people spoke only Breton, a Celtic language unrelated to French, or some French-based local dialect. Except for a handful of Protestants and Jews, who made up no more than 3 percent of the population, almost everyone was at least nominally Catholic—although no more than a third of the population routinely went to Mass.

However, that homogeneity is misleading. France has always been far more diverse than such statistics suggest and is even more so today.

As international relations scholars rightly point out, the nation-state is a relatively new institution—most date it from the Treaty of Westphalia in 1648. For our purposes here, the development of the **nation**—the psychological sense of being part of a country—is more important than the creation of the powerful state, which is covered in the next chapter.

If we looked at the early eighteenth century rather than the first decade of our new millennium, we would find a country in which most people identified with their region (*pays*) rather than with France as a whole. They spoke dozens of only somewhat related languages. People from the Languedoc (literally where people used *oc* instead of *oui* to say "yes") would have a hard time understanding Parisians and vice versa.

By the 1850s most people undoubtedly thought of themselves as French. Nonetheless, it took mass access to elementary education and then to the radio before the regional dialects began to give way to a common language with differences restricted largely to accents, as in the United States and Great Britain.

From 1850 to 1950 France experienced significant immigration. Some came as political refugees; others simply sought a better life. Whatever their reasons for coming, by the 1950s, people with names like MacMahon, Blum, Zola, Poniatowski, Sarkozy, and Mendes had long filled French political and intellectual life.

And, as Le Pen's consistent success since the late 1980s suggests, France also has a far more varied population today. In the aftermath of his shocking second-place showing in the 2002 presidential election, analysts frequently made the case that 20 percent of the population has non-French roots, which includes those earlier waves of mostly European immigrants and, now, even more people whose families have come from what is called the third world.

In short, since the 1950s, another wave of immigration has occurred, this time mostly from former French colonies in North Africa, sub-Saharan Africa, the Caribbean, Southeast Asia, and the Pacific Islands. As of 1998 just over 7 percent of the population were born outside of France, but many immigrants have had children while living in France, which probably puts the minority population at about 10 percent of the total. The exact number is unknown, since quite a few people are in France illegally and thus not included in official counts.

In at least one respect, Le Pen is right about these immigrants being different from earlier generations of people who moved to France. As noted above, most earlier immigrants came from Europe; they learned French quickly and adapted to French culture in a generation or less. The more recent immigrants have assimilated far more slowly; some have not even begun to learn French. One sign of how poorly integrated members of minority groups are is the fact that in 1998, only one of France's 36,560 cities and towns had a nonwhite mayor. In 2006 the government passed a law making it harder for poorly educated immigrants to enter the country and requiring people who do take up residence in France to learn the language and respect republican values.

The New French Revolution

If you watch French films from the 1950s, you will see a country with a far lower standard of living than the United States or Great Britain. Homes without inside toilets or running water, for instance, were still quite common. France was known for the quality of its food, philosophers, and artists. However, its industries lagged far behind the American and other major European powers. To cite but one statistic, the French economy grew by a total of 5 percent between the two world wars, a figure that left it farther and farther behind its main competitors, all of which did better economically despite the Great Depression.

The quaint but inefficient France of a half century ago is gone. As Hans Koning put it, "forget the clichées about a French scene consisting of berets, loaves of fresh bread, long lunches, intuition, improvisation, and bad telephones."[1] Bad telephones were an important part of the recent French past. When I moved to Paris to do research for my Ph.D. dissertation in 1972, I knew I would need a telephone to arrange interviews. The wait to get a phone installed was over a year. Otherwise, I would have to go to the post office or a café and use expensive pay phones, and, of course, I couldn't receive calls. So, I had to find an apartment that already had a phone, the rent for which was almost twice what a comparable, but phoneless, one would have been.

Today, France is one of the four most affluent countries in the world, trailing only the United States, Japan, and Germany. It is a pioneer in many cutting-edge industries. It is a world leader in rocket design and aircraft manufacturing. French companies built the first high-speed trains that can travel at more than two hundred miles an hour. French technicians even invented the first machine that automatically picks up dog droppings from streets and sidewalks. In contrast with the statistic cited earlier, from 1945 until the mid-1970s, the French economy grew by an average of over 5 percent *each year*, a figure topped only by Japan.

Crude measures of economic growth hide changes "at the human level" that were already so sweeping and so visible by the 1960s that the Irish journalist John Ardagh wrote a book entitled *The New French Revolution*.[2] You can see the change in the French themselves. An improved diet has produced French men and women who are inches taller and pounds thinner than their grandparents. And their phone service is second to none. In fact, France Telecom invented the Minitel—small computer screens that almost everyone has that tie into the phone system and provide almost all the information a person would need—long before the invention of the World Wide Web.

Per capita gross national product (GNP) measured using the World Bank's purchasing power parity (PPP) method is our best single indicator of the overall wealth of a country. French, German, and Japanese citizens all had roughly the same standard of living at the start of this new millennium, although all trailed the United States. The gap between them and the United States is not as great as has been suggested, since PPP statistics fluctuate with changing conditions such as the value of a country's currency. But there is no doubt that France is one of the four or five wealthiest countries on the planet.

In 1940 close to a third of all French workers were farmers. Now, agriculture employs only 3 percent of the workforce, about the same tiny percentage one finds in most advanced industrial countries. And, as is typical of a **postindustrial society**, almost three workers in four are employed in the service sector.

France has its own "Silicon Valley" surrounding the new town of Sophia Antipolis just outside of Nice on the Mediterranean coast, where more than a thousand companies employ tens of thousands of people. And it is very typical of France's economic growth since the end of World War II that the new city and its university were planned through a joint venture between the government and the private sector, with the regional authorities playing the leading role.

France has its share of economic problems. Unemployment has hovered around 10 percent since 2000 and had been as high as 12 percent in the 1980s and 1990s. Unemployment was particularly high among poorly educated young people, adding to the frustration in both the white and minority communities.

Many of the huge industrial firms, dubbed "national champions" by former president Valéry Giscard d'Estaing, are struggling, especially those that were nationalized under Mitterrand and then privatized again later. Given the centralization of the business and educational worlds, France has been slow to develop the entrepreneurial small businesses that sparked the 1990s boom in the United States. Nonetheless, such business leaders now exist in substantial numbers and have been in the workforce long enough to develop the expertise and resources to set up new high-tech firms in Sophia Antipolis and beyond.

However, the difficulties should not keep us from understanding that France has one of the richest and most dynamic economies in the world. In addition, the country's extensive social service system, which is covered in more detail in Chapter 8, provides a strong "safety net" for the underprivileged. Despite the legendary (and filthy) *clochards* (bums) who sleep along the banks of the Seine in Paris, there are very few homeless people. Health care and higher education are virtually free. The French government does spend about half of the nation's GNP (compared with about a third in the United States and two-fifths in the United Kingdom). The key difference lies in the social service programs. Although it is impossible to find definitive statistics about such spending, average French citizens get a lot for their money.

The European and Global Contexts

Political scientists still draw a sharp distinction between comparative politics and international relations. The former deals with political life inside a country's borders. The latter explores how states interact with each other. That dividing line makes less and less sense these days.

Although this book focuses on the traditional domain of comparative politics, it also considers France's role in the world. France's international stature has long been an important and controversial domestic political issue. Its failure to withstand Germany's 1940 invasion led to the collapse of the Third Republic. Eighteen years later, its inability to contain the twin rebellions in Algeria brought down the Fourth Republic.

As is the case in any country, the transition from one government to the next often brings with it shifts in foreign policy. That was certainly true in France when de Gaulle returned to power in 1959 and charted a more independent foreign policy that stressed restoring French grandeur.

But important changes occurred in less spectacular but still significant ways when one conservative politician replaced another in the presidency. Thus, when de Gaulle resigned, he was replaced by Georges Pompidou. Pompidou was one of the first supporters of European integration during the 1920s and was thus more open to expanding the membership and the powers of what was then called the European Community.

Globalization

The book also concentrates on how international forces affect France, in part through what is frequently but loosely called **globalization**. There are dozens of definitions of globalization, which is a good sign that it is an important but still ill-understood concept.

Many observers see globalization as primarily an economic phenomenon that is increasingly integrating the world into a single, interconnected market. I will use the term more broadly and include other ways in which the world is "shrinking," including the spread of an American-dominated culture, telecommunications, and even politics.

Those global forces are making it harder and harder for leaders to control their own country's destiny. The most obvious example of this in France is that Mitterrand tried to move France markedly leftward in the 1980s at a time when most other Western countries were run by conservatives. His policies required borrowing billions of dollars at a time when global interest rates were extremely high. In short, within two years it had become clear that his desire to "reconquer the domestic market" was a financial disaster, and he had to abandon almost all of his egalitarian goals.

France is by no means a pawn of the businesses and others who are leading the way to globalization. Because it is a rich and powerful country, it can resist global trends more readily than can a smaller or poorer country in Europe, let alone a country in the third world. But, globalization is having a powerful impact on France nonetheless.

Until recently, comparativists tended to view political life through many lenses, one of which saw it as pitting the power of society against that of the state (see Figure 2.1). The government could take on new powers only if it did so at the expense of the people—and vice versa.

Thus, traditional centralization made it impossible for French citizens to have a voice in how their children were taught or even what the school they attended was named. By contrast, the decentralization laws of the 1980s stripped the national government of power over education, welfare, zoning, and more and gave it to regional, departmental, and local governments, over which average citizens had far more influence. Now, as Figure 2.1 also suggests, global forces are constraining the ability of both average citizens and political leaders alike to shape public policies that could change the direction in which France is heading.

Before we consider how these global forces limit what any French government can do, it is important to note that because of the intellectual divide between comparative politics and international relations, we cannot measure the impact of globalization with any precision. Scholars have failed to develop methodologies that would allow us to calculate the influence of global forces with the statistical detail we can employ when studying topics within each of the subfields of political science, such as voting behavior or international trade.

Nonetheless, global forces are there. And, for France and its European neighbors, they operate on two levels. The first is globalization per se.

That is easiest to measure in the economy. France is highly dependent on foreign trade. Imports accounted for 25 percent of gross domestic product (GDP) in 2003; exports made up 26 percent. Both figures were up by between 3 and 4 percent since 1990. Although Germany, Japan, and the United States buy and sell more on the global marketplace, only Germany tops France on a per capita basis. When making domestic public policy France simply cannot afford to ignore trends in international finance or in the evolution of markets for everything from its wine to new computer software.

Figure 2.1	The Impact of Global and Domestic Forces on the State

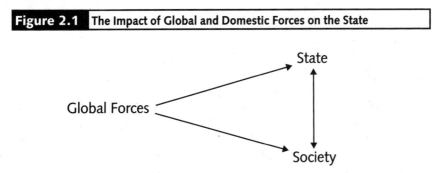

It isn't just the cutting edge of high-tech industry. There were 860 Mc-Donald's in France in early 2002, and the number continues to grow at about 30 per year. If you go to the corporate Web site (www.mcdonalds.fr), you will see that McDonald restaurants in France are not exactly the same as those in the United States. Beer is served. The coffee is better. It sells a version of a *croque monsieur*, a distinctively French version of a grilled ham and cheese sandwich. Drive-up windows are known as McDrive, and only about half of the restaurants have one. Still, they are the McDonald's that any American would recognize.

McDonald's is but the tip of the iceberg. Coca-Cola drinking is up and wine consumption is down among people under thirty. French pop culture increasingly resembles that of the United States or Great Britain. American movies are shown on almost half the screens in major cities. French teens dress more and more like Americans each year. The National Basketball Association (NBA) is wildly popular, although its games are not as widely watched on television as those of *les bleus*, the national soccer team. Rap music is at least as popular in France as in the United States. The words of French rap tunes may be French or Arabic, but the sound is the same as that heard on MTV in the United States. Of course, there is an MTV France.[3]

French protesters get a lot of publicity for their attempts to stem what they see as the disastrous consequences of globalization for the poor, the environment, and French traditions. The most famous of them, José Bové has led a movement to protest globalization with McDonald's as its focus. His followers even tried to tear down one restaurant. The government has vainly tried to limit the number of American films that are shown and American music that goes over the airwaves.

Perhaps most telling of all is the role of the **High Commission on the French Language,** created by de Gaulle in 1966. It alone has the power to determine which new words can be included in the language. In recent years, it has struggled to keep foreign—mostly English—words out. People may well want to say "le one man show," "le disc jockey," or "le hit parade," but the High Commission on the French Language insists on *spectacle solo, animateur,* and *palmarès.* The commission has fined American Airlines for issuing English-language boarding passes at Charles de Gaulle airport and has hauled a furniture store owner into court for advertising his "showroom," rather than his *salle d'exposition.* In 1998 "the law resulted in 8,000 linguistic inspections, 658 warnings, 255 cases to the public prosecutor, and 124 rulings won."[4] In practice, almost everyone ignores it.

The fact is that most French men and women are accepting most aspects of our increasingly interdependent world as fully and as enthusiastically as their American, British, German, or Italian counterparts. Activists like Bové may resist those aspects of globalization that seem to assault symbols of French grandeur, such as its language, films, or food. But they have had little choice about and shown little resistance to changing the way the economy is structured and, for that matter, popular culture in almost all of its forms.

The same holds for a tradition that has only recently been abandoned. Until early in the 1990s, the government insisted that children had to be given the name of a saint or a figure from classical history in order to receive the extensive benefits it offers families. Breton or Occitan or German names were forbidden. Richard Bernstein of the *New York Times* tells of a friend whose first and middle names were Mignon Florence, which was double trouble. Not only was Mignon not on the list of approved names, the people at the registry office were convinced that, as a girl, she should have been Mignonne. Later, her teachers insisted that she spell her name that way. Officially, she had to assume the name Florence, which she did until the rules were relaxed when she was an adult.[5] The rules had to be relaxed because there were so many immigrants with names like Zinedine or Fatou.

France has also had to face one of the world's most daunting political problems—terrorism—and had to do so long before September 11. Until recently, terrorism mostly revolved around domestic politics, most notably the actions of the Secret Army Organization, created in the late 1950s to try to block Algerian independence and then to assassinate de Gaulle. There have also been periodic bombings by fringe groups in Corsica and Brittany who seek independence from France.

For the last thirty years, most terrorism has had its roots in politics outside its borders. France has not only welcomed immigrants in general, but it has also had a liberal political asylum policy over the years. Many activists from the Middle East and elsewhere have settled there. That has meant that on numerous occasions, political scores for conflicts elsewhere were settled there too. When I was in France in 1972, the Israeli secret service killed a Palestinian terrorist not far from my apartment. Since then, various groups, most frequently from Algeria, have staged terrorist attacks in France. Now it appears that appalling conditions in Paris's working-class suburban slums have given rise to Islamic militants, including Zacharias Moussaoui, who was sentenced to a life sentence for his role in the 2001 terrorist attacks in New York and Washington.

Europe

The most important and most visible way that global forces affect France is through the impact of European institutions. France belongs to all the major ones, including the North Atlantic Treaty Organization (NATO), the Organization for Security and Cooperation in Europe, the Western European Union, and the Organization for Economic Cooperation and Development. However, it is the **European Union (EU)** that has the greatest impact and that is concentrated on here and in Chapter 9.

Idealistic and visionary French leaders were among those who founded the European Coal and Steel Community and the European Economic Community (EEC) during the 1950s, the predecessors of today's EU. De Gaulle, however, had doubts about them and preferred what he called a Europe of Nations (Europe des patries) in which national interests would be privileged.

During his decade in office, he drastically reduced France's commitment to NATO and almost destroyed the EEC. Since his resignation, successive French presidents have brought their foreign policy more in line with that of their Western allies, and more important for the purposes here, they have been among the leaders in every effort to increase the size and power of the EU.

The EU is a complicated organization, and analyzing those complexities in any detail is beyond the scope of this book. It is enough to note that it exercises many powers that were once held by politicians in Paris (or London or Berlin). Few French politicians openly say that they have ceded some of their sovereignty to the EU, but that is what they have done. Most of the EU's authority is over the economy, but it is beginning to have an impact on social, judicial, and foreign policy as well. Among its policies and actions that have limited what French politicians and citizens can do are:

- France no longer sets tariffs and duties on imports.

- People, goods, and services flow freely across its borders, as freely as they do between American states or Canadian provinces.

- Goods that meet any country's safety and quality standards may be sold in France.

- All professionally qualified workers (except for lawyers) who have been certified in any EU country may work in France.

- The euro has replaced the French franc. The European Central Bank has taken on the macroeconomic responsibilities previously exercised by the Bank of France.

Conclusion

It is tempting to jump ahead and consider these and other, more explicitly political, aspects of contemporary France. However, it is important first to take a step back and consider how these aspects of the environment of the French political system emerged over a period of five centuries or more.

Key Concepts

centralization   18
dirigisme   20
globalization   24
nation   21
postindustrial society   23

Key People, Entities, and Events

Questions for Discussion

1. France shares many characteristics with most industrial democracies. What are they? What makes it different from similar countries?

2. There is no doubt that globalization is affecting France. Is that true of your country? Whatever your answers, what are the differences between it and France? How would you account for them?

3. France has long been one of the most centralized countries in the world. How do you think that has affected French politics? Why and how is your country different from France in that respect?

3

History I
The Long Term

In discussing systems analysis in Chapter 1, I stressed the impact of history in determining the basic parameters of political life in any country. Events in the past do not determine everything that happens today. If that were so, there would be no reason to study political science.

Nonetheless, we ignore the past at our peril. Policymakers who fail to take history into account often find themselves fighting losing battles against their fellow citizens who are more wedded to their country's traditions than they are. Students who do not include historical trends in their analyses of current events often miss the key reasons why a country uses a particular election system or has as many political parties as it does.

History is especially important in the case of France for two reasons. First, its past is filled with events that over much of the last two hundred years have been crucial in the making of both its turbulent political life and the "normal" state of affairs discussed in Chapter 1. Second, the French argue about the nature of their history more than do people in most other countries. Debates over such turning points as the Revolution of 1789 or the events of May 1968 filter down from academic historians and find a major outlet in the popular press and broadcast media. In other words, disagreements over events that occurred decades and even centuries ago are part of the division between the Left and Right today.

French history is also, not surprisingly, long and quite complicated. As a result, two chapters are needed to cover it all. This one covers the broad sweep of French history over the last millennium. Chapter 4 concentrates on the years since de Gaulle returned to power and founded the Fifth Republic.

This chapter is not organized in strictly chronological order, although a series of tables draw attention to the most pivotal events. Instead, the chapter focuses on two broad sets of trends.

- Four major transformations that created the broad contours of modern French political life, including its ideological divisions

- A "traditional syndrome" that paralyzed the Third and Fourth Republics for more than three-quarters of a century and, ultimately, contributed to their downfall

Four Transformations

In 1967 Seymour Martin Lipset and Stein Rokkan published a long and dense chapter showing how the alignment of parties in western Europe could be explained by the divisions left by four great changes that occurred over the previous five hundred years.[1] In Chapter 6, I argue that their case is no longer as convincing in explaining the shape of the French (or any) party system today. Here, however, I actually want to take their line of reasoning one step farther than they did and show that the great transformations shaped much of French political life, not just the nature of its political parties and voting patterns.

As the text and comparative boxes in this chapter suggest, each transformation but the first left France deeply divided. What's more, the French frequently had to deal with more than one of these momentous issues at the same time, leaving it with the political equivalent of multiple and overlapping geological fault lines.

Creating the Nation and State

As noted in Chapter 2, the nation-state is a relatively new institution, consisting of two separate building blocks. The state consists of the institutions that exercise power over a particular geographical unit. Some of those institutions are formal parts of the government; others may not be, as seen in the discussion of the iron triangle in Chapter 7. The nation is a psychological concept, referring to the sense of belonging to or identification with that geographical unit and its state. Thus, in a nation-state, I am more likely to think of myself first and foremost as an American than as a Virginian.

In France both the state and the nation developed quite early. Unlike the transformations discussed below, the French reached a broad consensus in support of a strong and centralized state that, ironically, may well have magnified the impact of the divisions left by the other three.[2]

It is possible to identify a single date that marked the creation of certain countries, such as July 4, 1776, for the United States. There is no such day for France. Instead, more and more of the territory we now think of as France came under the authority of the king during the first half of the last millennium. By the time of Henri IV's reign (1589–1610), the country had grown to include almost all of the territory that is in France today.

Table 3.1	Events in French History before 1945
Year	Event
987	Hugh Capet crowned king of the Franks
1520 onward	Wars of religion
1643	Louis XIV enthroned
1648	Treaty of Westphalia
1789	The Revolution
1830	Failed revolution
1848	Revolution and creation of the Second Republic
1870–1875	Defeat in war with Germany; creation of the Third Republic
1939–1945	World War II and collapse of the Third Republic

That does not mean that the state in general or the monarchy in particular was very strong. The state had few responsibilities, and most historians think that the nobles had more power than the king.

That imbalance began to end during the long reign (1643–1715) of **Louis XIV**. By that time, the state had had to become more powerful, largely because of the wars of religion that swept Europe in the 150 years following the Reformation. Not only was France embroiled in conflict with other increasingly powerful states, but it had to fight a civil war that pitted Catholics and Protestants against each other (see the next section and Table 3.1).

Fighting those wars forced the king to recruit, equip, feed, and pay more soldiers than the monarchy had ever needed before. That could only be done by developing a political infrastructure of officials whose primary loyalty was to the king, which could not be taken for granted as far as the nobility was concerned.

Although earlier kings had begun expanding the state's impact, most historians claim that the real turning point occurred under Louis XIV. Among other things, he created a new group of officials, the *intendants*, who would carry out the king's policies and raise revenues in local jurisdictions. Meanwhile, Louis had the enormous Palace of Versailles built and required the nobles and their entourages to spend the bulk of the year there, further undercutting their influence back home.

The trend toward a strong and centralized state was reinforced by the Revolution that began in 1789 and ended only with the defeat of Emperor Napoléon Bonaparte in 1815. Some of the early revolutionaries wanted to return to a more decentralized and weaker state, but they lost out to the Jacobins and others who made the state even more centralized and powerful than it had been under the absolute monarchs of the seventeenth and eighteenth centuries. So, too, did Napoléon, who created the prefects (*préfets*), the civil servants who controlled political life in the then ninety departments, and the École polytechnique, the first of the grandes écoles whose mission was to train civil servants. From then on, few influential politicians from any point on the political spectrum objected to a state in Paris that controlled public education and civil administration while raising almost all the tax revenues spent by governments at all levels.

It was another half century or more before most people came to make the nation the primary object of their political identity or loyalty. Because we do not have public opinion polls or other data that reflect what people thought before the 1940s, we cannot tell for certain when that sense of nationality became the norm, but it may well not have happened until the early part of the twentieth century and the mass diffusion of radio.

What we do know is that most French citizens became quite nationalistic in the century following the Revolution. They may well have thought of themselves as Lyonnais or Provençal first. But, as their willingness to fight and die in the many wars France fought suggests most were quite loyal and nationalistic.

Religion

The second transformation has already been mentioned—the conflicts over religion that broke out shortly after Martin Luther began the Reformation by posting ninety-five theses on the door of the Castle Church in Wittenberg on October 31, 1517. In fact, there were three conflicts. First, there were the international wars fought largely over religious issues, which, as just mentioned, played a vital role in creating the modern state. Second, many countries, including France, also fought bloody civil wars that pitted Catholics against Protestants. Finally, even after those wars were over, most European countries still had lively debates over the role the church should play in political life—if any. The second and third of these conflicts concern us here.

France is an overwhelmingly Catholic country today. That was not the case in the aftermath of the Reformation. The new Protestant sects had a wide following, especially in the middle classes, the towns, and other areas that had a history of hostility toward the clergy. At their peak Protestants made up somewhere between one-fifth and one-fourth of the total population. John Calvin (real name: Jean Chauvin), who gave birth to one of the stricter Protestant sects, was French even though his beliefs had their greatest impact elsewhere.

The rise of Protestantism was a political threat to the monarchy. The king got much of his income from the church, and the clergy played a central role in carrying out what little public policy there was. What's more, a concordat reached with Rome in 1516 gave the monarchy all but total control over the French church, including the selection of bishops.

By the late 1560s the appeal of Protestantism in general and Calvinism in particular had begun to ebb. The government took the offensive, most notably with the St. Bartholomew's Day massacre of August 24, 1572, when as many as six thousand Protestants were killed in Paris and provincial cities.

The crisis deepened when a Protestant, Henri IV, took the throne. Most Catholics refused to accept him as a legitimate king. In order to try to restore order in the divided country, he issued the Edict of Nantes in 1598 that gave

State and Nation

The British state developed at about the same time as the French. However, it has never been as powerful or as centralized as the French government even though Parliament has been the sole source of sovereignty for several centuries. The national identity of the British has also been blurred by the existence of strong feelings of regional and, some would say, national loyalty in Wales, Scotland, and Northern Ireland.

German national identity and nationalism developed at about the same time as they did in France. However, there was no German state until 1871. That combination of ardent nationalism and statelessness contributed strongly to German aggressiveness after the Second Reich was finally created under Prussian domination.

The founders of the United States consciously decided not to build a strong state. Although the U.S. Constitution, passed in 1787, did concentrate more power in the federal government's hands than the Articles of Confederation allowed, the founders and most Americans since then have sought to minimize the impact the state has on people's lives. Americans also identify strongly with the United States, which is rather surprising, given the fact that it fought a bloody civil war and, since then, has absorbed wave after wave of immigrants.

On July 14, 2000, the French celebrated their national holiday—Bastille Day—in style, with a long lunch. This "incredible picnic" stretched more than 600 miles and ran through 337 towns and cities, from Dunkerque in the north to Prats-de-Mollo, along the French-Spanish border in the south.

Protestants the freedom to practice their religion and to control towns in which they were in the majority.

Henri IV was assassinated in 1610, and another period of turmoil followed. He was succeeded by his nine-year-old son, Louis XIII, who was raised Catholic by his mother. When Louis XIII turned twenty-one and took full control of the country, he and his close advisers, Cardinals Mazarin and Richelieu, began a counteroffensive against Protestantism. That continued under Louis XIV and culminated with the revocation of the Edict of Nantes and the emigration of most of the Protestant Huguenots to North America. Small pockets of Protestantism remained, but France was once again an overwhelmingly Catholic country.

For our purposes, the key to this phase of French history is the close identification between the church and the crown and their shared conservatism. In other words, when the third transformation occurred—the demand for democracy—opposition to the monarchy inevitably became intertwined with opposition to the political clout of the church.

From then on, the conflict was not between Catholics and Protestants but between the pro- and anticlerical communities. Both were Catholic, but **anticlericals** opposed the church's involvement in political life; most of them were also not particularly observant. During the nineteenth century, village priests vied with schoolteachers (named by the state and thus normally anticlerical) for the sympathies of people they worked with. The anticlericals ultimately achieved their goal of separating church and state in 1905. However, the debate between the two camps continued, typically over whether the national government should give financial and other support to parochial schools. Into the 1980s, "religiosity" remained the single best predictor of the way people voted. The more often a person went to Mass, the more likely he or she was to vote for the Right; less observant Catholics voted overwhelmingly for the Left.

Democracy

Democracy is even newer than the nation or state. There were a handful of democracies in the Greek city-states of antiquity, and some claim that Poland and a few other countries had democratic systems during the Middle Ages. However, democracy as we know it emerged only in the late eighteenth century, if by the word we mean a country in which political leaders are chosen through free, competitive, and fair elections; basic civil liberties are guaranteed, and the rule of law is respected by all. Many political scientists also think a democracy requires a capitalist economy and a civil society, but others argue that a democracy could exist without them.

Democracy was not established easily anywhere. France's attempt to create and sustain a democracy was particularly difficult. In all, France has tried five different republican regimes, and it was only in the late 1960s or early 1970s that one could argue that a democracy was securely in place.

Religion and Politics

The fallout from the Reformation had very different effects in Germany, Great Britain, and the United States.

The German division between Catholics and Protestants turned out to be one of the main reasons the country did not unify over the following three-and-a-half centuries. The peace agreements that ended the wars of religion, most notably the 1648 Treaty of Westphalia gave each state's ruler the right to determine its religion. When Germany did unify, it had large groups of Catholics and Protestants. Although there are some political differences between them, religion is not a major political issue today.

Henry VIII moved all of England into the new and official Church of England in the late sixteenth century, in part so he could get divorced and remarried. The Church of England is still the established church. Many believe that someone of another religion cannot become either prime minister or king. The state-owned BBC begins each morning with "Prayer for the Day" on the radio. The Church of England runs most elementary schools, and all schools have religious education. However, that curriculum, like most aspects of religion in the United Kingdom, stresses tolerance and ecumenicalism.

Many American colonies were founded by religious groups and thus had established or official religions—Puritans in Massachusetts, the Society of Friends (Quakers) in Pennsylvania, and Catholics in Maryland, for example. However, the First Amendment to the Constitution denied Congress the right to establish any religion. By the early nineteenth century, the remaining states with official religions disestablished them. Religious issues often influence American politics, as in the debate over abortion or President George W. Bush's faith-based initiative. However, they have nothing like the influence they have had historically in France and Germany.

Though France is religiously and culturally diverse these days, it is still very much a Roman Catholic country. Here, a Parisian baker's wife displays All Saints' Day cakes and cards to commemorate a holiday in which the devout reflect on the lives of saints, and their sacrifices for their faith.

France's democratic history begins with the great Revolution of 1789. There were many reasons why the Revolution occurred. In part, it reflected the growing economic and military weakness of the Bourbon monarchy following the death of Louis XIV. In part, it reflected the growing number of educated middle-class men who, like their counterparts throughout Europe, demanded political as well as economic freedom. In part, it reflected the anger of the poor in the cities and in the countryside, who were furious about their declining standard of living, which left many on the brink of starvation.

Protesters stormed the Bastille prison in Paris on July 14, 1789. A new constituent assembly took control of the country shortly thereafter. Later that year, the nobility relinquished its political power, and the largely unelected National Assembly passed the famous **Declaration of the Rights of Man**. In 1791 King Louis XVI accepted a new constitution that called for an elected legislative assembly and a constitutional monarchy. That only delayed the inevitable. In 1792 the monarchy was abolished. That year also marked the beginning of the shift toward rule by more radical and violent revolutionaries, who executed the king, his family, and hundreds of nobles. As many as forty thousand more alleged supporters of the monarchy were killed in the Terror during the next two years. By the time **Napoléon Bonaparte** became consul and then emperor in 1799, there was nothing democratic left about the First Republic.

After Napoléon's defeat at the Battle of Waterloo in 1815, the Bourbons were restored to the throne. In 1830 France became a constitutional monarchy, in which the legislature had far more power than the king. Don't make the mistake that there was much democratic about the regime either, however. Only 0.5 percent of the population—the very richest men—were allowed to vote. By contrast, the Great Reform Act of 1832 in Britain expanded the suffrage to include about 10 percent of all men.

The monarchy never firmly reestablished itself, and it began to lose support not just among the middle class but among the growing number of industrial workers as well. Finally, revolutions broke out in much of Europe in 1848, and after a few skirmishes in Paris and other cities, the monarchy collapsed and was replaced by the Second Republic, which did not even last as long as the first one.

Its constitution had two historical "firsts." To begin with, France became the first country to adopt universal manhood suffrage. Second, it called for a powerful, elected president, which turned out to be its undoing.

To the surprise of many, **Louis-Napoléon Bonaparte**, the great-nephew of the first emperor, won an overwhelming victory in December of 1848. Within three years, he had held a number of plebiscites, or referenda, the last of which abolished the republic and installed him as the head of the Second Empire.

Support for a republic, however, was what market researchers call "embedded." No matter how much repression the imperial authorities employed, the ideals of liberty, equality, and fraternity were not going to disappear. So, when the empire weakened in the 1860s, middle-class and working-class opposition reemerged. The empire was toppled, however, largely because of its own foreign policy mistakes, which led to the disastrous war with Prussia in 1870, during which the emperor was captured.

It was another five years before the **Third Republic** was firmly in place. It never had a formal constitution, but most scholars date its birth from November 30, 1875, when key laws were enacted involving the responsibility to parliament of the prime minister and his cabinet. And, although it survived until World War II, it could hardly be considered a success, a theme that is explored in detail in the concluding section of this chapter. Here, it is enough to note that although it may have been, as President Georges Clemenceau put it, "the form of government that divides us least," the French were still very divided.

In 1875 a majority of French politicians probably would have preferred restoring the monarchy. However, they could not agree among themselves on which pretender to the throne to choose, and conservative republicans ended up dominating the Third Republic for much of its life.

The Third Republic always struggled to cope with powerful movements on the Right, which sought to destroy it. They were most visible and powerful in the years surrounding the start of the twentieth century and then again during the Depression. The first period revolved around the **Dreyfus Affair**. Alfred Dreyfus, a respected Jewish army officer, was framed on espionage charges. Many Catholics and other conservatives simply took his guilt for granted and then took the next logical step of assuming that a regime that would allow a Jew into the upper ranks of the military had to be replaced. When evidence that Dreyfus had been framed became impossible to ignore, their intransigence only mounted. The republic survived, but not easily.

The same thing happened in the 1930s. By then, the Catholic, royalist, and imperial supporters who made up the anti-Dreyfusard movements had turned into permanent antidemocratic organizations, the most important of which was Action française. Once the effects of the Great Depression hit, the stakes of politics mounted. Hitler and Mussolini took power in Germany and Italy. The Left showed signs of uniting to resist the Nazis and the Fascists. In France, support for Action Française and the other neo-Fascist movements boomed. The republic survived, but just barely.

It wasn't just the Right that posed threats to the republic. Although rarely in power, the Left deepened the antagonism of the regime's critics. In 1884 a left-leaning National Assembly passed the Loi Ferry, which established free elementary schools for all children. This may not seem like a controversial act, but it was enacted in large part to undermine the influence of the church by teaching republican and anticlerical positions to the young. Indeed, it is often said that the schoolteacher and the priest were the two most important—and antagonistic—political figures in most French villages and towns.

Later, the Left took its revenge after the Dreyfus scandal ended. During the first decade of the twentieth century, it outlawed some of the main teaching orders, including the Jesuits. Then, in 1905, it passed a law disestablishing the Catholic Church thereby formally separating church and state.

These and other ideological divisions also had an indirect effect that ultimately led to the collapse of the Third Republic. Because there were so many political parties with so many different points of view, it was hard for Third Republic governments to enact public policies that might have helped modernize the economy and, then, in the 1930s, confront a rearmed and aggressive Nazi Germany. So, when Germany attacked in 1940, France fell in a matter of weeks and the **Chamber of Deputies** voted to end the Third Republic and create the **Vichy regime**, which collaborated with the Nazi occupiers.

However, an obscure general, Charles de Gaulle, called on the French to defy the Germans and Vichy and continue the war. Gradually, the Resistance grew and played a major role in defeating the Germans, generating a new generation of potential leaders in the process. There was new hope for democracy when the French Resistance and Allied troops forced the Germans out in 1944.

After two years of a **provisional government**, the politicians ended up adopting a constitution very much like that of the Third Republic. Knowing that the **Fourth Republic** would then lapse into traditional ways of doing things, de Gaulle resigned the prime ministry. Although few people in France opposed democracy, per se, the Gaullists and others on the right and the Communists on the left opposed the Fourth Republic and, among them, routinely won a third of the vote. The Fourth Republic suffered from the same kind of stalemate in policymaking as the Third (discussed in more detail in the next chapter) before it was put out of its political misery in 1958.

The Industrial Revolution

The **Industrial Revolution**, the final transformation, began while France was still struggling with the conflicts over religion and democracy. Prior to the late eighteenth century, most people lived on the land, and most manufactured goods were made in small workshops owned by skilled artisans. In the eighteenth and early nineteenth centuries, the ability to make machines and harness more and cheaper energy made it possible for businessmen in the United States and Great Britain to begin mass production in factories.

The Industrial Revolution that followed had two main effects for our purposes. First, it ushered in modern capitalism and generated unprecedented wealth for the owners of those new businesses, who became a political force in their own right. Second, it turned the growing number of men and women who worked in the new factories into little more than "cogs in the machine." Their mounting frustration and anger led many of them to create labor unions and to back socialist parties, which sought a more equal distribution of that wealth and the political power that came with it.

Democracy

France adopted the first declaration of human rights and was the first country to give all men the right to vote (although women only gained the suffrage after World War II). However, it did not achieve a widely supported and stable democracy anywhere near as quickly or as easily as the United States or Great Britain.

In the United States and Britain, democracy developed more gradually over the course of the late eighteenth and nineteenth centuries. Both countries had their share of conflict along the way, including the Civil War in the United States. However, it is safe to say that by 1900 neither country faced much opposition from groups that would abolish democratic rule. One reason for that was that they were both able to reach broad agreements on each of Lipset and Rokkan's four transformations before they had to deal with the next.

Germany, of course, had an even harder time than France in establishing a secure democratic regime. There are many reasons for that, one of the most important of which is the link between the nationalism that grew out of the difficulties in creating a German state and the rise of Hitler and the Nazi Party.

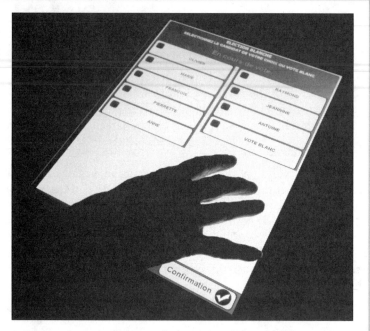

In France, as in the United States, long-standing democratic institutions, such as voting, meet twenty-first-century technology. In this photo, Nicole Rivoire, the mayor of Noisy-le-Sec, demonstrates an electronic touch screen voting machine in time for the 2007 presidential elections. The machines were used in eighty-two voting districts.

France did not industrialize as quickly as Germany, Great Britain, or the United States. The rise of modern capitalism divided the French deeply nonetheless. Not only did it split France in two, but each camp—Left and Right alike—itself was divided.

France was one of the first countries to develop a large socialist movement. During the last half of the nineteenth century, just about all socialists were revolutionaries, although they were divided into many different factions with sharply different ideologies and strategies. By the end of the century, most had become supporters of the ideas developed by Karl Marx and Friedrich Engels.

At about the same time, some socialists, often called social democrats or revisionists, began to argue that they could achieve their goals through reform rather than revolution by winning a parliamentary majority and enacting radical legislation. The revolutionaries and reformers were able to coexist in a single party, the **French Section of the Workers' International** (**SFIO**), until the Bolshevik revolution brought Marxists to power in Russia, the first time socialists had ever won control of a country. On Christmas 1920, most of the radicals broke away to form a new party, the French Communist Party (PCF), both to bring revolution to France and to support the new and struggling Soviet Union.

The capitalist camp was split as well. Some supported the kind of laissez-faire, free market version of capitalism that most Americans, in particular, assume is the only way such an economy could or should be run. Others, however, drew on the French dirigiste tradition and thought the state should play a major role in managing the economy. Until the end of World War II, this division was not as important as the one in the working class, because, in practice, most right-of-center politicians were more interested in sustaining France's traditional economy based on small businesses and farms. It did, however, become extremely important during the provisional government from 1944 to 1946 and again during the first quarter century of the Fifth Republic, because the Gaullists drew on the dirigiste tradition in, as the general put it, "marrying France to its century."

The Traditional Syndrome

This history of overlapping conflicts affected all parts of French political life.[3] Together, they produced a political syndrome that plagued the Third and Fourth Republics and was the backdrop against which de Gaulle conceived of his very different regime. Like a medical syndrome, this political one was an interconnected series of "maladies" that operated like a vicious circle on the dysfunctional system discussed in Chapter 1. As suggested in Figure 3.1, it had five main components.

The Industrial Revolution

The Industrial Revolution divided all European states. Until the rise of Hitler, Germany had strong social democratic and Communist parties. Capitalists who favored a free market had been less influential than business leaders, who believed in using the state to spur and secure economic growth ever since the forced industrialization of the late nineteenth century.

That has not been the case in the Anglo-American democracies. Great Britain has had a strong Labour party, but Marxists have never had much of an impact. Similarly, the dominant Conservative party has by no means been as dirigiste as the Gaullists, but it had never been an outspoken advocate of market practices until Margaret Thatcher became prime minister in 1979.

The United States has never had a strong socialist movement. At its peak, the Socialist Party won slightly under one million votes. More important, free market capitalism is the only economic model with any significant support in American political culture.

While French factories produce cars, precision tools, and aircraft, a significant portion of French industry is devoted to luxury goods—wine, perfume, and high fashion—that utilize pre-industrial hand finishing processes. Here, a worker in the Louis Vuitton factory puts the finishing touches on one of many leather handbags to be sold to celebrities and wealthy clients.

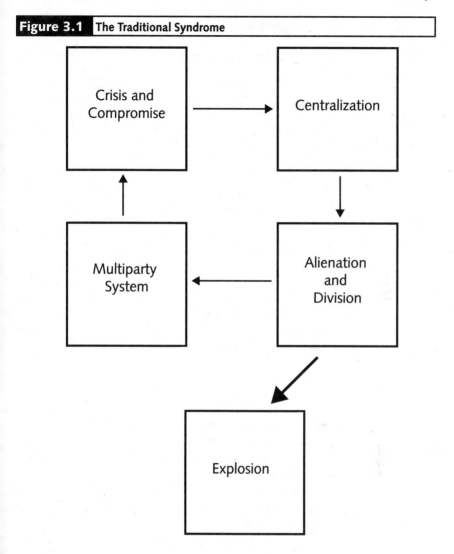

Figure 3.1 The Traditional Syndrome

The Multiparty System

Because France never reached anything approaching a consensus on three of the four transformations and the issues they raised, it had a large number of "political families" and, in turn, political parties. With the exception of the Communists, French political parties were as decentralized and undisciplined as those in the United States, not the well-organized machines one found at the time in Great Britain.

The exact number and nature of the parties changed dramatically from year to year. However, the situation after the 1951 legislative elections is typical enough to provide a general picture of the problems the multiparty

Table 3.2	Legislative Election Results, 1951
Party	Seats
Communists (PCF)	102
Socialists (SFIO)	106
Radical Socialists	75
Democratic and Socialist Union of the Resistance (UDSR)	16
Christian Democrats (MRP)	87
Independents and Peasants (CNIP)	95
Gaullists (RPF)	120

system posed. Six parties won between 75 and 120 seats each. Other small groups had a handful of representatives in the Chamber of Deputies (see Table 3.2).

On the far left were the Communists. As noted earlier, they had split off from the SFIO in 1920. Of all the Communist parties in western Europe, the PCF was the closest to (and someone would say most dominated by) the Soviet Union. Its members were by no means all well-informed, committed Marxists. Instead, the PCF got the bulk of its support from the working class, where anger and frustration with the capitalists was widespread. The Communists had also played a major role in the resistance against German occupation and had been in the cabinet from 1944 to 1947, until Cold War tensions made them unacceptable to the mainstream parties and to France's powerful ally, the United States.

Next came the SFIO, the reformist Social Party. There was no love lost between the PCF and SFIO. The Socialists were still bitter about the PCF's behavior in the 1920s and 1930s, when it attacked the SFIO as viciously as the "bourgeois" parties. Meanwhile, the SFIO itself was beginning to shed its remaining radical views and members and become a party used to being in the government both at the national and the local level.

After the SFIO, it becomes harder to array the parties on a single left-right continuum. It is jokingly said that the Radical-Socialists (as that party was officially known) was neither. It had been radical before the Industrial Revolution, when to be on the left meant being for the republic and being anticlerical. The term "Socialist" had been added for what we would today call public relations purposes when the party was formally created in 1901. In fact, most **Radicals** (as they were commonly known) were local notables who were ferociously anticlerical and procapitalist.

The **Mouvement républicain populaire (MRP)** was one of the Christian Democratic parties that emerged after World War II in most European countries with a substantial Catholic population. Many progressive Catholics had participated in the Resistance against the Germans and sought their own political outlet after the war. The party, of course, was strongly proclerical. Otherwise, it took positions that ranged from the center left to the center right on social and economic issues. As the 1950s wore on, the MRP turned more conservative, although it would never move as far to the right as its Italian or German counterparts.

The **National Center for Independents and Peasants (CNIP)** was made up of a loose grouping of local notables, very few of whom were either independents or peasants. Most did represent rural areas. Most, too, were pro-clerical and conservative on social and economic issues. In other words, unlike the Radicals or the MRP, the Independents and Peasants (also sometimes called the Moderates) were unambiguously to the right of center.

The **Rally of the French People (RPF)** was a new party created by de Gaulle's supporters after the general resigned the prime ministry when the Fourth Republic was created. The Gaullists were opposed to the Fourth Republic, and some critics saw them as the inheritors of the Bonapartist tradition that preferred strong and even authoritarian leadership to a democracy. Officially, de Gaulle was retired and writing his memoirs at his country home at Colombey-les-deux-églises. In fact, he was very active politically, using his weekly trips to Paris to take verbal potshots at the republic he despised because it was so weak (see the next chapter).

Crisis and Compromise

France used a fairly standard version of the British-style parliamentary system under both the Third and Fourth Republics. Between elections, prime ministers and their cabinets remained in office as long as they retained the support of a majority of the members of the Chamber of Deputies on critical votes of confidence.

Under the Fifth Republic, France has normally had such a parliamentary majority. However, it never did during the Third and Fourth Republics.

As shown in Table 3.2, a typical parliament had six or more parties with a roughly equal number of seats, three or four of which would be needed to form a majority. Given their ideological differences, that would be difficult under the best of circumstances. However, at times, as in 1951, there were parties that either refused to join a coalition (the Gaullists) or that would not have been accepted by the other parties (the Communists).

That meant that the parties of the center left and center right were critical to the creation of any government. Tiny parties like the Union of Democrats and Socialists for the Resistance (UDSR) or the handful of members who represented France's colonies typically held the balance of power.

To make matters even more complicated, the Radicals and the Moderates, in particular, were filled with notoriously ill-disciplined and ambitious politicians. Some of them would be willing to sabotage a colleague's cabinet on the assumption that they would get a better post in the next government or the one after that.

A not very useful habit developed that Philip M. Williams labeled **crisis and compromise**. A government would be formed to address a particular issue regarding, say, economic policy but bring together politicians who disagreed

Maigret chez le ministre

The famed mystery writer Georges Simenon wrote seventy-five novels and twenty-eight short stories about the Parisian detective Inspector Maigret (Simenon was Belgian and wrote between sixty and seventy pages a day). Only one dealt with politics, *Maigret chez le ministre*.[a]

Simenon never mentions any political party by name, and his disdain for politicians leaps from every page. It is must reading for anyone interested in Fourth Republic political life, as are his other novels, and in French society before the return of de Gaulle.

Note: Published in English as *Maigret and the Calame Report* (New York: Harcourt, Brace, Jovanovich, 1969).

sharply on another area, such as aid to parochial schools. Politicians usually tried to avoid dealing with controversial issues (which, of course, also happened to be the most important ones). As Williams put it of Henri Queuille, a perpetual minister who served briefly as premier, "Queuille believed that the art of statesmanship is to postpone issues until they are no longer relevant."[4] But once an issue from some area they disagreed about had to be addressed, the government fell. The Chamber of Deputies rarely passed a vote of no confidence; the fatally weakened government resigned before it legally had to.

That cabinet crisis would be followed by an often lengthy period of negotiations that finally led to a compromise that allowed the next cabinet to be formed. The typical cabinet lasted about nine months; the interim period averaged six weeks.

In most parliamentary systems, the prime minister or president can dissolve the legislature and call for new elections at almost any time. President MacMahon had done that in 1877 in the hope of having a royalist majority win so that the monarchy could be restored. Instead, republicans won a decisive victory and were so incensed by the president's actions that they established an informal rule that the Chamber of Deputies would never be dissolved or premature elections held. To make certain that was the case, the members of the Chamber and the Senate, which formed an electoral college to choose the president, normally opted for a senior politician with no remaining ambitions or controversial views. As Georges Clemenceau (later to be become president himself) once put it in stating how he had voted, "I always vote for the stupidest."

France was in the midst of one of those government crises when the Fourth Republic collapsed, discussed in more detail in the next chapter. From 1954 on, the most vexing issue facing France was the rebellion in Algeria. As opposition to the use of torture and other policies grew, the mainstream parties were split between factions that wanted to prosecute the war with full vigor and those that wanted to negotiate with the rebels.

That made it impossible to form a strong government when France needed one most. For the first two-thirds of 1957, Radical prime minister Maurice Bourges-Manoury conducted discrete, informal negotiations with the Arabs but was then defeated when the white settlers threatened demonstrations to protest the talks. It took five weeks before the politicians could agree on another Radical, Félix Gaillard, who took office at the head of an even weaker government on November 5. He resigned on April 15, 1958, following the air force's controversial bombing of a rebel base in neighboring Tunisia. Four weeks later, it seemed likely that the little-known MRP deputy, Pierre Pflimlin, would get the job next because he was prepared to negotiate with the Arabs. On the night of May 12–13, the white settlers and dissident officers staged a coup in Algiers and prepared to move on to France itself. Gaillard's caretaker government was in no position to stop them.

The Third and Fourth Republics did not always teeter on the brink of disaster. However, even during periods of relative calm, the repeated crises and compromises did not lend themselves to effective policymaking. The Chamber elected in 1951 seems to have spent more time debating peasants' right to distill liquor than what their colonial, foreign, or economic policy should be.

To make matters worse yet, the mainstream politicians did actually agree on one thing—what France should not do. In the terms of eminent Harvard professor Stanley Hoffmann, the dominant politicians agreed on a "republican synthesis" to prop up a "stalemate society."[5] They accepted French society as it was and saw no need to modernize a country still dominated by its agricultural sector and small towns. To the degree that industry was created and urban areas grew, little of the needed infrastructure of schools, homes, or roads followed. This was especially true during the Third Republic and was one of the reasons why France lost so quickly and so decisively when Germany attacked.

Centralization

In the absence of effective parliamentary institutions, what power there was devolved to the centralized bureaucracy. The top civil servants of the *grands corps* were recruited, then as now, largely from the Parisian upper middle class. Before the formation of the ENA in 1946 and the revolution in bureaucratic culture it sparked, the civil servants shared the politicians' lack of enthusiasm for social and economic change, because their friends and relatives were the people getting rich from France's inefficient businesses.

Even more important than the impact of centralization on policymaking was its effect on the society as a whole. Education policy was made in Paris. Students studied under a uniform curriculum in schools whose main job was to prepare them to take national exams, which alone determined if a student passed or failed. Similarly, the prefect ran departments and most towns and cities as if they were his personal fiefdom. Prefects were discouraged from

developing close ties with people under their jurisdiction and were transferred every two or three years so that those ties could not develop.

In addition, the civil service was run on the basis of explicit and extremely
rigid rules. Instead of exercising the discretion and flexibility Americans expect from their civil servants, the French bureaucrats seemed to mechani-
cally apply rules that had been invented for every imaginable turn of events.

In sum, the extreme centralization posed three problems. First, it stifled
innovation in both policymaking and implementation. Second, as the soci-
ologist Michel Crozier put it, the state loomed as a massive metaphorical
stone wall that citizens felt they bumped their head against all the time.[6] Finally, it led to a cynical kind of irresponsibility in which civil servants and
citizens alike found illegal or immoral ways of getting around the bureaucracy and its rules if they wanted to get anything accomplished.

An Alienated Culture

The first three components of the syndrome had a lot to do with the fourth—
an alienated political culture. I cannot describe the French political culture
with much precision before the 1960s. Public opinion polling was only introduced in the late 1930s, and few pollsters asked questions that probed the
kind of basic values and assumptions that make up a political culture.

Before the advent of modern survey research, the conventional wisdom
was that the French were more interested in politics and more divided ideologically than the mass publics of most other democracies. Path-breaking research in the 1960s showed that, in fact, they were not noticeably more
engaged than the Americans, the British, or the Germans. Some polls
showed that as many as a third of the population were part of what political
scientists called "the swamp" (le marais), because they were so ill informed.
French voters were also less likely than their counterparts to identify with a
political party. In 1956 a study of men drafted into the army showed that far
more knew who won the Tour de France bicycle race that year than who was
prime minister. However, politically active people did have more consistent
and more polarized views on issues at least than Americans did.[7]

The cultural problems extended beyond ideological division. In France
today, most people think the Fifth Republic is a legitimate regime. They may
want to change some of its institutions and practices, but few serious politicians or analysts advocate abandoning it in favor of a new form of government altogether. That was not the case under the Third and Fourth
Republics, when opposition to a given government or on a single divisive
issue often turned into demands to do away with the republic altogether.

Just as important for our purposes was a widespread and deep sense of
alienation felt by French men and women of all ideological stripes. Again,
we do not have enough polling data to document that alienation with any
precision. However, nonquantitative research by anthropologists and others
showed a France in which many people were "defensive individualists,"
who tried to protect themselves and their families from others, including the

state. People often referred to politicians disparagingly, using the third-person impersonal pronoun, *on*, usually with a sneer.

Explosion

The combination of the ideological divisions, ineffectual government, centralization, and alienation was a political powder keg. For understandable reasons, few people felt they could effectively work to redress their grievances within the party and parliamentary systems. Similarly, the bureaucrats did not seem to be open to legitimate input from below. As Crozier put it, this **bureaucratic phenomenon** led people to get ever more angry and frustrated, because the system never got at the root cause of any problem.

Eventually, they could not take the frustration any longer and exploded, giving rise to the massive waves of strikes and protests that have been such a prominent feature in French history since the days of the Revolution. Like everything else in the system, these explosions did little but let people vent their fury, because the system always returned to crisis and compromise.

But if Crozier and others are right, these were not just political patterns but served as a paradigm for all social relations. For example, the shift from repressed anger to explosion was common in the schools. If students felt that their teacher was doing a good job in preparing them for the exams, they grudgingly accepted a classroom experience they loathed. If, however, the students felt a teacher was not doing a good job, it was a different story altogether. In that case they might engage in a wild demonstration called a *chahut* (probably derived from the words for screaming cat), which political scientist William Schonfeld graphically described:

> Students might constantly talk with one another, get up and walk around the room whenever they feel like it, and if the teacher should call on them to respond to a question, they would answer disrespectfully—e.g., Teacher: "When you mix two atoms of hydrogen with one atom of oxygen, what do you get?" Pupil: "It rains," or "merde." Or the students might jeer at the teacher in unison, call him nasty names and run around the classroom. In certain classes, wet wads of paper will be thrown across the room, landing and then sticking on the wall behind the teacher's desk. Or there might be a fistfight, with the winner ejecting the loser from the room, while the other pupils stand around cheering for one or the other of the pugilists. With some teachers, the students might bring small glass sulfur bombs into class, which would be simultaneously broken, creating such a stench that the teacher is usually driven into the hall while the pupils stay in class, happily suffering the odor. Finally, students might bring a tent, camping equipment, and food into their class and, during the lesson, set up the tent, prepare lunch for each other, and then eat it—the teacher being powerless to help.[8]

Conclusion

As the years wore on, the costs of maintaining politics as usual kept mounting. The Third and Fourth Republics were certainly regimes whose legitimacy and effectiveness were sapped by the vicious circle of the traditional syndrome. They were systems that, under the best of circumstances, produced only incremental change and often were not able to do that much.

Key Concepts

alienation   48
anticlericals   35
bureaucratic phenomenon   49
crisis and compromise   45
democracy   35
Industrial Revolution   39

Key People, Entities, and Events

Bonaparte, Louis-Napoléon   37
Bonaparte, Napoléon   37
Chamber of Deputies   39
Declaration of the Rights of Man   37
Dreyfus Affair   38
Fourth Republic   39
French Section of the Workers' International (SFIO)   41
Louis XIV   32
Mouvement républicain populaire (MRP)   44
National Center for Independents and Peasants(CNIP)   45
provisional government   39
Radicals   44
Rally of the French People (RPF)   45
Third Republic   38
Vichy regime   39

Questions for Discussion

1. France had a difficult time developing a democracy—or any other kind of stable regime—between 1789 and 1958. Why do you think that was the case?

2. How did the problems outlined in the discussion of the traditional syndrome complicate political life and make the Third Republic "the form of government that divided us the least?"

3. How did France's difficulties from the Revolution onward contribute to its growing weakness internationally?

4

History II
The Fifth Republic

The many overlapping themes in Chapter 3 made it too difficult to present the material in chronological order. This chapter has only one theme—the development of what I call normal politics in Chapter 1. This chapter, then, is presented chronologically through an exploration of the five men who have served as president and what happened during their terms in office.

De Gaulle: Routinizing Charisma

After the Liberation, few leading postwar politicians wanted to return to the disgraced crisis and compromise of the Third Republic, and no one seemed to want the disgraced politicians of the 1930s to return either. But a series of decisions eerily reminiscent of those made when the Third Republic itself was created led to exactly that.

The Unlamented Death of the Fourth Republic

Charles de Gaulle wanted a new republic with a strong executive. In his first radio appeal calling on the French people to resist the German occupation and the Vichy regime, he had blamed the collapse of the Third Republic on the divided parties and resulting weak leadership of the 1930s. The inability of parliamentary leaders to act consistently and coherently had been one of the main reasons the French had not rearmed and otherwise prepared for the German invasion. His first act on returning to France as soon as the Allied victory in Normandy was secure in June 1944 was to give a speech in Bayeux in which he called for a "national arbiter" who would be the personification of France and the national will and who would be able to rise above the partisan fray, forge the unity that had been so tragically missing in the 1930s, and restore France's lost grandeur.

The Communists, Socialists, and the new parties and politicians who emerged from the Resistance wanted to go in exactly the opposite direction. They agreed that a constituent assembly should be elected (with women voting for the first time) as soon as possible after the Liberation. In the elections held that October the parties most involved in the Resistance received just over half the vote and an overwhelming majority of the seats. However, de Gaulle was the unquestioned leader and everyone assumed that he would remain prime minister. By the beginning of 1946 it was clear to de Gaulle that what he called "the regime of political parties" had returned, and he abruptly resigned at the beginning of a cabinet meeting on January 20, 1946.

The Communists and Socialists then forced through a draft constitution that abolished the presidency and the Senate. The MRP opposed it, and the draft was defeated in a referendum in May. Another constituent assembly was elected that June and wrote another new constitution that shared the key characteristics (and many would say flaws) of the Third Republic—the lower house would have all the key powers and could not be dissolved. It was approved in a referendum, and the Fourth Republic came into existence on December 21, 1946.

The Fourth Republic was not an abject disaster. Along with the provisional government, it was responsible for a speedy recovery from the wartime destruction, the creation of the **National Planning Commission,** and the introduction of an extensive social service system, all of which are discussed in later chapters.

However, the Fourth Republic soon developed the same problems as the Third. The Communists, Socialists, and MRP kept their progressive "tripartite" coalition together until the Cold War began in earnest. It fell apart in 1948, after which, none of the other parties would even consider including Communists in a governing coalition. The Socialists and MRP had to turn to the political parties and politicians that had been such a problem before 1940. Their task became even more difficult after the Gaullists formed their own political party to contest the 1951 election and subsequently refused to participate in governments.

The past repeated itself. Twenty-one prime ministers came and went in less than twelve years, returning France to a political life in which no government could govern effectively.

As was the case with the Third Republic, foreign policy failures were to be the downfall of the Fourth. This time, however, the disasters started far from home. Unlike the United Kingdom, Fourth Republic France did everything it could to hold on to its colonial empire in Asia, Africa, and the Caribbean.

The first crisis occurred in **Indochina** (today's Vietnam, Laos, and Cambodia). The Japanese had seized the peninsula during World War II, and a strong nationalist resistance led by Ho Chi Minh developed among the Vietnamese against the occupation. After the Japanese defeat, the French reoccupied the colony instead of granting it independence.

Now, Ho and his Viet Minh had to resist the French. Meanwhile, the nationalist movement turned Communist, which made Vietnam a battleground in the Cold War as well as in its struggle for independence from colonial rule. A full-scale war broke out between French troops (aided by the United States) and the Viet Minh. It culminated in a disastrous French defeat in 1954 at **Dien Bien Phu**. French troops withdrew, and a peace conference was held that divided Indochina into separate independent countries.

Rebellions in France's North African colonies broke out almost immediately after the withdrawal from Indochina. The wars did little to convince most politicians that trying to hold on to the remaining colonies was a losing battle.

The most important of these wars occurred in **Algeria**. Algeria was crucial because it was home to about a million white people from France and Italy who had settled there after France took control of the country in 1830. As a result, many French citizens and politicians considered it an integral part of France.

Not surprisingly, France was ill-disposed to grant independence to Algeria when the **National Liberation Front (FLN)** took up arms in 1954. Instead, the French forces responded with brutality, including the use of torture against women as well as combatants.

Once it became clear that at least some politicians were prepared to negotiate with the FLN, the *colons*, or settlers, took to the streets as well. In short, Paris faced two opposing revolutions, one from the FLN, which wanted Algerian independence, and the other from the white minority, which insisted on Algeria's remaining French.

As noted earlier, the nomination of Pierre Pflimlin to be prime minister brought the army into the political debate. On the night of May 12–13, 1958, the settlers and the army took power in Algiers and ten days later seized the island of Corsica, a French possession off the coast of Italy. Rumors swirled that the paratroopers were preparing to attack the mainland.

De Gaulle played an ambiguous role in these events. One of his operatives went to Algeria and was in close contact with the Committee of Public Safety, set up by the rebellious officers. At least one of the leaders, General Raoul Salan, called for de Gaulle's return to power, and that quickly became a goal supported by most of the settlers. As the crisis deepened, a growing number of deputies came to the conclusion that de Gaulle was their only alternative to a military coup.

The general did not act quickly. Before Pflimlin's nomination, he had refused President René Coty's request to form a government. He continued to bide his time as the crisis deepened and made it clear that he would assume the prime ministry only if he were granted extraordinary power to rule by decree for a period of up to six months, during which he would draft a series of constitutional amendments. The leading mainstream politicians agreed at the end of May, and de Gaulle was elected prime minister on June 1, 1958, by a vote of 329 to 224 (see Table 4.1).

Table 4.1	Key Events in French Politics, 1944–2007
Date	Event
1944	Liberation
1946	Fourth Republic created, De Gaulle resigns
1958	Fifth Republic created
1968	"Events" of May and June occur
1969	De Gaulle resigns
1981	Mitterrand elected
1995	Chirac elected
2007	Sarkozy elected

De Gaulle and Charisma

Before continuing the narrative, it is important to understand just what Charles de Gaulle was like. He was born in Lille in northeastern France on November 22, 1890. His father taught philosophy and literature at a Jesuit high school, and young Charles took an early interest in history, which turned into a powerful sense of duty to his beloved France.

De Gaulle first lived out that commitment to serve his country through the military. He graduated from the military academy at Saint-Cyr and immediately joined an infantry unit. In 1916, during World War I, he was wounded and captured and spent the rest of the war in a prisoner-of-war camp, where he wrote his first book.

During the 1920s and early 1930s he held a number of positions on military staffs, served in the Rhineland and in Lebanon, and taught at Saint-Cyr. During the 1930s, he wrote three books urging France to modernize its army and became well known as a reformer within military circles, although his ideas were rejected by most soldiers and politicians.

At the outbreak of World War II, he was a colonel and was shortly promoted to brigadier general. On June 6, 1940, Paul Ramadier, one of the few politicians who agreed with de Gaulle, appointed him under secretary of state for war.

Eleven days later, when it became clear that Marshal Philippe Pétain would become prime minister and surrender to the Germans, de Gaulle left for London to rally support for the beleaguered France. The next day, he made his first radio address to the French people on the BBC. Over the course of the next four years, he became the symbolic head of a growing resistance movement both inside and outside of the country. When his troops helped the Allies liberate France in the summer of 1944, he was the obvious choice to become head of the provisional government.

De Gaulle was a complicated man. He was reserved and rarely showed emotions in public, except toward his retarded daughter. His haughty, aloof manner led many to dislike him personally and not trust him politically. But whatever his faults, it was clear that he was a person of integrity who stood for his principles even at the darkest hours of the war.

Some found him power hungry and manipulative. He certainly was stubborn and hard to work with, which drove President Franklin D. Roosevelt to distraction during the war. But, if he was power hungry and manipulative, it was to further his goals for France rather than to enhance his personal power and prestige.

Some questioned his commitment to democracy. His desire to use the referendum, have a directly elected president, and curb the powers of parliament flew in the face of French republican traditions. Doubts were also cast about his commitment to democracy because of his family background and military career. Nonetheless, de Gaulle never wavered from his commitment to a government chosen through direct election.

De Gaulle was a **charismatic leader** in the way Max Weber originally used the term, if not in the way it is loosely used today. For Weber, charisma is:

> the authority of the exceptional and personal *gift of grace* the entirely personal devotion to and confidence in revelations, heroism, or other qualities of leadership in an individual. This is "charismatic" rule as exercised by the prophet or, in the domain of politics, by the chosen war lord, the plebiscitarian ruler, the great demagogue, or the leader of a political party.[1]

In that sense, de Gaulle was definitely an exceptional, charismatic leader whose authority was qualitatively different from that of the vast majority of other politicians. As is the case with all such leaders, his charisma lay in a hard-to-pin-down mix of his ideas and the force of his personality.

But de Gaulle was also an unusually successful charismatic leader. During the Third and Fourth Republics France had a tradition of turning to what Stanley Hoffmann called **heroic leaders** when the country faced a particularly difficult crisis. The politicians would temporarily abandon crisis-and-compromise politics and turn to a strong leader, who was given the authority to deal with the problem at hand. They had most recently done so in 1954 when Pierre Mendès-France was made prime minister to shepherd France through a peace process following the debacle at Dien Bien Phu. But Mendès-France, like all the heroic leaders before him, was not given the opportunity to make his exceptional leadership the norm. As soon as the crisis was over, he was forced to resign—just like any other prime minister.

De Gaulle, however, was adept at conventional politics and was able to take advantage of the unusual circumstances that brought him back to power. As discussed in more detail in Chapter 7, he did not simply revise the constitution, he rewrote it, giving rise to an entirely new Fifth Republic. Among other things, it strengthened the power of the president and prime minister at the expense of the lower house of the parliament, now known as the National Assembly. De Gaulle did not get everything he wanted. He could not persuade the other politicians to accept a directly elected president

Charisma

The impact of de Gaulle's unusual form of charismatic leadership can perhaps best be seen through two comparisons, one with France's neighbor Italy, the other with China, some eight thousand miles away.

In the 1950s, Italy also had a fragmented party system and rotating prime ministers, although all of them came from the Christian Democratic Party. In part because it had no leader of de Gaulle's stature, Italy's instability continued well into the 1990s before the Christian Democrats imploded. Since then, Silvio Berlusconi (prime minister until his defeat in the 2006 election) has been the dominant force in Italian politics, but given his personal hunger for power and the scandals that have touched his business and political life, no one would confuse him with de Gaulle.

Even more important, France is one of the few countries in which a charismatic figure left an institutional legacy and a base of political support that allowed more "normal" politicians to rule effectively after the original leader left the scene. Contrast that with China. Mao Zedong was at least as charismatic as de Gaulle until the last decade of his life, when he allowed his personal vanity and political views to undermine most state and party organizations during the Great Proletarian Cultural Revolution, which left the country in chaos and at times seemed to put the very existence of the Communist regime in jeopardy.

In this photo, charismatic leader and World War II hero Charles de Gaulle greets supporters. Perhaps his greatest achievement as president was the way in which de Gaulle was able to convert his popular support into support for the regime and institutions of the newly minted Fifth Republic, despite the turbulence of the 1960s, the crises in Algeria and Indochina, and the student unrest of 1968.

and had to accept one chosen by an electoral college of more than 80,000 elected officials. Still, it was not a tough choice for the outgoing prime minister of the Fourth Republic to become the first president of the Fifth Republic which was, after all, his creation.

And he used the powers the new constitution gave him.

The constitution allowed him to name a prime minister and cabinet members, who did not have to be members of parliament (MPs). In a snub to the deputies, he appointed the main author of the constitution, **Michel Debré**, to be the prime minister. Debré was neither an MP nor a member of the political class that had dominated the Fourth Republic. Debré's career was completely dependent on de Gaulle's. Four years later, de Gaulle dismissed Debré, marking the first time since the 1870s that a president removed a prime minister.

The constitution allowed the president and prime minister to send certain types of legislation directly to the people in a referendum, a power de Gaulle often used throughout his decade in office. He used it first to settle the Algerian dispute. Shortly after taking office, he went to Algeria and announced, "je vous ai compris" (I have understood you). Most white Algerians took that as evidence that he supported the cause of French Algeria. In fact, de Gaulle soon started talks with the FLN aimed at granting the colony independence. Knowing he could not get legislation authorizing the talks, let alone approving independence for Algeria, through the parliament, de Gaulle held referenda instead. As he would do throughout the 1960s, de Gaulle turned each referendum into a vote on his rule in general by insisting that he would resign if the "yes" vote was not overwhelming, a tactic many critics said threatened democracy.

Finally, de Gaulle did something else no president had done since the 1870s—he dissolved parliament and forced early elections. As noted in Chapter 1, de Gaulle was nearly killed in an assassination attempt in 1962. He then went to the people and informed them of something they already knew. His successor would not have his extraordinary power or authority. Therefore, he was scheduling a referendum that would authorize the direct election of the president so that his successors would have the broadest possible popular mandate as a substitute for his charisma.

The mainstream politicians balked. Recall that Louis-Napoléon Bonaparte, the only other president who had been popularly elected, used his election as a springboard for creating the Second Empire. Many Fourth Republic politicians thought that de Gaulle's tactics, including the use of referenda, were too much like those of the Bonapartes and thus put democracy in jeopardy. Indeed, the Constitutional Court ruled that the referendum violated the provisions under which one could be held.

De Gaulle responded by dissolving the parliament and holding the referendum anyway. He won both the referendum and the legislative elections and, then, added insult to injury by naming **Georges Pompidou**, who had never even run for elected office, to succeed Debré at the Hôtel Matignon, the official residence of the prime minister.

In so doing, de Gaulle avoided a mistake made by most dynamic leaders who fail, in Weber's terms, to routinize their charisma. They do not make provisions for the succession to the next, more "normal" generation of politicians. In this case, de Gaulle did so in three ways. First, he gave the next president new powers, most notably the support that comes from direct election. Second, he made it clear through his own actions that even though the constitution was ambiguous about the exact powers of the president (again, see Chapter 7), the presidency was to be the dominant institution in the new republic. Finally, by identifying the new regime with himself, he was able, in essence, to convert some of his own popularity into support for the regime itself.

It was a good thing he did so, because after 1962 de Gaulle turned out to be anything but an effective, let alone a charismatic, leader. He was forced into a runoff against Mitterrand in the 1965 presidential election when the little-known Jean Lecanuet denied him a majority on the first ballot. Then, a candidate of the Left, which agreed to support the single candidate mostly likely to win on the second ballot, came close to winning the legislative elections two years later.

De Gaulle's stiffest challenge came with the protest and strike waves of May and June 1968, which are covered in more detail in the next chapter. He was initially caught off guard and proved unable to stop the growth of the movement until it had paralyzed the country. Eventually, he was able to bring it to a halt, but only by soliciting the support of the generals who had tried to overthrow him because of Algeria and by invoking public fear of a Communist takeover. Once he did seize the initiative and dissolve parliament, his supporters won an overwhelming majority in the new Assembly. However, it was now clear that France could be governed without de Gaulle and could perhaps be governed better without him.

His career ended less than a year later. In April 1969, De Gaulle called for a referendum on minor constitutional changes. As he had in all previous referenda, he announced that he would resign if the French did not back him overwhelmingly. Instead, they defeated the referendum by a narrow margin.

De Gaulle resigned the next day.

In his ten years in office, de Gaulle accomplished a lot. Nothing he did had a greater impact than the system that grew during his term and a half as president. After 1968, all talk of the need for fundamental constitutional reform or a new republic disappeared.

In 1971, for instance, Rice University's John Ambler found that only 5 percent of those included in a typical poll believed that the system needed major change. Similarly, he found that the average Fifth Republic prime minister had the support of 59 percent of the people compared with only 31 percent under the Fourth Republic. As important, two-thirds of the electorate believed that "the people who govern" pay attention to average people.[2]

Pompidou and Giscard: Steps toward Normality

De Gaulle was right. His successors did not have his massive popular support and the authority that came with it. In fact, the dour and taciturn Pompidou, who was elected president in 1969, had no charisma at all. See Table 1.1.

Perhaps as a result, Pompidou and his somewhat more popular successors presided over a country in which politics became more and more routine and the stakes of political life decreased.

Pompidou (1911–1974) did not set out to have a political career. He was educated at the École normale supérieure, a school that trains people to be university professors, which the young Pompidou became in the late 1930s. Although an early supporter of European integration, he was not politically active during World War II. He entered political life after the Liberation as de Gaulle's personal secretary, and when the general resigned the prime ministry, his young protégé took a position with the Rothschilds' investment bank.

De Gaulle named him prime minister after he fired Debré in 1962. At that time, Pompidou was still a political neophyte. Surprisingly, the poet turned banker became a top-notch politician. More than anyone, he was responsible for the creation of the Gaullist political party (see Chapter 6), which has been the most powerful force of the Center Right since the 1960s.

The only major policy change under Pompidou involved Europe. Because he was more pro-European than the general, he refused to veto requests by Denmark, Great Britain, Ireland, and Norway to join the European Economic Community.

As president, Pompidou retained most of de Gaulle's domestic priorities. He continued de Gaulle's commitment to rapid economic growth and modernization. And, since the first generation of ENArques were reaching the peaks of their careers, he appointed ever more civil servants, both current and former ones, to top jobs.

It is impossible to tell how much more would have changed under his presidency had he served a full term. Unfortunately, he contracted cancer in 1973 and died the next year.

There was no obvious orthodox Gaullist to succeed Pompidou. The former prime minister Jacques Chaban-Delmas ended up as the candidate of the official Gaullist party. But he was outvoted by more than two to one in the first round by the far more popular and telegenic **Valéry Giscard d'Estaing** (1926–). Giscard then beat Mitterrand by a mere 0.4 percent of the vote on the second ballot.

Some observers thought that Giscard, would restore a degree of the charisma that Pompidou had lacked.[3] Born in Germany to a prominent political and intellectual family, he was almost a generation younger than Pompidou. He was a graduate of both the ENA and the École polytechnique, the second most prestigious grande école. The young Giscard was first elected to parliament in 1956 and led a small group of centrist politicians who rallied to the Gaullist camp in 1962, providing it with enough seats to form the first stable parliamentary majority in French history.

The thirty-six-year-old Giscard was rewarded with one of the top jobs in French politics, head of the Ministry of Finance. Although squarely to the right of center, Giscard developed a reputation as a reformer, most notably with the publication of his book *French Democracy*, which called for the opening up of the stalled society and its bureaucracy, discussed in Chapter 3.

As president, Giscard at first gave signs that he would continue as a reformer. He met with immigrant garbage collectors at the Élysée Palace and blocked construction of an expressway along the left bank of the Seine. Both acts were symbolically important to the veteran activists of 1968. He also dramatically raised the minimum wage and pensions and oversaw passage of France's first capital gains tax.

But most observers do not consider his presidency to have been a success. Giscard took office just as the impact of the OPEC oil embargo reached its peak. During the first thirty years after World War II, referred to as *les trente glorieuses*, economic growth had averaged over 5 percent per year. During Giscard's presidency, it dropped to about 2 percent.

His term in office thus coincided with France's first postwar recession. More was involved than just the statistics associated with an economic downturn. Critics on the left, in particular, worried about *la crise*, as they dubbed the economic malaise that gripped the country.

To make matters worse, his government faced its share of scandals. Many political figures close to Giscard and Pompidou were implicated in real estate speculation schemes in Paris and other major cities. Giscard accepted a gift of diamonds from the corrupt and dictatorial Emperor Bokassa of the Central African Empire (now the Central African Republic).

In short, whatever their personal strengths or weaknesses, both Pompidou and Giscard were more conventional politicians than de Gaulle because circumstances required that of them. That was especially true of Giscard, whose presidency coincided with the most serious economic downturn in postwar history.

One anecdote sums up the situation. By the late 1970s, Giscard and his prime minister, Raymond Barre, were desperate to come up with anything that would spur economic growth. As a result, they fell for an absurd scam presented to them by a con man into which they invested a few million francs from the public treasury. He claimed that he had invented an *avion renifleur*, literally a sniffing airplane that could detect underground deposits of oil and natural gas. Of course, it didn't work.

Mitterrand: The U-Turn

The turn toward more normal politics was even more evident under Mitterrand, at least after the first two years of his first term.

The Right maintained its parliamentary majority in 1978 only because the Communists and Socialists could not re-create the electoral alliance that had almost brought them to power in 1973 and 1974. By the time Giscard's term was over in 1981, it was the Right that was internally divided. Both Giscard and Chirac, his former prime minister, ran a bitter campaign against each other on the first ballot. Even though Giscard actually outpolled Mitterrand, the Left as a whole got slightly more votes than the Right. More important, Mitterrand did far better than the Communist Georges Marchais, who quickly joined the left-wing bandwagon to support Mitterrand on the second ballot, which Mitterrand then won by about 3 percentage points. Mitterrand immediately dissolved the National Assembly. This time, the Socialists won a majority of the seats, the first time a single party had ever done so. Although it did not need to, it gave the much weakened Communist Party four cabinet posts in the new government.

No one expected Mitterrand's presidency to mark an even greater turn toward normal politics. He came to office with an ambitious plan for a "rupture with capitalism" to "regain the domestic market" from imports. Mitterrand always had a reputation for being an opportunist and an elitist, and many observers doubt just how committed he ever was to socialism. Nonetheless, his Socialist and Communist colleagues were committed to nationalizing industries, reducing the number of hours in the workweek, redistributing wealth, decentralizing the state, and more.

Furthermore, his victory marked the first real transition in power away from the Gaullists in the twenty-three years since the Fifth Republic was created. Most political scientists think such transitions are vital for building support for new democratic regimes. In regard to France, however, there were few concerns about the stability of the Fifth Republic's institutions. After all, Mitterrand himself, who had once been a staunch opponent of the new republic, now made it abundantly clear that he planned to make use of all the presidential powers available to him.

Four things, however, forced Mitterrand and his Socialist colleagues to adopt a more moderate approach to governing.

First, they were going against an important global trend. Between 1979 and 1982, Britain, Germany, and the United States all elected conservative leaders who were interested in giving new life to the private sector, not nationalizing more industries. Meanwhile, the international financial markets were struggling in the aftermath of the second OPEC oil shock following the Islamic revolution in Iran in 1979. France had to borrow a lot of money to pay for the government's expensive programs. By 1982 interest rates reached 20 percent. Minister of Finance **Jacques Delors** (1925–), convinced Mitterrand that he had to abandon his most radical and ambitious programs. The

François Mitterrand

François Mitterrand was born in 1916 in Jarnac, a small town in southwestern France. His family was wealthy, conservative, and Catholic. The young Mitterrand studied political science and law in Paris beginning in 1934.

His early political career is clouded in mystery. There are reports that he joined many of his fellow law students in attending demonstrations led by Fascists and royalists in the 1930s. He was a civil servant in the collaborationist Vichy regime for much of World War II, although he always claimed he was secretly working for the Resistance at the same time. After the war, he formed a small political party that sought to attract former members of the Resistance of all political stripes. He was a regular member of Fourth Republic cabinets and was widely viewed as an opportunist with few political principles, to the point that he apparently staged an assassination attempt on his own life to try to bolster support.

A very different Mitterrand emerged in the Fifth Republic. He was one of the firs prominent politicians to oppose de Gaulle and call for a unified Left to defeat the general, which he came close to doing in the 1965 presidential election. Six years later, he took over the moribund Socialist Party, moved it dramatically toward the Left, and turned it into the most dynamic force in French politics at the time.

After two failed attempts, Mitterrand was finally elected president in 1981 and was reelected seven years later. His plan to introduce radical economic reforms foundered in the wake of the downturn of the early 1980s. For the rest of his presidency, Mitterrand tried to govern as a leader who stood above the partisan fray. In the late 1980s he was diagnosed with prostate cancer and was barely able to function during the last three years of his second term.

When he died, in 1996, his wife, his mistress, and his illegitimate daughter all attended his funeral.

government then engaged in a political U-turn, which left it unwilling and unable to continue its rupture with capitalism.

Second, in 1986, something that Debré's team of constitution writers apparently did not anticipate happened. Because presidents then served seven-year terms, whereas the National Assembly served only five, eventually one party or coalition would control the presidency while its opposition had a majority in parliament. Until 1981, no one had really had to worry about this situation, because the Right won every election. Then, in 1981, Mitterrand dissolved the Assembly, thus avoiding the problem when the Socialists won the ensuing election.

By 1986, however, the Socialists' support had plummeted. Elections had to be held. The Socialist Party (PS) adopted a new electoral law (see Chapter 6) to minimize its losses. Nonetheless, the Socialists suffered a crushing defeat, losing fully a quarter of their seats.

France was going to be stuck with cohabitation for at least the two years Mitterrand had left in his term. According to the constitution, the president of the republic nominates the prime minister, whose government has to retain the support of a majority in the Assembly (see Chapter 7). The ever-wily president could have tried to appoint an independent technocrat. Instead, he named Jacques Chirac (1932–), his most serious rival and head of the Gaullist Rally for the Republic.

During the next two years, Chirac repealed some of the Socialists' reforms, including reprivatizing many of the industries the government had taken over. Meanwhile, Mitterrand portrayed himself as "president of all the French" in much the way de Gaulle claimed he did.

Mitterrand succeeded by winning 54 percent of the vote in his second ballot contest with Chirac in 1988. As he had done in 1981, he dissolved the Assembly, and new elections were held. The Socialists and their allies won a plurality of the seats, but could not govern on their own as they had from 1981 to 1986. Mitterrand and the three prime ministers who served during the next five years endorsed the policy of not pushing for more nationalizations or privatizations, thus taking the most controversial issue of the 1980s off the political agenda.

The third blow to Mitterrand's approach to governing came about because Mitterrand's image was damaged. Serious allegations about his cooperation with the Vichy regime, which collaborated with the Germans during World War II, surfaced. More important, a number of scandals involved people quite close to him. Former prime minister Laurent Fabius, for instance, was accused of negligence in allowing HIV-tainted blood into the health system. Former defense minister and sitting president of the Constitutional Council, Roland Dumas, was accused and later found guilty of taking hundreds of thousands of francs in bribes.

Finally, Mitterrand was old and ill. When he ran for reelection in 1988, he was seventy-two years old. More important, he knew he was suffering from cancer, although his illness was rarely discussed in public. The first rumors surfaced in the early 1990s, and by the time legislative elections occurred in 1993, he was obviously very ill, which undoubtedly contributed to a surge in support for the Right, which ushered in two more years of cohabitation. This time Mitterrand chose the less dynamic Gaullist Édouard Balladur to be prime minister. He was clearly a lame duck president. Mitterrand died less than a year after leaving office.

Chirac: From Normal to Banal

Jacques Chirac's two terms as president were remarkable only because they were so much like Mitterrand's second one. That is, perhaps, not very surprising for three overlapping reasons.

First, France went back into a period of cohabitation for the last five years of his first *septennat*, or seven-year term. Chirac and his prime minister, Alain Juppé, called legislative elections a year early in 1997 in part because of economic hardships they anticipated as France prepared to adopt the euro. Whatever their hopes, the decision was a disaster. The Socialists, led by Lionel Jospin, won a convincing victory.

Second, the ideological distance between the Left and the Right had narrowed considerably. Chirac, for instance, objected to the Socialists' goal of creating hundreds of thousands of new jobs by reducing the workweek to thirty-five hours. The Gaullists also opposed an intriguing new law that requires that women make up half of all candidates in contested elections using proportional representation (see Chapter 7). But the parties largely agreed on the major economic issues, including the elimination of nationalizations and the need to reduce the costs of France's extensive social service system.

The final and perhaps the most important reason for both the continuity and dissatisfaction with both coalitions was that France was being governed by politicians who had been around for a long time and were, frankly, thought by many to have run out of ideas. Chirac, for instance, had been a fixture on the political scene since 1963.

The 2002 elections changed things considerably, however. For the first time, presidential and parliamentary elections were both scheduled to be held at almost exactly the same time that spring. After considerable wrangling, the party leaders agreed to hold the presidential elections in late April and May with the legislative ballots to follow six weeks later.

Almost all observers expected the race to be a rerun of 1995 with Jospin and Chirac facing off against each other on the second ballot. A record sixteen candidates ran on the first ballot, very few of whom had a chance of winning even 10 percent of the vote.

As the campaign progressed, the voters deserted the major candidates in droves. When the first ballot votes were counted, one of the pollsters' predictions held true. Chirac came in first but with less than 20 percent of the vote. The pollsters got the more important part of the first ballot wrong, however, since Le Pen edged Jospin out for second place and the right to run against Chirac in the decisive round of voting.

Jospin resigned as prime minister the day after the first ballot, and Chirac appointed the little known senator Jean-Pierre Raffarin as interim prime minister to head a caretaker government that would stay in office through the legislative elections in June. The demoralized Socialists mounted a lackluster campaign. Parties loyal to Chirac won almost 400 of the 577 seats, whereas many leading Socialists were defeated, including Martine Aubry, whom many expected to succeed Jospin as head of the PS. The National Front held on to much of its vote from the presidential election, but because the center-right parties refused to cooperate with it on the second ballot, it did not win a single seat. Chirac then appointed Raffarin to a full term as prime minister, and all the signs pointed to the Right's being able to hold on to power for the full five years of the presidential and parliamentary terms (the presidential term was reduced from seven to five years as the result of a constitutional amendment passed in 2000; the amendment took effect with the 2002 election).

However, the landslide did not translate into an effective government. The newly renamed **Union for a Popular Movement** should have been able to pass sweeping reforms. In late June 2002, Raffarin introduced his plans for the next five years. They included proposals to decentralize more power to regions and departments, introduce a degree of privatization to state monopolies, and slow down the move toward the thirty-five-hour workweek. Nonetheless, the shift back to total control by the Gaullists almost certainly led to less change than there was in the United States, for instance, following the narrow victory by George W. Bush in 2000.

The Center Right's sweeping victories in 2002 have not continued in local and regional elections, nor have public opinion polls reflected such popularity since then. Raffarin proved to be an ineffectual prime minister who could neither stimulate the economy nor mute protests, especially over a new law that forbids students to wear overtly religious symbols to school, including Muslim headscarves.

When the Gaullists lost badly in the 2004 regional elections, Chirac reshuffled his cabinet and replaced Raffarin with **Dominique de Villepin,** who had been foreign minister during the tumultuous and discordant period before the start of the Iraq war the year before. Although de Villepin is often criticized for his role in that debate by people in the United States and the United Kingdom, he was widely seen as a rising star who, along with **Nicolas Sarkozy,** had the inside track for the Gaullist presidential nomination in 2007. However, de Villepin fared little better than his predecessor. He could do little to stop a violent wave of demonstrations by Muslim youth in 2005 and took most of the blame for the failed bill that would have allowed employers to fire anyone under twenty-six who had been on the job for less than two years.

Neither Gaullist government did much to improve the three policy areas that were at the top of most people's list of key issues—unemployment, education, and health care costs.

Meanwhile, the new Socialist leader François Hollande gave the party new energy and led it effectively in local and regional elections after 2002. In 2005 and 2006, he was eclipsed in the polls by his partner (they had been together for many years and have four children), **Ségolène Royal,** who was chosen to be the Socialist candidate in 2007.

The Next Generation

The 2007 elections brought about dramatic changes in France. Most of its leading politicians passed from the political scene. Younger politicians replaced them, including some who were not drawn from the Parisian elite, which has dominated French politics since de Gaulle's return to power.

Those politicians will have more than their share of difficult problems to deal with, only some of which can be anticipated today, such as dealing with the country's growing diversity or its accelerating integration into a more

Normal Politics

People tend to find high drama in their own country's political life: the Florida re-count, the turmoil inside the Labour Party resulting from Prime Minister Blair's decision to join the invasion of Iraq, the election of the first East German to be chancellor of the Federal Republic.

In fact, the stakes of politics are not all that high in any stable democracy, however passionate and heated the debate may become at any given moment. That's the case because almost everyone understands and accepts the fact that alternation in power from one side to the other is normal, despite how unhappy any of us might be with the team in power. We also understand and accept that our regime—the rules of the game—are good enough and are not likely to change substantially for the foreseeable future.

That was not true in France in 1958 or 1968. Twenty-three years passed before the Gaullists lost an election. Since then, French politics has been characterized with transitions in power as smooth as those from Clinton to Bush, Major to Blair, or Schröder to Merkel.

Normal politics.

Plus ça change.... The front-running candidates in the hotly contested 2007 presidential election—the Socialist Ségolène Royal and the conservative Nicolas Sarkozy—get ready to face off in the only televised debate of the 2007 elections, an event that drew an audience of more than 20 million viewers. The two candidates represented very different agendas and directions for France.

unified Europe. That said, we should not expect dramatic departures from the policies and procedures we have seen in the last thirty years or so— French political life has developed routines that are too deeply ingrained and widely accepted for that. The options that President Sarkozy and his team have to address are considered in the conclusion of the book.

Key Concepts

Key People, Entities, and Events

Questions for Discussion

1. No western democracy has had an easy time in the last fifty years. But compared with your country, does French political life seem more filled with conflict or less? Why or why not?

2. Few democracies have had a leader as influential as Charles de Gaulle. Why do you think that someone of his stature emerged in France rather than in any of the other European countries?

3. No leader after de Gaulle had his charisma. Yet, each successive president ruled effectively. Why was that the case?

5

Political Culture and Participation

This chapter and the next explores how the French people think and act politically. It starts with a discussion of how the French have become ever more like their counterparts in other industrial democracies in the nearly half century since the creation of the Fifth Republic. But it also examines the complicated world of French political parties and elections, which is in some ways very different from what we find in other democracies.

Political Culture

The first and perhaps most important area to consider is French political culture. As noted in Chapter 1, any country's political culture can be thought of in two main ways:

- The values and assumptions that people have toward the institutions and enduring issues in political life that shape the way people think, leading them to rule out certain options and lean toward adopting others

- The impact of history on the way average citizens think and act politically

French political culture is particularly important because it has changed so much in the last forty years. As pointed out earlier, French political culture under the Third and Fourth Republics was characterized by alienation and ideological divisions, which contributed mightily to the political crises that ultimately destroyed both republics.

Discussed here is how and why the culture changed.

Social scientists learn about a country's political culture primarily by conducting in-depth surveys of a representative sample of adults that tap what they think and why they think that way, and anthropologists, in particular, spend time doing "participant observation," in which they live in a community and build on the informal contacts they develop and conversations they engage in to paint a picture of those values.

Each type of study has its strengths and weaknesses. Public opinion surveys give a more accurate image of what the society is like, but the nature of both face-to-face and telephone polling means that the interviewers can only scratch the surface of people's belief systems. The anthropological approach yields "deeper" and more nuanced conclusions, but it is all but impossible to extrapolate from a handful of interviews done in a handful of communities to a country as a whole.

In fact, it's not necessary to explore these competing methodologies in any more depth, since neither of them has yielded much data. France was not one of the countries included in the classic civic culture study in 1959, which pioneered survey-based approaches to political culture. Italy was included instead, because the study's authors, Gabriel Almond and Sidney Verba, believed that because France was going through a regime change, responses to their questionnaires would tap far more than just enduring cultural values. A few political scientists did include some of the questions developed in that study in their research in the 1960s and 1970s, but the questions have largely been dropped from the work of the major polling agencies since then. Similarly, a number of social scientists did anthropological studies in rural France during those same years, but there has been little of that type of research in recent years.

Cultural Change

That said, French culture has changed dramatically under the Fifth Republic. And that is unusual.

It is one of the axioms of social science that cultures change slowly. That is hardly surprising, since the **agents of political socialization** tend to reflect the continuing impact of political tradition. In France, these include the family, which in almost every society tends to pass on values, ranging from party identification to basic ideological preferences, from one generation to the next. Much the same is true of school and church. To be sure, the two institutions imparted different values over the last two centuries, but those they did promote reflected long-standing definitions of what it meant to be on the left and the right. Finally, the French media did little to change preexisting values. The national radio network (France had little television before 1958) was largely apolitical, and people who read newspapers chose those that largely reinforced their political views.

Nonetheless, there are times when political cultures do change relatively quickly. That was the case in France after 1958, as it was in Germany after World War II or in South Africa following Nelson Mandela's release after twenty-seven years in prison.

First, there are now few open opponents of the regime and none in any of the major political parties or interest groups. That was not the case in the early years of the Fifth Republic, when such prominent politicians as François Mitterrand and Pierre Mendès-France wrote books about the need to move on to a sixth. However, since the late 1960s or early 1970s, polls have consistently shown that at least three-quarters of the population accept the basic institutions and operating principles of de Gaulle's republic. That consensus holds for some policy areas, including the broad contours of foreign and economic policy. What's more, the consensus in support of the republic has held firm even during the hardest economic times following the OPEC oil embargo in 1973–1974 and the long-standing slump of the 1980s and 1990s.

Although the evidence is skimpy, it seems to be the case that attitudes toward the republic do not carry the ideological baggage of earlier regimes. Thus, before 1958, being for a republic meant favoring a strong legislature and weak executive and the separation of church and state. Today, by contrast, republicanism has a far broader and more inclusive meaning that anyone who supports basic democratic principles (for example, one person one vote, competitive elections, basic freedoms) can endorse.

The single best indicator we have of that can be seen in Table 5.1, which presents responses to the same question asked by the French Society for Public Opinion Research (SOFRES) on four occasions between 1978 and 2000. Although directly comparable data from other countries are not available and although this question is "harder" to answer yes to than many used in such studies, it does show the steady growth in support for the Fifth Republic, if not for democracy in general.

Second, there has been a significant reduction in ideological differences and political tension. To be sure, the Fifth Republic has seen one of the largest protest movements of all time—the events of May and June 1968—which seemed to threaten the very existence of the republic. However, within a few years of the "events," support for anything approximating revolutionary change on the part of the Far Left had evaporated. More recent polls have shown that most people cluster around the Center, Center Left, and Center Right, whereas fewer and fewer take positions on either extreme. Indeed, surveys from the 1990s show a declining number of people who think that the very terms "left" and "right" hold any meaning whatsoever.

Third, moderation and the acceptance of the regime have been particularly pronounced among two groups whose doubts about democracy plagued the Third and Fourth Republics. Observers probably read too much into the support given to the Communist Party and its affiliated trade union, the General Confederation of French Labor (CGT), after World War II. Few supporters were well-informed Marxists, and far fewer were revolutionaries. Instead, the PCF tapped into a subculture in which many workers were more generally alienated from mainstream French society and politics. But as they began to benefit from the newfound prosperity and the appeal of

Table 5.1	Support for the Fifth Republic, 1978–2000	
Year	Functioned well (%)	Not functioned well (%)
1978	56	27
1983	57	25
1992	61	32
2000	71	21

Notes: Nonresponses excluded.

SOFRES (the French Society for Public Opinion Research) asked the following question in national surveys a number of times: "The Constitution of the Fifth Republic went into effect in 1958. If you had to render a judgment on how its institutions have functioned since then, would you say that they have functioned well or not functioned well?"

Source: Adapted from Olivier Duhamel, "Confiance institutionnelle et defiance politique: la démocratie française," in *L'état de l'opinion 2001*, ed. Olivier Duhamel and Philippe Méchet (Paris: Editions du Seuil, 2001), 75.

communism faded, more and more workers became part of the broad-based support for the regime, even if they had initially opposed de Gaulle's return to power. Much the same is true of devout Catholics, many of whom had rallied to the anti-Republican movements of the 1930s. They found it easier to endorse the new regime, which had been created by a devout Catholic whose symbol, the Lorraine Cross, was clearly patterned after the Roman Catholic one.

Even more important, the number of workers and Catholics has declined precipitously. One poll conducted to study the 1997 parliamentary elections discovered that only 22 percent of the population could be considered working class. The same survey found that just 16 percent of the population still called themselves "regularly practicing Catholics," and only 10 percent attended Mass weekly. More than a third of the people who were born before 1920 described themselves as regularly practicing Catholics, whereas only 6 percent of those born after 1970 did.

Fourth, it may just be that the political culture actually did not change all that much. The conventional wisdom has it that the French were highly politicized and deeply divided when de Gaulle returned to power. The large number of demonstrations with antiregime overtones and the stridency of the partisan press certainly reinforced that belief. However, in 1958, in the first in-depth survey conducted in France, the political scientists Philip Converse and Georges Dupeux discovered that the French were no more "politicized" than their American counterparts.[1]

Beforehand, there was ample reason to think that the French were more divided and contentious. After all, the country had just gone through the twin rebellions in Algeria and had barely avoided a military coup. By contrast, the United States was in the midst of one of the most tranquil periods in its history, when most people seemed to be more interested in "making it" than making political waves.

From that perspective, the Converse and Dupeux data were quite startling. The French were only slightly more likely to have belonged to a political organization or to have attended political rallies. Contrary to general expectations, they were less likely than Americans to have tried to persuade others how to cast their vote. More than twice as many Americans regularly read a newspaper. When the researchers combined responses on attitudes toward a range of issues, they found that the French were not more polarized than the Americans.

Later research confirmed that the French were not more politically engaged than other Western electorates. As many as a third of the voters were part of what some French pollsters called le marais (literally, the swamp), who placed themselves in the middle of the left-right spectrum largely because they did not have clear positions on any major political issues.

As will be seen shortly, the French are by no means in agreement on every issue, nor have unruly protests disappeared from the political scene. However, the admittedly indirect evidence available suggests that they have developed one important set of values that they share with citizens in just about every stable liberal democracy, including support for the rule of law.

On the one hand, many people remain frustrated about the government's stances on issues ranging from European integration to the quality of health care they receive. And a significant proportion of those dismayed men and women will take to the streets to vent their anger and try to change public policy.

On the other hand, such dissatisfaction with specific public policies rarely—if ever—spills over into demands for a new republic or other constitutional order. It is as if the vast majority of French citizens have drawn an invisible line in their heads. Although everyone believes it is perfectly legitimate to question the policies and proposals of a given government or party, they have come to view the regime as effective and legitimate, and protesters no longer see a need to turn their unhappiness into opposition to it. It is, of course, perfectly legal to call for a Sixth Republic or the restoration of the monarchy. The point is that such demands have lost almost all of their political appeal, and people who make them are now consigned to the political fringes, very much unlike the situation before 1958.

In the most comprehensive book on public culture and participation in industrial democracies, the University of California at Irvine's Russell Dalton finds a mixed pattern.[2] French men and women were more to the left on some political issues and protested more in some ways. However, in regard to national pride, they fall right in the middle of the citizens in the thirteen countries Dalton studied. Ninety-five percent of them approved of democracy, and more than three-quarters agreed that democracy was the best form of government. When all is said and done, the French were typical of the electorates with whom they are most frequently compared.

Why Did It Happen? Political Chickens and Eggs

In their path-breaking study of political culture, Almond and Verba joined many of their contemporaries in stressing how belief in democracy, a sense of political efficacy, and other values are needed to sustain a liberal regime. And, more than forty years of further research around the world has only confirmed that they identified an important causal connection.

However, the situation in France and many other countries suggests that the picture is far more complicated and that the "causal arrows" operate in both directions. All the evidence suggests that most French voters have *in principle* supported democracy in one form or another much of the time since at least the beginning of the twentieth century. There have been periods, most notably the 1930s and 1940s, when antidemocratic sentiments grew. Nonetheless, the number of Fascists on the far right and antidemocratic Marxists on the left never approached a majority of the population.

Although we do not have the kind of evidence we would like, it may well be that the success of democracy under the Fifth Republic helped cause the kind of culture Almond and Verba assumed was needed to give rise to democracy in the first place.

Taking into account, again, the huge holes in the evidence, it is likely that several of those broader political changes discussed in Chapter 4 had an impact on French political culture. The first change in this respect lies in the behavior of the Fifth Republic's two most influential politicians—de Gaulle and Mitterrand. During de Gaulle's eleven years in power, he succeeded in convincing most right-wing voters that a return to the old parliamentary-based republic would inevitably lead to a return to the chaos of earlier years. Then, Mitterrand, after taking over the Socialist Party in 1971, led the party to power by presenting himself as a politician who could use the levers the new republic gave its president to aid the working class and the Left in general. In short, people from virtually every subculture came to the conclusion that the system worked well enough to warrant their approval.

Many scholars also argue that the social and economic changes discussed in Chapter 2 also contributed to cultural change. Note that it would be hard to document this impact even if good data were available, since few people are aware of how social and economic changes contributed to their adoption of new values. Put in the simplest terms, urbanization, improved standard of living, and the spread of a mass popular culture have made the French increasingly like each other, including politically. This is especially true among people under forty-five or fifty who have lived their entire lives in the modern, affluent, globally open France. And, again, although many individuals may not have consciously made these calculations, there was a widespread sense that the new republic had played a major role in creating the "new France" in the first place.

Culture and Democracy

In the Bush administration's arguments for invading Iraq and toppling the Saddam Hussein regime, you would have heard one rationale that suggested that Iraqis freed from totalitarian rule would immediately flock to democracy.

The historical record—including that of France—suggests otherwise. Of course, there are Iraqis who relish a democratic future for their country. But if we look at countries as different as Germany, India, and Japan, strong and all but unshakeable support for democracy only grew gradually after signs that the regime could govern and provide tangible results to its citizens. The same is almost certainly true of France, where a democratic culture took centuries to firmly take root and then only after the successes of the Fifth Republic.

The Communist Party is alive and well and still attracting supporters in France. Young attendees of the annual Communist Party fair in 2004 sit under a banner proclaiming that Karl Marx is not dead.

Continuing Divisions

We should not paint too placid a picture of public opinion in France. The public and politicians may have shed any desire for revolution or regime change. However, as in any country, that does not mean that there is a lack of conflict on specific policy issues or the positions of political parties and individual candidates, especially at election time.

But here, too, there have been important changes. The first set we will consider is in keeping with the broader cultural shifts discussed above. The second, however, shows new areas of contentious and deeply rooted conflict, even if the disputes are not likely to expand into regime-threatening violence.

Left and Right. France is the country in which the terms "Left" and "Right" were first used. They emerged during the first years after the storming of the Bastille in 1789, when deputies in the National Assembly who favored the most radical change sat on the left side of the chamber, and those who wanted to retain and, later, restore, the monarchy sat to their right.

Since then, the connotation of the two terms has changed. As noted in Chapter 3, during the nineteenth century, being on the left meant supporting democracy, free market capitalism, and the separation of church and state. In the twentieth century, support for the working class, socialism, and more egalitarian social policy was added to the definition of the Left. Opposition to these goals led people and parties to be classified as on the right.

Thus, as discussed in more detail in the rest of this chapter, practicing Catholics, the upper classes, and the self-employed have traditionally voted overwhelming for the Right, and anticlericals, members of the working class, and public sector employees have cast their ballots disproportionately for the Left.

Given the social changes discussed in Chapter 2, these issues and the traditional definition of left and right have become less and less important to most French citizens, especially younger people. A person's self-location on the left-right scale, class affiliation, and degree of religious practice are still among the most powerful predictors of how he or she will vote. Nonetheless, tensions surrounding these issues and their very centrality in French political life have declined considerably since the 1960s.

The most systematic recent polling about the left-right cleavage shows that well over 90 percent of French voters are willing and able to identify themselves as being either on the left or right or in the center. However, that self-placement is only weakly correlated with positions on key issues facing France.

Postindustrial Issues. One of the reasons that the left-right division may be less important today than it was a generation ago is that the issues that most divide the French have little to do with the positions traditionally taken by the major parties.

Some issues have actually contributed to the diminished importance of left and right as traditionally defined and to the fragmentation of the party system since the "big four" of two left-wing and two right-wing parties (to be discussed in the next chapter) have not done a particularly good job of addressing them. I only touch on them briefly here, because they are all dealt with in considerable depth in the rest of this chapter and the next one.

Environmentalism. When I was studying the French Far Left in the early 1970s, I would never have predicted that the environment would become a major issue. But, as in most of Europe, it has become so. Not only do people recycle and "buy green" more than ever before, environmentalism has spawned a number of green political parties, the most important of which are now part of the political mainstream. Few people oppose protecting the environment. Thus, the very conservative city of Caen in Normandy turned its downtown into a pedestrian mall, expanded its already copious parkland, and beautified the banks along the Orne River. To be sure, the municipal leaders of Caen were more interested in business opportunities than the more politicized Greens would have been, but their policies reflect the fact that environmentalism in its various forms is here to stay. The one difference between the Left and the Right is the speed at which the leftist groups want to implement environmental reforms and regulations.

Race. This is potentially the most explosive issue in France today. As we have already seen, France is much more racially diverse than it was even twenty years ago. And as discussed shortly, anger toward and fear about the new immigrants and their children spawned the National Front. The Socialists have publicly opposed racism, but to the degree that such opposition has been real, it has come from independent organizations such as SOS-Racisme. It should also be pointed out that the racism of the twenty-first century is not the same as the anti-Semitism or fascism of the 1930s. It by no means threatens the regime, but it has attracted a significant number of people who used to be on the left (see Chapter 6).

Europe. What France's role in Europe should be divides public opinion in ways that also splinter the traditional Left and Right. In some ways, the debate over Europe overlaps with that over race. However, as seen in the referenda on the Maastricht Treaty in 1992, to be discussed in detail in Chapter 9, and on the European Constitution in 2005, leading politicians on both the Left and the Right were to be found in each camp. What's more, the closeness of the two votes shows a more even split in attitudes toward European integration.

Globalization. To average citizens, globalization is probably the least important of these issues. However, for elites such as business executives and public intellectuals, it is important and has provoked more opposition than in any other country. To some degree, there are concerns about how global trends will threaten the independence of the French economy. However, more people are probably concerned about its potential effect on French culture. Much of it comes from people on the left, many associated with the Greens. But there are also conservatives, including a former cabinet minister, who are just as fearful and critical. To cite but one example, a French author published a book on French and American culture and argued that the French had a lot to learn from American culture; he was roundly criticized from all sides.

Participation beyond the Ballot Box

Voting is the most important political act most citizens engage in because it determines who will be in power. For most citizens, it is the only thing they do politically. However, many citizens also participate in two other and, sometimes, overlapping ways.

Protest

A Country of Demonstrators. The conventional wisdom among both academics as well as mass media pundits is that the French take to the streets often and do so with more venom and more danger to the regime than other Western populations. To be sure, there have been times when popular protests did seem to put the regime—let alone the government of the day—in jeopardy.

But that is no longer the case. As the vast majority of French people came to accept the Fifth Republic as legitimate, protests increasingly concentrated on specific issues alone.

1968 and Its Diminishing Impact. The events of May 1968 were discussed in Chapters 1 and 4 as one of the most important turning points in French political life. At the time, many observers (including this author), thought they opened the door to a rebirth and redefinition of a radical Left that could, yet again, transform political life in France.

As also noted earlier, we were wrong.

There is no denying the size or importance of the month-long wave of protests. Somewhere between 6 million and 8 million people participated. France was the only country where trade unions and their members joined radical students in the streets. Together, they paralyzed the country for more than two weeks.

That there were protests in France should come as no surprise. This was the height of the 1960s New Left, which was inspired by a number of issues in every country. However, for France, like the United States, Vietnam was an important part of the mix.

Political Protest

Comparative research has begun to suggest that over the last century or so, French protests have not been all that different from those in other countries, at least as far as their real or potential impact on the regime is concerned.

Still, protests in France are not the same as they are in other countries either. They are more colorful, and their leaders probably call people to stage protests more often.

The United States actually sees far larger protests, as during the civil rights movement or the run up to the war in Iraq. Generally, though, demonstrations in the United States or Great Britain are much calmer. The Rally to Save Darfur in summer 2006 drew close to 100,000 people who wanted to take a stand for a place most Americans could not find on a map, but it felt more like a picnic than a protest.

A young woman dons the classical robes, the tri-colored ribbon, and the Phrygian cap of Marianne, the symbol of the French Republic at a 2006 protest in Toulouse against the job contract law, which sent thousands of students and young people into the streets to protest.

But just as important were political issues growing out of a decade of heavy-handed Gaullist rule, or so the protesters thought. Indeed, it was the seemingly brutal response to relatively minor protests that initially brought the students support from both the unions and many middle-class voters, especially those in Paris who watched events unfold from their apartment windows.

Whatever the exact mix of causes, the massive wave of protests topped anything that occurred in the other democracies, including the United States, which was by far the most deeply involved in Vietnam. And many of the millions who participated in the marches and strikes called for drastic reforms, including **autogestion**, a form of self-managed socialism.

What matters here is that there were limits to how far the overwhelming majority of the protesters were willing to go. I watched the events from afar as a leader of student protests on my American campus who was also taking his first course in European politics with a very conservative professor—one of the three people to whom this book is dedicated. I thought some sort of nonviolent revolution or, at least regime change, was possible.

What I discovered four years later when I interviewed activists in the most prominent political group to emerge from the "events" was that they all assumed that autogestion and the other sweeping reforms they proposed could be enacted through the existing institutions of the Fifth Republic.

In other words, even the most left-wing people in France had drawn a psychological barrier that accepted the regime as legitimate, albeit run by the wrong people who had the wrong priorities.

Protest Today. Almost forty years have passed since May 1968. France still has more than its share of protests, most of which reflect the issues raised in the section on postindustrial divisions above. Students, railroad engineers, fishing boat crews, airport staff, and many others have struck and protested, occasionally disrupting life for millions for a day or so. However, the protests have never come close to reaching either the size or the impact of those of 1968.

In fact, there have been so many protest movements over the last four decades that it is all but impossible to document or even categorize them all. Two from 2005 and 2006 should suffice to illustrate the point made about 1968.

First, for a decade or more, the unemployment rate for young people has hovered around 20 percent. It is much higher among minorities. Frustration is particularly pronounced among men and women of North African origin, some of whom are third-generation French citizens.

During the summer of 2005, two young men of North African origin were accidentally killed while trying to escape from the police. Because the deaths occurred during France's vacation period, when nothing political of any sort normally occurs, nothing much happened until the fall.

But that September, when police stopped to check the identification of a group of teenagers in the poor, Parisian working-class suburb of Clichy-sous-Bois, that frustration boiled over. A spontaneous demonstration that really should be called a riot broke out the next night. A few cars were burned, and twenty-seven young people were arrested. The day after, twenty-nine cars were burned, and fourteen more rioters were taken into custody.

Then the protests spread to almost every part of the country that had a significant North African population. By the time the protests died out in mid-November, almost 9,000 cars had been burned and almost 3,000 young people arrested.

Second, early that year, the government introduced a bill for the First Employment Contract (CPE). It would allow employers to hire young workers at a below-standard wage while permitting them to fire those employees with relative ease. In short, the young workers would not enjoy the extensive social benefits available to their elder colleagues.

Needless to say, young people were not enamored of the proposed law. Protests mounted. On March 13, 2006, as the bill was nearing final consideration in the National Assembly, rallies were held in all of France's large cities. The organizers said a million people showed up; the authorities put the figure at closer to 500,000. The protesters could not stop passage of the bill, which President Chirac signed into law at the end of that month. In so doing, however, he did call on the parliament to pass a new version of the law that would soften its provisions, for instance, by limiting the probationary period to one year.

The protests against the CPE were far more typical of the kind of "inside the system" dissent than the riots of 2005. Very few protest movements in recent years have been violent. Very few have been spontaneous explosions like those in the impoverished suburbs that surround almost every French city.

Interest Groups

In one of the first attempts to come up with concepts for comparative politics as a whole, Gabriel Almond and his colleagues distinguished between interest articulation and aggregation. The former was the province of **interest groups,** or organizations that defended and promoted the positions of a relatively limited segment of the population. The latter involved organizations—mostly political parties—that had the desire and the capacity to compete for control of the government as a whole. The topic of the next chapter is political parties and elections, the key "aggregating" institutions. Here, the text focuses on interest groups, which, in France, often serve to channel the frustrations discussed in the preceding paragraphs.

Like most advanced industrial democracies, France has a wide range of interest groups. Some are local, such as the Citizens of Caen, which tries to rally support from residents of the city who are concerned that its urban renewal policies benefit only the wealthy. Some are national, such as SOS-Racisme, which has helped organize opposition to racism for more than two decades.

As with protest movements, it would not be possible to cover all of them in a book such as this. Therefore, only the two types of interest groups that have had the most impact during the Fifth Republic so far are discussed: trade unions and big business.

Labor. Trade unions have been the major organizations representing the interests of the working class since the mid-nineteenth century. Many have had close ties with left-wing parties, but most have concentrated their own efforts on improving the wages, working conditions, and benefits of their members.

France is unusual in that it has a fragmented trade union movement. In addition to the unions, discussed here, that try to organize the traditional working class, there are equivalent bodies for farmers, upper-level managers, and students. Four labor groups stand out.

General Confederation of French Labor. Once all but dominated by the Communist Party, the CGT has the strongest base of support among the dwindling number of manual workers. Once also the most militant of the unions, it tried to keep the events of 1968 in check. Until the Communist Party all but collapsed after the demise of the Soviet Union, the CGT did little its political allies in Moscow would have objected to.

Force Ouvrière (Worker's Force, FO). FO was created in 1948 when many on the anticommunist left abandoned the CGT. The split, of course, was part of the impact of the Cold War on all of French politics, as we saw in Chapters 3 and 4. Until the 1990s, FO was a minor force on the union scene. However, since then, it has become more militant and could well be the largest union in France at this time. Its base has traditionally been among civil servants.

French Confederation of Catholic Workers (CFTC). As its name suggests, it was the workers' wing of Catholic Action, a wide array of interest groups established by the clergy and laity to bring Catholics in a variety of social groups together. Historically, it was the most moderate of the unions, but it gradually radicalized during the 1960s. With the defection of the CFDT (see the next paragraph), it seemed to be in permanent decline during the 1970s and 1980s. In the last decade or so, however, it has enjoyed something of a comeback. Its religious side is not always obvious, except, for instance, in its continued opposition to opening stores on Sundays, ostensibly so workers can be guaranteed a day off.

French Confederation of Democratic Labor (CFDT). The CFDT initially split from the CFTC, which its leaders felt was too moderate and too heavily based on the Catholic community. Among the unions, the CFDT was the major beneficiary of the events of 1968 because it had been the strongest supporter of the protests and autogestion.

Given that French workers have so many unions to choose from, it would be reasonable to conclude that the labor movement is quite strong. The opposite is closer to the case.

Strikes can have a disruptive impact on life. To cite but one example, I arrived at Charles de Gaulle airport with a group of students. We had four hours to make our connecting flight to Geneva. We were lucky to have that long a layover because customs officials who had to check our passports were having a "work by rule" protest in which they did only what their contracts absolutely required them to do. What would normally have been a twenty-minute line took us three hours to get through.

The weakness of French unions lies, first, in their declining membership. All four of them claim close to a million members. That figure is grossly exaggerated. The best estimate is that about 5 to 7 percent of the workforce is unionized, a figure that is declining rapidly. Indeed, one study suggests that fewer workers are unionized in France than in any industrial country.

French unions are also weak because they are divided. Typically, three or four of them are represented in a single workplace or bargaining unit. And, since the unions do not usually get along with each other very well, that makes bargaining with management all the more difficult, especially in a country that does not allow what Americans call a "union shop" in which holding a job is contingent on belonging to a union.

Business. French business paints a very different picture. It has trade associations, chambers of commerce, and small business groups. But as discussed in Chapter 7, one of the most important features of French political life is the close contact that big business executives have with the civil service and the political elite, especially the Gaullists.

The critical organization here is the Movement of French Entrepreneurs (MEDEF). MEDEF was created in 1998 and replaced the old General Confederation of Bosses, which *only* represented big business and had a certain haughty and stodgy reputation. Today, MEDEF represents about 750,000 companies, 70 percent of which have fewer than fifty employees. Nonetheless, its main impact lies in the informal contacts its members have with what I call the iron triangle in Chapter 7.

It should also be pointed out that, in a country where a surprisingly small number of women have risen to the top of political life, MEDEF chose Laurence Parisot as its president in 2005. She is the chief executive officer (CEO) of an old and private family furniture manufacturing firm. That may not seem as if she is part of the elite grandes écoles graduates who dominate the top firms, again as discussed in Chapter 7. However, her education and outlook are much the same as her colleagues who went to ENA and other such schools.

Conclusion: The People and Normal Politics

This is the first chapter that looks at politics in France today from an analytical perspective. It is also the easiest one in which to see the sense in an argument about French politics becoming "normal."

Whether the focus is on culture or nonelectoral forms of participation, the French regime has become more legitimate and public opinion more consensual. Politics in the streets remains colorful, but it remains well within the parameters one would expect of a well-established liberal democracy.

That argument is more nuanced in the chapters to come. Nonetheless, even in the next chapter, on the bewildering French party and electoral systems, the preponderance of the evidence leads me, at least, to decide that France remains "normal."

Key Concepts

agents of political socialization   69
autogestion   79
interest groups   80

Questions for Discussion

1. Before 1958, few political scientists saw France as having a culture that could easily sustain democracy. Given the discussion in Chapter 3, why do you think that was the case?

2. Since 1958, French political culture has changed dramatically so that it has become more like those of most other successful democracies. Given what is discussed in Chapter 4, why do you think that was the case?

3. Despite all the cultural changes, French political participation remains more fragmented (and some would say more colorful) than that in many other countries. Why is that the case? And, what differences does it make for the way France is governed?

6

Political Parties and Elections

Elections—and hence **political parties**—are at the heart of all theories of liberal democracy. In defining democracy most people start with basic personal freedoms and the rule of law. Nonetheless, every definition of the term that I am aware of includes the free and competitive elections that determine who governs.

That is the case because parties and elections offer average citizens the most important way to have an impact on the political choices facing France or any other democracy. To return to the terminology developed by Gabriel Almond and his colleagues in the early days of the systematic study of comparative politics, interest groups discussed in the preceding chapter "articulate," or give voice to, the needs or positions of relatively narrow or marginalized sectors of the total population, such as women, workers, or winemakers. Political parties, by contrast, "aggregate" the interests of much larger social, economic, ethnic, or ideological segments of the electorate as part of their effort to win control of the government, something interest groups rarely try to accomplish.

In other words, political parties are among the most important institutions "linking" average citizens with decision makers at the national, regional, or local level. At least according to democratic theory, the most important of those links goes "upward" as a vehicle for voters to directly or indirectly shape the composition of the government and its public policy. Thus, voters choose candidates who most support their own point of view, and the winners reflect the values and opinions of the majority of the population. The links also run "downward," since parties influence public opinion not only during election campaigns, when they are most visible and active, but also during the periods between them, when they are developing and publicizing their stands on public policy in general.

No party or party system, of course, links the people seamlessly with policymakers. As in any country, the French parties do not—and cannot—completely mirror public opinion. Only a few voters have consistent and well-developed views on anything but the most important issues facing the country. Similarly, parties do not always faithfully implement the platforms they ran on once they reach office.

Still, whatever its imperfections, the electoral process offers the citizens of a democracy their best opportunity to hold the men and women who govern them accountable. If nothing else, they can use elections to "throw the bastards out," something the French voters have done in most elections since 1981. Usually, too, an election also offers some direction for the policies of the government and parliament. Often, it is hard to tell what the "mandate" the voters give the politicians actually consists of. However, at major turning points, such as the 1981 Socialist landslide in both presidential and legislative elections, politicians can—and do—interpret the results as a mandate for the kind of sweeping change they called for during the campaign.

Bucking the Trends ... at Least for a While

According to most recent interpretations, political parties in North America and western Europe have not been linking citizens and policymakers very well in recent decades. American political scientists, in particular, have been writing about the "failure" of their political parties since the early 1970s. They cite several developments in the organization and behavior of political parties, which Otto Kirchheimer first analyzed in an article on what he called **catch-all parties** in 1966.[1] These parties have shed most of their hundreds of thousands of devoted and motivated activists and strong stands on most major issues. Instead, they conduct their election campaigns primarily through television, a medium in which handsome candidates and short sound bites have largely replaced detailed positions on public policy as the main way of attracting voter support. In other words, political parties have become a different type of organization, run by telegenic national leaders who, in turn, stress vague slogans rather than traditional ideologies.

If the critics are right, catch-all parties have brought a number of problems in their wake. Given their desire to appeal to as broad an electorate as possible (and literally "catch all" the voters) parties have lost the ability to take strong stands and, thus, help the voters adapt to political change through the enduring realignments that have produced mandates for major and lasting policy innovations so often in the past. Instead, parties have become principle-less machines that try to stay one step ahead of—and then manipulate—public opinion to their short-term advantage. Catch-all parties may dominate political life, but they are not very popular among the electorate, since fewer and fewer people identify strongly with them and, in most countries, the turnout rate on election day has been declining steadily since the 1970s.

For the first thirty years of the Fifth Republic, the French party systems went against these trends, or, as Frank L. Wilson put it, they "refused to fail."[2] Most of the major parties grew stronger, not weaker, on just about every indicator political scientists use to assess them, from depth of popular support to effectiveness in government. From 1962 on, a left-wing and a right-wing bloc, consisting of two parties each, won a durable and disciplined majority in each election and presented the only serious candidates in presidential contests.

Those blocs, or coalitions, are still the largest force in French electoral life. However, since the mid-1980s, the party system as a whole has undergone the same kind of transformation we have seen in most other industrial democracies. The party system has begun fragmenting again, which we can see most notably in the 2002 presidential election in which sixteen candidates ran on the first ballot, none of whom won even 20 percent of the vote. Turnout has declined steadily, reaching a low of 60.7 percent on the second ballot of the 2002 legislative election. Voters have grown more skeptical and cynical, as reflected in the growing reluctance to think in the traditional terms of left versus right, discussed in Chapter 5. Behaviorally, we see it not only in the growing abstention rate but in their voting the incumbent coalition out of power in every parliamentary vote since 1981 and, when they do vote, increasingly opting for new and smaller parties.

Those changes and their causes are explored in the rest of this chapter. However, first, a brief description of the major parties, their positions, and their bases of support is in order, leaving the 2007 election largely to Chapter 11.

The Major Parties

As discussed in Chapter 3, the French party system has historically been highly fragmented and almost always favored the extremes, therefore making a majority coalition all but impossible to form. Since 1962, however, elections have been dominated by no more than four parties, all of which wanted to form lasting parliamentary majorities as part of a left- or right-wing coalition.

The Gaullists

Some observers used to call the British Conservative Party the "natural party of government," because it has held power for most of the last century and a half. The same could be said for the Gaullists (see the box on names and acronyms). With various coalition partners, the Gaullists governed France for the first twenty-three years of the Fifth Republic, shared power with the Socialists for nine of the years between 1981 and 2002, and from then on returned to power on their own.

On Names and Acronyms

The French party system can be truly bewildering. Not only are there many parties, but they come and go, merge and split. To make matters even more complicated, they change their names and acronyms almost as frequently.

To make things as clear as possible, I will rely on generic names for the parties and avoid acronyms whenever possible.

In essence, the Gaullists have gone through three major phases:

- From 1958 until 1976 the Gaullists were the embodiment of de Gaulle's vision and hopes for France and were led by many of his closest colleagues.

- In 1976 the Gaullists went through their fourth reincarnation since 1958, renaming themselves the **Rally for the Republic (RPR)** and became primarily a vehicle to support Jacques Chirac's presidential ambitions.

- Between the 2002 presidential and legislative elections, it merged with most of its traditional coalition partners to form the **Union for the Presidential Majority** and has since been renamed the **Union for a Popular Movement (UMP)**.

In 1958 we would not have expected this outcome. General de Gaulle detested political parties. He thought they were the main source of the weakness of the Third and Fourth Republics because they divided the French and made the pursuit of unity and grandeur impossible. He once even quipped that a country that had over 300 kinds of cheese would also have the same number of political parties.

De Gaulle did launch a party, the Rally of the French People to contest the 1951 election. Although it did well, it did not do well enough to end the crisis and compromise the rotation of governments, which became the norm after de Gaulle resigned the prime ministry in 1946. What's more, many of the party's deputies began playing the parliamentary game of seeking ministries in the next cabinet, which angered de Gaulle even further, and he disavowed electoral politics for the 1956 election, which turned out to be the Fourth Republic's last.

His reticence about political parties was easy to see during the six months after his assumption of power in May 1958 and the drafting of the constitution for the new republic. The leading architect of the new constitution, Michel Debré, was a long-time admirer of the British system in which disciplined majority parties allowed cabinets to govern with a minimum of disruption from the House of Commons. Debré and de Gaulle both understood that there was little likelihood of such a majority ever taking hold in France. Therefore, they included quite a few new provisions in the constitution that limited the power of the National Assembly while expanding that of the executive, provisions that are explored in more detail in the next chapter.

At the same time, their experience in office from 1944 to 1946 had shown that not even de Gaulle could govern without substantial support in parliament. So, reluctantly, de Gaulle accepted that people who supported him and his new republic had to have an organization for candidates to contest opponents entered in the 1958 election, in which the voters chose the first National Assembly for the new republic.

The newly formed Union for the New Republic (UNR) did surprisingly well. De Gaulle had disbanded the Rally of the French People following the 1951 election. That did not mean that the Gaullists were inactive. From his position at the Rothschild investment bank, Pompidou coordinated the work of a team of the general's confidants in anticipation of a time when they would be able to return to power.

Still, the Gaullists were ill-prepared organizationally compared with the other parties, since the UNR was formed on October 1, 1958, and elections were held just seven weeks later. It had only about 30,000 members, and not all the local notables who campaigned under its banner in 1958 were totally loyal to the general and his ideals.

The party actually did not do all that well on the first ballot, winning less than 20 percent of the vote. The Gaullists did, however, take advantage of the restored two-ballot electoral system (to be discussed later in the chapter) to win 212 seats, far more than any other party (see Table 6.1).

The UNR did well because of a combination of de Gaulle's personal popularity and widespread public concerns about the dangers facing the country. The new party, however, was by no means unified on any of the issues on the political agenda, beginning with Algeria. As noted in Chapter 4, the general opted to grant Algeria its independence against the wishes of many in his own party, let alone those that supported his government during the first years of the new republic.

Although only about fifteen members of parliament quit the Gaullists over Algeria, the party's leadership did change. By 1962 most of the early and hard-line Gaullists had been replaced by men like Pompidou, who realized that the party had to position itself near the political center if it was going to survive de Gaulle's departure, which was bound to occur sooner rather than later. Therefore, they built an organization with strong support from conservative politicians who had strong local power bases. They also succeeded in attracting young activists, like Jacques Chirac, who had been part of the modernization of les trentes glorieuses.

The polling evidence is skimpy. Nonetheless, it does appear that people continued to vote for the Gaullists, not because of the general, but because of the prosperity and stability their government provided. As Jean Charlot put it:

Table 6.1	Results of Parliamentary Elections among Major Parties, 1958–2007								
	PCF		PS		Center		Gaullists		National Front
Year	Votes (%)	Seats (no.)	Votes (%)	Seats (no.)	Votes (%)	Seats (no.)	Votes (%)	Seats (no.)	Votes (%)	Seats (no.)
1958	19.1	10	15.5	47	41.0	215	17.6	212	—	—
1962	21.8	41	12.5	66	26.5	84	36.4	269	—	—
1967	22.5	73	19.0	121	12.6	41	37.7	242	—	—
1968	20.0	34	16.5	49	10.3	33	43.7	354	—	—
1973	21.2	73	20.4	101	12.4	31	34.5	261	—	—
1978	20.5	86	24.7	117	—	—	43.9	274	—	—
1981	16.2	44	37.6	281	—	—	40.0	150	—	—
1986	9.7	35	31.9	210	—	—	42.0	274	9.9	35
1988	11.3	27	35.9	276	—	—	37.7	258	9.8	1
1993	9.2	23	20.3	70	—	—	39.5	460	12.4	0
1997	9.9	37	28.6	282	—	—	39.5	257	15.1	1
2002	4.8	21	24.1	140	—	—	38.5	386	11.3	0
2007	4.3	15	35.5	212	—	—	45.6	345	4.3	—

Note: Dashes = not applicable. The major parties listed include their allies, because these parties were not major contenders in these elections.

Public opinion accepted some of the specific contributions of Gaullism not necessarily associated with de Gaulle himself, namely the authority of the state; political stability based on an institutional regime far removed from the old French parliamentary tradition; and policies of independence in East-West relations, of moderation, and of economic expansion. As far back as 1962, the image of the Gaullist party as revealed in public opinion polls was no mere reflection of de Gaulle's image.[3]

In fact Pompidou and his colleagues turned the Gaullists into France's first catch-all party and attracted an electorate that drew support from all sectors of society. As his decade in office wore on, de Gaulle's personal popularity declined considerably. Nonetheless, support for the governments that ruled in his name grew.

In retrospect it is now clear that de Gaulle lost his personal magic after 1962. That year, he succeeded in winning the referendum on the direct election of the president; dissolved the National Assembly, whose leaders opposed the plebiscite; and with his new allies, the Independent Republicans (see the next section), swept to victory at the polls with France's first coherent parliamentary majority in history. His style was to turn every legislative election and referendum into a vote on his rule as well as for the office or on the issue that ballot supposedly was about. Put simply, as noted earlier, he claimed that if he did not get an overwhelming majority of the vote for his position, he would resign, something few people were willing to risk in the late 1950s and early 1960s.

By the time the first presidential election took place at the end of his first seven-year term in 1965, that demand for personal support no longer held much sway among voters. Initially, most observers expected him to overwhelm the little-known centrist Jean Lecanuet and François Mitterrand, who was the candidate of all the parties on the left. De Gaulle started his campaign late, and did not work as hard as his competitors. As a result, he won a shockingly small share of the first-ballot vote—45.7 percent. De Gaulle was forced into a runoff with Mitterrand. Although he won it easily, the election was the first clear sign that de Gaulle's personal popularity was declining and that the Gaullist party, not the general himself, held the key to the Center Right's future.

That was certainly the case in the two legislative elections held while de Gaulle was still in office. In the regularly scheduled 1967 race, the Gaullist machine was on center stage in the first election, in which a reasonably united Left ran against a reasonably united Right. The Gaullists came in first, winning almost a third of the vote and a comfortable majority with the Independent Republicans, their coalition partners. During the events of May and June 1968, many observers thought de Gaulle had lost control and that Pompidou was the one Gaullist politician who exercised any significant leadership. Still, it was de Gaulle's personal appeal and attack on the Communists after he dissolved the National Assembly that led to a victory for the renamed Union for the Defense of the Republic (UDR) in elections held at the end of June. It was, however, to be a swan song for de Gaulle himself. When he issued his usual "support me or else" ultimatum before a referendum on some minor constitutional reforms he proposed the following year, the voters said no and, as noted in Chapter 4, he resigned as soon as the results became known.

De Gaulle had replaced Pompidou as prime minister after the 1968 election, claiming he was "putting him on reserve for the republic." When de Gaulle resigned, Pompidou was the obvious person to run as the Gaullist candidate for president and won the election handily. During his five years in office, the less than charismatic Pompidou relied even more heavily on the Gaullist party machinery. Even more important, the party began to soften many of its stands on some of the issues that the general believed strongly in, most notably by supporting Britain's application to join the then European Economic Community, or Common Market, in 1972.

The party was thrown into organizational disarray when Pompidou died of throat cancer in 1974. This time, the strongest center-right candidate was Valéry Giscard-d'Estaing of the small but powerful Independent Republicans. The UDR hierarchy supported the resistance hero and former prime minister Jacques Chaban-Delmas, who trailed throughout in the polls and came in a distant third on the first ballot, which eliminated him from the runoff ballot two weeks later. That happened in part because a number of Gaullists, including the forty-two-year-old Jacques Chirac, supported Giscard from the beginning. Chirac was rewarded with the prime ministry, but his relationship with Giscard was never a comfortable one. Chirac resigned two years later and imposed his leadership on the tattered Gaullist party.

He renamed it the Rally for the Republic and engaged in a wide-ranging purge of the party leadership. By the time of the 1978 legislative election, the old Gaullist "dukes" had lost their positions as party leaders; half of the new leaders, hand-picked by Chirac, were also new to the movement. Not surprisingly, the party controlled by Chirac became primarily a vehicle for his presidential ambitions, which were finally achieved in 1995.

The RPR thus became more like British Conservatives and other secular center-right parties. It did not drop all of its traditional Gaullist goals. For instance, it never abandoned the Gaullists' long-standing support for France's nuclear weapons program. Similarly, while the government did privatize many companies nationalized by the Socialists when Chirac was prime minister between 1986 and 1988, it never rejected a state-driven capitalist economy in favor of the market to the degree that the British Conservatives did.

The most recent stage in the Gaullists' evolution came in 2002. Once Le Pen edged out Jospin for second place in the first ballot of the presidential election, all the other parties at least grudgingly supported Chirac against a rival many took to be racist and a threat to democracy. Chirac seized on the opportunity to broaden the Gaullists' base by convincing many of the leaders of the coalition of parties Giscard had put together to merge with the RPR and create the Union for a Popular Movement after the 2002 elections

The new party did little to develop a formal program during its first months in existence. It held its first national congress ("convention" in American terms) that November, where it adopted a bland "charter of values," which it listed as "liberty, responsibility, solidarity, nation, and Europe." Most observers expected the new party to continue supporting the slightly neoliberal positions.

Its candidate for the presidency in 2007, Nicolas Sarkozy, took over the party in 2004. In the three years before the first ballot of the presidential election, Sarkozy tried to define the UMP as a party that could maintain order in the poorest suburbs (see Chapter 5), continue to support economic development in the high-tech arena, and maintain a Gaullist commitment to a strong and independent foreign policy.

The Giscardiens

The second major party is even harder to define than the Gaullists. Like their more powerful allies, the **Giscardiens** have changed the party's name on a number of occasions. The party has always been a loose coalition of quasi-independent parties rather than a disciplined and unified machine like the Gaullists. The creation of the UMP in 2002 has given it a very tentative future.

Like many others, I have chosen to use the label Giscardiens to describe the second largest center-right party in honor of its founder and senior spokesman, Valéry Giscard d'Estaing. Giscard is part of a family with a long tradition of political activity on the center right. As a teenager, he participated in the Resistance near his home town of Clermont-Ferrand in central France. After the war, he graduated from France's two most prestigious grandes écoles, the National School of Administration and the École polytechnique (see Chapter 7) and later did further graduate study at Harvard University. Giscard was first elected to parliament in 1956 as a member of the National Center of Independents and Peasants. Most of its members were neither independent nor peasants but were a loose collection of local notables who mostly represented small town and rural constituencies.

Most members of the Independents and Peasants reluctantly supported de Gaulle in 1958, once they became convinced that he was the only alternative to a military coup. Most of Giscard's colleagues, however, also had deep misgivings about de Gaulle and his new republic, including what they thought was de Gaulle's heavy-handed use of power, the authority given to the executive, and the decision to grant independence to Algeria. The overlapping decisions to hold the referendum on the direct election of the presidency, fire Debré, dissolve the National Assembly, and hold new elections in 1962 proved to be the last straw for many of these politicians, who were responsible for the first and only successful vote of censure (no confidence) in the first fifty years of the Fifth Republic.

Giscard was part of a small minority that supported de Gaulle throughout the difficult first few years of the republic. When the Assembly was dissolved and early elections called in fall 1962, he launched a new party, the **Independent Republicans**, which won enough seats to guarantee the Gaullists the first secure majority ever in the history of republican France. Giscard himself was rewarded with the post of ministry of finance, which he held until he won the presidency himself twelve years later.

During that time, he developed a deserved reputation as a technocrat and a modernizer and was thus squarely in the heart of the Gaullist community as far as economic policy was concerned. He and his colleagues were always loyal to their larger coalition partner—at least when they had to be as on votes of censure. Giscard succeeded in keeping his party at a distance from the Gaullists by using more liberal and less nationalistic rhetoric.

The Independent Republicans never really defined a program and identity of its own. Rather, it served as a party that centrist politicians could be comfortable joining as an alternative to the Gaullists once they realized that they had to cast their political lot with the then-majority coalition (the reasons for this are made clear when the electoral system is discussed later in this chapter).

As president, Giscard struck a more informal tone than his often imperious predecessors by, for instance, inviting a group of mostly African garbage collectors to the Elysée Palace for a meeting. On balance, however, he continued basic Gaullist policies in support of economic modernization, including using the ample powers of the state to encourage the creation of "national champion" firms in major industries that would be competitive in European and national markets. His term in office largely coincided with the uncertain economic times following the OPEC oil embargo of 1973–1974. The resulting recession, increased inflation, and high unemployment limited what Giscard was able to accomplish. His personal popularity plummeted and he was defeated for reelection by Mitterrand in 1981.

The Giscardiens remained a "political magnet" that attracted centrist politicians who could not bring themselves to support either Mitterrand's Union of the Left (see the next section) or join the Gaullists now dominated by Chirac. The infusion of these new factions with their ambitious leaders proved to be a mixed blessing.

On the one hand, it did broaden support for the Giscardiens, who renamed themselves the **Union for French Democracy (UDF)** in 1974. On the other hand, the party turned into an organization whose message was increasingly diluted and became so ill-disciplined that it was hard at many critical junctures even to call it a party. That was especially true in the 1990s, when the aging Giscard became more of a senior statesman than an active politician who intervened on a daily basis.

During the 1990s, it also became harder to determine just how popular the party was. In 1993 and 1997, it ran a list of joint candidates with the RPR; in other words, only one candidate from the partner parties contested each seat. Similarly, in the 1995 presidential election, the UDF supported outgoing RPR prime minister Édouard Balladur, rather than running their own candidate.

The party splintered in 2002 even before the shocking results at the first round of the presidential election. Because Chirac was a reasonably popular incumbent, UDF officials knew that they had next to no chance of fielding a candidate who could come in first or second in the initial ballot and thus stand a chance of winning. Indeed, the UDF had not stood a chance of reaching the second ballot of a presidential election since Giscard's defeat in 1981.

Nonetheless, two different UDF leaders got the five hundred signatures from elected officials needed to place their names on the ballot. François Bayrou represented the official UDF, and Alain Madelin—who at one point seemed as if he would become a major national leader—represented his wing of the organization, Liberal Democracy. Together, they won only 12.7 percent of the vote and came in fourth and tenth place, respectively.

The Liberal Democracy Party ran its candidates as part of the UMP coalition in the ensuing legislative elections and claimed 63 of the coalition's 357 deputies. It officially joined the formal UMP organization that fall, even eliminating its Web site. The rump UDF's slate of candidates, led by Bayrou, won just under 5 percent of the vote and twenty-one seats, which left it nine short of the thirty needed to create a formal party group in the National Assembly.

As the 2007 election loomed on the horizon, the UDF gained new hope. Neither of the main candidates, Sarkozy and Royal, had broad appeal (see Chapter 11). On the center right, that left room for Bayrou to challenge Le Pen for third in the presidential race and gave new life to the UDF in the legislative elections to follow.

The Socialist Party

The other two parties with the greatest impact on the Fifth Republic are on the left. By far the most important of these is the **Socialist Party (PS)**.

Had this book been written in the early 1970s, it would have been hard to predict that the Socialists would be that influential. The PS's predecessor, the French Section of the Workers' International had a long and storied history. However, its fortunes had been sagging for years, and its candidate barely won 5 percent of the vote in the 1969 presidential election. After the debacle at the polls, the SFIO formally disbanded and recreated itself as the PS, but its fortunes still seemed bleak. Indeed, it was only when the veteran (but not very left-wing) Mitterrand took over the new party in 1971 that it began a decade of growth that brought it to power in the 1980s.

The SFIO had its unusual name because it began life in the nineteenth century as part of the Second Workingman's International, a partnership of socialist parties that had been inspired by the writings of Karl Marx and Friedrich Engels. Like all members of the International at the time, the SFIO was convinced that the Left could achieve its goals only through revolutionary means. With the dawn of the twentieth century and the spread of democracy into more of Europe, some Socialists, dubbed revisionists or democratic socialists, became convinced that serious change to the capitalist system could be achieved through legislation passed in parliament.

Like most of the parties in the International, the SFIO became a tension-filled organization as the revisionists and orthodox Marxists battled for control. Their struggle came to a head following the Bolshevik victory in Russia in 1917. Lenin and his supporters created a Third International of parties that were simultaneously loyal to Moscow and committed to revolutionary change in their home countries (see the next section).

For fifty years or more, the two dominant parties on the left barely spoke to each other. There were brief periods when they cooperated, as during the Popular Front of the 1930s and the Liberation governments a decade later.

Distrust between them continued for the first decade of the Fifth Republic, even though political realities forced them to cooperate at the ballot box. But by the end of the 1960s, it had become clear to leaders of both parties that neither could win an election without the other.

At the time, there was still widespread hostility toward the Communists and therefore a widespread fear of the possible consequences of their participation in a cabinet. However, Mitterrand's success in rejuvenating the PS and in attracting the new social groups to it helped him undermine those concerns.

In July 1972, the PS, the PCF, and the small Left-Wing Radical Party agreed on a momentous and sweeping Common Program. In it, they agreed to a series of projects they would pursue if they were to win the next legislative elections. The planks of the program focused on the nationalization of nine major industrial firms. At the same time, Mitterrand ran the 1973 and subsequent election campaigns in ways that made it clear that there was no way that the PCF would be anything more than a junior partner in a government dominated by the PS.

In 1973 the PCF actually slightly outpolled the PS on the first ballot. However, given the Socialists' greater ability to appeal to middle-of-the-road and independent voters, they won about forty seats more than the PCF in the new Assembly. In 1974 Mitterrand played on his personal popularity and the very real chance that he could get elected to persuade the PCF to support him on the first ballot and not run a candidate of its own. In 1978 the two parties could not agree on how to update the Common Program, which probably cost them the legislative election.

Then, in 1981, Mitterrand outpolled aging PCF leader Georges Marchais by 10 percentage points on the first ballot of the presidential election and then won the legislative elections held a few weeks later by 20 percentage points. The PCF has never come close to challenging the PS's hegemony on the left since then.

Although it won control of both the presidency and the parliament easily in 1981, the experience of governing did not go all that well for the PS. As discussed in more detail in Chapter 8, the Socialists immediately began a program that nationalized even more industries than the Common Program anticipated, decentralized power to subnational units of governments, increased the minimum wage and other benefits, began reducing the length of the workweek, and gave workers more of a say in the way their enterprises were run. Unfortunately for Mitterrand and his supporters, these were expensive projects that forced the government to borrow massive amounts of money at a time when interest rates were unusually high throughout the Western world and when the balance of power in Europe and North America was tilting toward the right. A sharp economic downturn ensued, forcing the Socialists to make a dramatic U-turn two years later when for all intents and purposes they abandoned all the radical plans in their 1981 platform.

Since then, the party has struggled to find an ideological orientation. It has resisted pressures from some militants to move the party leftward. It has not, however, moved as far to the middle as New Labour in Britain, the Democratic Leadership Council in the United States, or the Social Democrats in Germany. The party, thus, has consistently supported European integration and improved relations with the United States, but it has not endorsed such promarket reforms as the privatization of nationalized industries or abandoned such pro-working-class policies as the reduction of the workweek to thirty-five hours.

Similarly, the party's electoral fortunes have ebbed and flowed since then. sically, Mitterrand was able to win reelection in 1988, but other than that, party has only been able to win legislative elections they entered as part of the opposition and has not won a presidential race since 1988.

The two elections of 2002 were especially hard on the PS. As mentioned earlier, Le Pen edged out Prime Minister Lionel Jospin for a spot on the second ballot of the presidential election, which devastated internal party morale. The dispirited party then dropped below a quarter of both the total vote and the seats it won in the legislative elections. What's more, many of its most popular leaders lost, including Martine Aubry, whom many expected to replace Jospin as de facto party leader.

Since June 2002 the party has been engaged in deep soul searching as it tries to figure out why it did so poorly and what it should do next. By 2006 its fortunes had rebounded in part through a series of victories at regional and European elections.

More important was its decision to choose new leaders, who came in a unique combination. Shortly after 2002, the party selected François Holland as its First Secretary. He thought about running for president in 2007 but lost out to his long-term partner (they have four children) Ségolène Royal, who was the first woman to be a major candidate for the Elysée.

The Communist Party

The last major party probably will not remain one for long. The French Communist Party routinely won between one-fifth and one-quarter of the vote as recently as the 1970s. Since then, however, the party has been in a precipitous decline both because of its internal problems and because of difficulties brought on by the collapse of communism in the Soviet Union and Eastern Europe.

As noted in the previous section, the tensions between revolutionaries and reformists within the SFIO were intense even before World War I. They reached a boiling point after the Bolsheviks seized power in Russia in October 1917. The Bolsheviks claimed that, because they won the first successful socialist revolution, they should have the right to take over the Second International. When the reformists resisted that demand, Lenin and his colleagues created the Third International (Comintern) for revolutionaries who supported the Bolsheviks and their desire for worldwide revolution. In the next few years, the Bolsheviks provoked splits in existing Socialist parties. In France the provocation occurred on Christmas Day 1920, during a congress (convention) of the SFIO.[4]

The early PCF—like the other Communist parties around the world—attracted revolutionaries of all ideological persuasions and was not a particularly disciplined party. During the early 1920s, however, the Bolsheviks forced them to become completely loyal to Moscow and to mirror the organizational structure and policy goals of the Communist Party of the Soviet Union. The PCF struggled during the 1920s but made its first major breakthrough during strikes after the start of the Great Depression and then in the victory of the Popular Front in 1936. It solidified itself as a major political force when it joined the Resistance against Nazi and Vichy rule following the German invasion of the Soviet Union in 1941. Because of its role in the Resistance, its ability to win as many votes as most of the other major parties, and its links with the trade union movement, the PCF was included in the provisional government and in the first cabinet under the Fourth Republic. The onset of the Cold War forced the PCF out of government and onto the political margins for the rest of the Fourth Republic and the first fifteen years of the Fifth. No party was willing to collaborate with the PCF, and it showed little or no interest in cooperating with other parties, especially the SFIO.

There are two popular but different interpretations of the PCF during those years. Both are largely accurate.

The first was developed largely by analysts on the right and viewed the party primarily through a Cold War lens. From this perspective, the PCF was totally dependent on the Soviet Union, which determined what it would advocate, who its leaders would be, and how it would be financed. Therefore, it was seen as the equivalent of its "fraternal party" in Moscow, an organization whose true goal was the overthrow of capitalism, democracy, and the Western alliance.

The second interpretation came from more sympathetic observers, who concentrated more on the millions of men and women who regularly voted for it and the hundreds of thousands who were party members. As these observers saw it, the PCF succeeded because it could build support in the vast working-class subculture and among the small number of intellectuals and others who harbored deep resentment against the leaders of both the Fourth and Fifth Republics. In short, the PCF did well, not because either its leaders or its followers were dedicated Marxists, but because it tapped the broader but less radical resentment toward those with power and wealth.

By the 1970s the PCF's strengths were beginning to turn into weaknesses, which started its gradual decline culminating in its disastrous showing in 2002. That year, the PCF candidate, Robert Hue, finished in eleventh place with only 3.4 percent of the vote, more than 2 percent behind the Trotskyist, Arlette Laguiller, who had never had more than a marginal impact in the four other presidential races she had entered. The PCF did only slightly better in the legislative elections, winning 4.8 percent of the vote. It did manage to capture twenty-one seats, largely because its votes are clustered in heavily Communist districts in the working-class suburbs of Paris and other major cities.

The PCF's decline occurred for a number of reasons.

First, the working class itself began to change as a political force. Its numbers shrank with the shift toward a postindustrial society in which the bulk of the jobs moved into the tertiary sector. Meanwhile, most workers were making more money and leading more comfortable lives than ever before, which made the radicalism of the PCF less appealing. At the same time, the workers who continued to fare poorly began to look for political outlets that seemed to provide economic and other forms of security, which led them to organizations like the National Front rather than the PCF (see the next section).

Second, the party was harmed by the political dynamics, which benefited the PS, as discussed in the last section. Among other things, its relatively conservative stance against the students (if not the workers) in 1968 convinced many who were drawn to the left that the Communists were out of date and that the PS, the French Confederation of Democratic Labor, the Greens, and the women's movements better represented what the Left should be like in the late twentieth century.

Third, the party was not helped by the fact that it had aging and not very creative leaders. For most of its history, the party had been led by two men, Maurice Thorez and Georges Marchais. Both were intellectually unsophisticated and unswervingly loyal to the Soviet Union. They also ran their party in an extremely centralized manner, which brooked no dissent from below. Both their dedication to Moscow and their unwillingness to allow even a minimal flow of ideas about the direction the party should take drove thousands of activists away, including some of its most creative intellectuals.

Finally, from the middle of the 1980s on, the PCF suffered from the domestic political fallout caused by the collapse of communism. To a minor degree, the PCF lost some support in the 1980s as a result of the resurgence of the Cold War and the general drift rightward in much of the West. However, the real damage began after Mikhail Gorbachev came to power and began instituting his program of reforms, including perestroika, glasnost, democratization, and new thinking in foreign policy. Marchais and his aging colleagues had qualms about what were very popular reforms in France. Even had the party's leaders been more open to change it seems unlikely it could have done much to stop what turned out to be a hemorrhage of voters and members after the Berlin Wall came down in November 1989, after which it never reached 10 percent of the vote in a national election.

The PCF's future is not completely dismal. Robert Hue, who finally replaced Marchais in 1994, is more dynamic, telegenic, and innovative. The working-class subculture has not disappeared and will not do so in the foreseeable future. And perhaps most important of all, the PCF is likely to continue receiving at least some of the "protest vote" that goes to parties on the left. Nonetheless, it is all but impossible to imagine how the party could return even to its relative success in the 1970s.

New Political Parties

A stable party system dominated by the "big four" was a rarity in French political life. It is unlikely to return soon, although either a left- or right-wing coalition is likely to win elections for the foreseeable future.

In other words, the power of the four major parties has been fragmented as the postindustrial issues discussed in Chapter 5 have emerged on the political center stage. The traditional parties have had a hard time coping with those new issues, and a number of new parties have taken support away from them.

These include at least two parties that seem likely to last—the **National Front** and the **Greens**. In addition, as has been the case since the 1870s, the country has given rise to a number of "flash" parties that burst onto the scene and do well for an election or two but just as quickly disappear.

The National Front. The National Front is the largest and most worrisome of the new political parties. In one sense, it is but the most recent incarnation of the French Far Right and thus harkens back to the Fascists, Bonapartists, and monarchists of earlier republics. But in another, equally important sense it is a wholly new phenomenon, reflecting the strains of a country that has experienced substantial immigration while integrating itself increasingly in a unifying Europe.

The National Front's origins do lie in the traditional Far Right. According to Jonathan Marcus, Defense Correspondent for the BBC World Service:

> It was established by the leadership of France's most important postwar neo-fascist organisation, *Ordre Nouveau*. Its aim was to create a nonviolent movement that would bring together the disparate and often feuding families of the extreme-right to amplify their message. The Front was also to be a "front" organization in the literal sense, providing a respectable political façade behind which the more traditional activist and street politics of the far right would continue.[5]

There was good reason to question the Front's commitment to the regime and democratic norms in its early years. Ordre nouveau was known for provoking street battles against its adversaries on the left. The new party's leader, Jean-Marie Le Pen, had been elected to parliament in 1956 and 1958 with the short-lived and right-wing Poujadist Party and then became a paratrooper in Algeria, where he participated in the torture of Arab prisoners and later lost an eye. His opposition to de Gaulle and the new regime cost him his seat in 1962 and he drifted further to the right and became the Front's most visible leader within a year of two of its creation.

In 1976 an assassination attempt on Le Pen ironically enhanced his image. He also enjoyed a windfall inheritance that made the National Front financially stable. The new circumstances persuaded Le Pen to soften the party's image in order to spread its appeal beyond the narrow social milieu in which the antidemocratic right had recruited following the end of World War II.

Since then, the Front has tried to strike a balance between the often-extremist views of its leaders and the more moderate positions needed to reach mainstream voters, and Le Pen and his colleagues have rarely made explicitly racist or antiregime remarks. However, they have used a lot of what American political scientists call "coded language," or phrases that almost everyone understands carry with them only slightly veiled racist and extremist overtones. Thus, the party has advocated putting an end to immigration and sending current immigrants "home," with the clear implication that it is referring only to nonwhite immigrants. Le Pen argued that the French should not support the country's victorious World Cup team in 1998 because it had so few "real Frenchmen" on it. Le Pen has also opposed further expansion of the EU's powers, again claiming that any new authority given to Brussels would dilute "real French" identity and influence.

In so doing, Le Pen and thus the Front began to touch some important raw nerves in French public opinion. Not many people were unhappy enough to want to get rid of the Fifth Republic or democracy altogether, but plenty of men and women were concerned about immigration and issues that eddied around it. For example, in the 1980s and 1990s, unemployment topped 10 percent and stayed there. Not surprisingly, many workers who lacked the kinds of technical and other skills to find jobs grew resentful of nonwhites who did, even though many of them were in jobs most French people had refused to take during the heady days of les trentes glorieuses. Many, too, worried about the presence of immigrants in marginal neighborhoods, fearing, for instance, that the largely male immigrant population would "threaten" young French women. In the 1990s new fears about immigrants emerged, as the Front and other parties fueled the notion that immigrants were disproportionately responsible for the growing crime rate, especially in working-class neighborhoods.

The Front made its first significant breakthrough in the 1983 municipal elections, when it won 20 percent of the vote and seats on the city council of Dreux. Dreux is a dreary, declining city with a growing immigrant population, located about sixty miles west of Paris. It was to become the archetype of the kind of community in which the Front would do well; it had high unemployment, crowded and increasingly diverse public housing projects, and mainstream politicians who could not or would not address the question of racism in a constructive manner.

Since then, its vote in national elections has risen steadily, although not spectacularly. It has always fared better in presidential than in legislative elections, because the electoral system used in the latter works to its disfavor for reasons to be considered later in the chapter. For now, it is enough to see that the Front has little chance of actually winning seats, which has led some people who might otherwise have voted for it on the first ballot to either abstain or vote for one of the mainstream right-wing parties. Even so, its worst showing in a legislative election since the success in Dreux has been 9.8 percent of the vote. As discussed later in this chapter, the manner in which presidential elections are conducted does not harm parties like the Front as much, and Le Pen has averaged about 15 percent of the vote in the last four contests.

In fact 2002 did not mark a tremendous improvement in the Front's share of the vote or in the likelihood that it could ever gain power on its own or in a coalition with other right-of-center parties. Le Pen won only 1.7 percent more of the first-ballot vote than he had seven years earlier (although it should be pointed out that his erstwhile lieutenant, Mégret, running on a similar platform, won another 2.3 percent of the vote). Then, in the legislative elections, the Front's vote declined to about its average in those contests.

As noted earlier, Le Pen's surprising first-ballot success reflected more the failure of the Left to run an effective campaign and turn out its voters than it did an accomplishment by the Front itself. That Le Pen could not even win 20 percent of the vote on the second ballot attests to just how limited the potential for the Front's growth is—at least for now.

Polls conducted at the time of the 2002 election did not paint a pretty picture. The Front did particularly well among older voters, workers with uncertain professional futures, small shopkeepers, and people who lived in "transitional" neighborhoods. The Front's voters came from all sectors of French society and it actually won its largest proportion of the vote in the northeast, the region of the country with the fewest nonwhite residents.

Still, depending on the question asked in a given poll, as much as half of the population did agree with at least some of the positions taken by the Front. The same polls, however, also show widespread rejection of the Front itself from almost everyone who votes for other parties. Thus, in April 2002, almost 80 percent of the population agreed that it was a party of the far right, and almost three-quarters believed it was racist. Sixty-eight percent believed the party to be a threat to democracy (although relatively few of its own voters did). A series of polls conducted between 1992 and 2002 found that no more than 20 percent of those questioned ever said that they agreed very often or fairly often with positions taken by the National Front.[6]

Finally, what kind of future can we predict for the Front?

On the one hand, there are signs that the party could face more problems in the not so distant future. To begin with, Le Pen was born in 1928. And although he was in remarkably good health when these lines were written in 2007, the party is going to have to choose a new leader sometime reasonably soon, and there is no obvious successor waiting in the wings. The one serious candidate, Bruno Mégret, quit the party to form the National Republican Movement, and it could conceivably threaten the Front's vote once Le Pen departs the political scene. Also, it is entirely possible that Front voters will get discouraged by the party's inability to become a serious contender for power or even win a single seat in the National Assembly in most elections and will begin drifting to the UMP or other mainstream parties that can and do win elections.

Still, for all its weaknesses, the Front has established itself as a permanent force in French politics and has far exceeded the support won by any of the other far right parties in western Europe in the last twenty years.

The Greens. The final enduring new party is the Green Party (*les Verts*), which represents the other end of the "new politics" dimension from the National Front. Although the party has done almost as well as its German colleagues at the polls and had a minor role in the Jospin government, it has received far less attention than its counterpart on the other side of the Rhine.

Like their colleagues elsewhere, the Greens trace their roots back to the birth of the modern environmental movement, itself a by-product of the New Left of the late 1960s and early 1970s. In France, early support for what became the Greens grew out of a series of environmental protests, most notably against the civilian and military use of nuclear energy and some notorious environmental accidents in the early 1970s. At about the same time, many activists in the far left Unified Socialist Party (PSU) who refused to join the PS but remained dissatisfied with the inability of the "1968 generation" to touch a widespread political nerve just a few years later began looking for other issues and partners to work with. The PSU struggled on as an autonomous party through the 1970s, and its leader, Huguette Bouchardeau, served as environment minister in the first Mitterrand cabinet.

The U-turn made by the PS in 1983 finally convinced the loose coalition of environmental and New Left activists that they had to form a political party, which led to the creation of the Greens in January 1984, just after their German colleagues won their first seats in the Bundestag. The French party did surprisingly well in the European elections held later that year, gaining about 3.5 percent of the vote, not much less than the German Greens had won the year before. The Greens have done slightly better than that in subsequent elections but have never topped 10 percent and thus have not had the kind of breakthrough enjoyed by the National Front.

The French Greens have never been as ideologically driven as the German party. In Germany the party's founders were inspired by a philosophy known as "deep ecology," which held that all the world's problems—and not just the environment—were interconnected and could be solved only in an integrated and cooperative manner. But like the Germans, the French Greens were internally divided, although their disputes were not as pitched and destructive as those between the "fundis" and "realos," that is, the more hard core and more pragmatic voters and party members. Rather, the French had two organizations—the Greens and Génération Écologie—each of which had ambitious leaders who disagreed over the wisdom of allying with the PS on the second ballot of legislative elections.

The two were able to agree on running a single candidate in each district in 1993, but without an agreement for mutual support with the PS for the second ballot, none was elected. In 1995 the Greens' Dominique Voynet was the only environmentalist presidential candidate but only because she was the only one able to collect the five hundred signatures from elected officials needed to get on the ballot. Two years later Voynet persuaded the Socialists to withdraw their candidates in favor of a Green on the second ballot in twenty districts. Six of them won. Voynet became minister of the environment and land use management in Jospin's government. She was joined three years later by Guy Hascoët, who became minister for economic solidarity. In 2001 Voynet resigned, and her position was taken by another Green.

In 2002 the party decided that the well-known but controversial Voynet should not run for president. Instead, after a series of false starts, the party agreed to support the veteran activist Noël Mamère who won 5.25 percent of the vote, coming in sixth. The Greens renegotiated their legislative election agreement with the PS and actually ran sixty candidates who were jointly supported by the two parties on the first round. Overall, the party slipped a bit from its 1997 total and, given the overwhelming defeat suffered by the Left as a whole, only three members were elected to parliament.

On the Margins. Candidates from other minor parties won 30.6 percent of the first ballot of the presidential vote and 11.5 percent of the first ballot of the legislative vote in 2002. They also won 11 of the 577 seats in the National Assembly. In practice, these parties and candidates do not represent a major force in French politics. The most popular of the minor presidential candidates won under 6 percent of the vote and none of the smaller parties even garnered 2 percent in the legislative elections. What's more, a number of them represented "flash parties," which are not likely to survive more than another election or two, if they last that long. Nonetheless, four of them are worth mentioning at least in passing.

The Revolutionary Communist League (Ligue communiste révolutionnaire) and Worker's Struggle (Lutte ouvrière) are competing wings of the Trotskyist movement, which split from orthodox communism in the 1930s. Both have been fixtures on the fringes of the French Far Left since they gained a degree of publicity during the events of 1968. For the next thirty years they never gained more than a handful of votes, but together they won almost 10 percent in the 2002 presidential election. That should not be seen as a harbinger of better things to come for either of these parties. Rather, they seem to have benefited from dissatisfaction among traditional PCF and PS supporters who cast a protest vote on the first ballot on the assumption that they would then cast what the French call a "useful vote" for Jospin on the second.

The Republican Pole was created to support Jean-Pierre Chevènement's presidential campaign in 2002. During the Mitterrand years, Chevènement had been one of the most prominent Socialist politicians, holding a number of key cabinet posts, including minister of defense. During the 1990s he came to oppose such critical PS policies as support for the Maastricht Treaty, decentralization, and the abandonment of many egalitarian social and economic goals. He therefore left the party in the mid-1990s and hoped to launch a more traditional left-wing alternative to it. He won 5.3 percent of the 2002 vote in the presidential election but only 1.2 percent in the legislative race later that spring. Chevènement has decided to keep the Republican Pole alive, but it is hard to see it developing a serious power base.

The Hunting, Fishing, Nature, Tradition (CPNT) Party is one of the more curious political organizations in a country known for its unusual politics. The party's name might suggest that it is another environmental party on the left. To understand this party, American readers have to drop their stereotypes of hunters as members of the lower classes who go out to bag a deer each fall, and British readers have to do the same with their image of "the hunt" run by upper-class men and women who chase down foxes on horseback with their packs of dogs. The French party is more broadly based and is inspired by European Union rulings against a French law that forbids any landowner with less than 150 acres to deny people the right to hunt or fish on their land. In fact, CPNT draws its support from people in rural France who have broader objections to the urbanization of French life and to the growing EU influence over national decision making. Many party leaders have histories on the far right, especially among those who have opposed European integration. Indeed, it is in elections to the European Parliament that it has scored the most success, and that is the only venue in which it has exercised any noticeable impact.

Declining Turnout

There is one other important change that is hidden in any discussion of what the parties stand for and how they have fared at the polls. There has been a noticeable decline in turnout for presidential and, especially, legislative elections.

In part, the decline reflects the fact that three recent legislative elections (1981, 1988, and 2002) came within weeks of two rounds of presidential balloting. Some relatively disinterested voters who suffered from "election fatigue" did not bother going to the polls for a third or fourth time. And American political leaders would be delighted by turnout that still hovers around 70 percent of the registered voters. Still, abstention and failure even to register to vote (perhaps as much as 10 percent of the electorate) have been growing at a time when the proliferation of new parties and candidates has actually given voters more—not fewer—options.

Nonvoting citizens in France are clustered in the same social and economic groups we find in all the industrial democracies: the less-educated, poorer, and younger segments of the population. Particularly worrisome are the young, since over 40 percent of the people under thirty-five did not vote in 1997, the most recent year for which data are available. The polls show that young people dislike all politicians and parties and hold them all responsible for France's continuing difficulties, especially the high unemployment rate, which has hit the young particularly hard.

It may be that today's young French men and women will be like young people in other countries and other times and start voting more regularly as they get older. However, there is little sign of that happening even for people in their thirties, and it is thus possible that much of an entire generation has been permanently turned off from participating in mainstream political life.

Who Votes for Whom?

Another way to understand the French party system is to explore the ways people vote. As in any country, there is more to the choices voters make than just the parties' positions and leaders discussed above. So an exploration of their choices provides a richer picture of the way parties and elections link people to the state—or don't, as the case may be.

People in Britain would believe that French voters vote a lot. In most of the United Kingdom, people vote only in parliamentary, local, and European elections (Northern Ireland, Scotland, and Wales do have elected regional assemblies). But to most people only parliamentary elections count. The French vote at those three levels as well. However, the available evidence suggests that local and European elections matter more to them for what might seem like contradictory reasons. Because so many French towns and villages (communes) are still quite small, whereas the United Kingdom has created larger and larger local jurisdictions, municipal elections are "closer to home" for many French voters. By contrast, given the far broader support for European integration in France and, perhaps, the greater impact of Europe on French life, its voters have shown more interest in European elections and used them as an opportunity to give new parties a voice in decision making. In addition, unlike their British counterparts, the French also vote in presidential and regional elections as well as when referenda are called, the most recent of which came up in 2000, when the president's term was reduced from seven years to five, and in 2005, when the proposed European constitution was rejected.

Here, the discussion concentrates primarily on the factors shaping how French voters make their choices in the two races that most shape domestic political life—legislative and presidential elections. These are not only the most important elections but also the ones for which the most extensive data are available. Even so, there are gaps in what we know and the picture painted in this section is "blurred" to a considerable degree because I have had to draw on studies of a number of different elections, which, in turn, rely on different methodologies.

That is not as serious a problem as it might seem. My goal here is not to focus on the variations from one election to another, many of which have already been discussed. Nor am I interested in subtle nuances in the forces determining how people vote, for which conclusions can be deeply affected by the methodologies different political scientists use. Rather, I am concentrating on the most important, long-term trends that have shaped French voting behavior for the last generation or more and are likely to endure long after this book is published.

The most obvious determinants of the way people vote are the attitudes they have about the key institutions, individuals, and issues in political life. As we saw in Chapter 5, the French voters have at least one thing in common with their counterparts in other democracies—few of them are all that attentive to politics and, therefore, few of them have a well-developed set of beliefs. Nonetheless, there are important links between what they do believe and how they vote, none of which should be surprising.

These links include two main considerations.

First is the voters' position on key issues, including where they place themselves on a spectrum running from far left to far right. Not surprisingly, people who said they were at least "rather to the left" were most likely to vote for one of the left-wing candidates on the first ballot of the 2002 presidential election.[7] Right-wing voters, similarly, voted for right-wing candidates. Similar findings emerged for party identification. The only exception to this rule is the Le Pen electorate. The National Front candidate received a disproportionate share of the vote from people who said they were neither on the left nor the right and from those who claimed "another" as a party identification (the TNS-SOFRES team did not include the National Front in that question). The pollsters also asked interviewees whom they had voted for in the first ballot of the legislative elections of 2007 and in the second ballot of the 2005 presidential election. Such "retrospective" questions are notoriously inaccurate; however, the same basic pattern emerged. Le Pen also got an unusually large number of votes from people who said they were "not interested at all" in politics, perhaps reflecting their overall dissatisfaction with mainstream political life.

Second are the types of people who were drawn to each camp. Religion remains one of the best predictors of how people voted. Thus, Jospin got 20 percent of the vote from those who claimed to have no religion, but only 9 percent from practicing Catholics. The results were almost exactly the opposite for Chirac and other prominent conservative candidates. If France has a gender gap, it is the opposite of that in the United States. Women were more likely to vote for the Right than the Left. By contrast, only Le Pen got a disproportionate share of the male vote. Unlike the United States or Great Britain, neither education nor occupation predicted how people voted very well. Finally, in what has to be a worrisome sign for the Left, Jospin and his left-of-center competitors fared best among voters over sixty-five.

Why This Happened

So far, the focus of this chapter has been on documenting trends—the clustering of the party system around major parties on the center left and right, its recent fragmentation, and declining turnout. Now, the chapter will turn to a discussion of why these changes have occurred. Two factors, the electoral system and leadership, stand out. Unfortunately, only the impact of the first can be demonstrated with any degree of precision.

The Electoral System

The architects of the Fifth Republic made two important decisions about how elections would be run. First, they decided to return to the unusual **single-member district two-ballot system** (*scrutiny uninominal à deux tours*) used under the Third Republic instead of the proportional representation of the Fourth Republic. Second, they did not include those provisions in the constitution but left them instead for "normal" laws, which could be changed, if desired, quite easily. In fact, governments have tinkered with its details over the years, and the Socialist government scrapped it altogether in 1986, but only in that year. Nonetheless, its basic operating principles and their impact have remained basically the same since 1958.

Observers were frankly surprised by the Gaullists' decision to return to the two-ballot system in 1958, because it had contributed to the fragmentation of the party system and the power of local notables throughout the Third Republic. However, in the changed circumstances of the Fifth Republic, it had almost exactly the opposite effect. By the middle of the 1960s, it had helped turn most legislative and presidential elections into contests between reasonably coherent coalitions on the right and the left, all but squeezing the once-dominant centrist parties out of existence.

This electoral system is actually simple even if its implications are not. For elections to the National Assembly, France is divided into 577 districts, including a handful in its remaining overseas possessions. Anyone who can collect a minimal number of signatures and pay a minimal deposit can run on a first ballot. If no one wins a majority of the vote on the first ballot, a second election is held a week later. As the law was originally written, a candidate who won at least 5 percent of the vote could run again on the second ballot; that minimum has since been raised to 12.5 percent. Candidates who do that well, however, do not have to run. They can withdraw (*désister*) and openly support another candidate. Whoever wins the most votes in the second round wins the seat, whether he or she wins a majority or not. Presidential elections operate the same way with two exceptions. First, the second ballot (there has always been one) is held two weeks after the first. Second, only the top two candidates are allowed to run on the second ballot, which means that the winner is guaranteed majority support from those voting.

To understand the impact of the electoral system, consider what happened in the third district of the department of Hérault in the 1958 and 1962 elections (see Table 6.2). On the first ballot in 1958, five candidates ran, a Communist (PCF), a Socialist (SFIO), a Christian Democrat (MRP), a Gaullist, and someone from the Far Right. The right winger was eliminated from the second ballot because he did not get the needed 5 percent. The other four candidates had the right to continue. The Christian Democrat realized he had no chance of winning and withdrew, urging his voters to cast their second-round ballot for the Gaullist. As the only right-of-center candidate

Table 6.2	The Electoral System in Action				
	Total votes, 1958			Total votes, 1962	
Party	First ballot	Second ballot	Party	First ballot	Second ballot
PCF	12,239	13,676	PCF	13,581	24,281
SFIO	12,284	15,244	SFIO	11,313	—
MRP	6,325	—	—	3,026	—
Gaullist	7,643	16,905	Gaullist	12,042	16,836
Far Right	2,744	—	—	—	—

Note: Dashes = candidate withdrew or did not receive 5 percent of the vote on the first round.

on the second ballot, the Gaullist won almost all the votes that had gone to the right winger and the MRP on the first ballot. Because the Socialists and Communists were barely on speaking terms, both candidates stayed in the race for the second ballot, creating a "triangular," or three-way, race. The two split the left-wing vote once again, and the Gaullist was able to carry the seat with only 36 percent of the vote.

The other half of the table shows the very different results in 1962, which are typical of the impact of the new electoral system in two ways. First, smaller parties got "squeezed" by the larger ones. The Far Right did not even bother to run a candidate, whereas the MRP saw its vote cut in half. Indeed, the first-ballot losses by the once-dominant centrist parties were so devastating that they ceased to exist as an autonomous, let alone prominent, force with the election of 1983. Second, the Left came to realize that its internal divisions all but ensured a Gaullist victory. So, in a number of districts like this one, the Communists, Socialists, and left-leaning radicals (not represented here) reached a tactical decision to jointly support the one candidate on the left who had the best chance of winning. In this district, the Communist candidate won almost the same number of votes that the two parties had won on the first ballot and carried the district easily.

In 1967 the Communists and a coalition of Socialists and Radicals known as the Federation of the Democratic and Socialist Left reached an agreement to run a single candidate on the second ballot in every district nationwide. The Gaullists and Giscardiens did the same. With but some minor exceptions and variations, the left- and right-wing parties have been able to work out similar second-ballot agreements ever since.

Since the 1980s, the number of triangular races has increased, because most National Front candidates have refused to withdraw and the members of the Gaullist-led coalition have refused to support any National Front candidates on the second ballot. And because the Front can only hope to come in first in a three-way race in a handful of districts and then only under the best of circumstances, it has never won more than three seats when the two-ballot system was used.[8]

Since the 1980s as well, there has been a proliferation of new parties, since the electoral system does not necessarily penalize minor parties at the first ballot. However, the dynamic that has led to the creation of left- and right-wing coalitions for the second ballot remains the same one that ensures that the four big parties and the smaller ones that work with them at least to some degree still win the lion's share of the seats.

The rule that only two candidates can run on the second ballot of presidential elections has only reinforced the division of the country into two broad coalitions—even when the specific events of a given election did not yield a "decisive" vote between a left-wing and a right-wing candidate, as was the case in 1969 and 2002. It is often said that the French opt for their first choice on the first ballot and then cast a *vote utile*, or tactical vote, on the second. Thus, a leftist might vote for a Communist or a Green candidate on the first round so that his or her true preferences could be on the record. However, two weeks later, that same person would willingly vote for whoever was chosen to represent the Left as a whole.

There have been two elections in which the first ballot did not produce a contest of left versus right for the second. The Left's failure to reach the second ballot following de Gaulle's snap resignation in 1969 led directly to the creation of the PS and then to Mitterrand's commitment to a unified Left on subsequent second ballots. Similarly, the splintering of the Left's first-ballot vote in 2002 led to another soul-searching within the PS and to a greater willingness on the part of left-wing voters to think tactically before casting their first- as well as their second-round ballots. Put simply, had even 200,000 people who voted for one of the seven other left-wing candidates cast their ballots for Jospin, he and not Le Pen would have survived to face Chirac on the second ballot.

Leadership

Far harder to document although no less important is the role a handful of key leaders played in reinvigorating the party system in the 1960s and 1970s and then in its growing fragmentation afterward. Ironically, some of the same people whose innovations made the French party system run counter to the "failure of political parties" trend early on were responsible for its falling into line with the other leading industrial democracies later on.

A remarkable group of politicians with few ties to the major parties of the Fourth Republic helped create the new and more dynamic institutions that have dominated the Fifth. Most notable here are de Gaulle, Pompidou, and Chirac, who created and then built the powerful Gaullist machine. Almost as important was Giscard d'Estaing, who provided the unexpected support that made the Gaullist majority coalition possible and then helped sustain it. On the left, much the same can be said for the Mitterrand team, which turned the moribund Socialist Party around and transformed it into the largest party in the country in less than a decade by forging an appeal aimed at the new middle class and by unifying the Left, at least for the second ballot. It could also be argued that the failure of the Communists and the other parties with deep roots in earlier republics made it possible for the group of largely new organizations to dominate from the mid-1960s on.

But the leaders who were a source of constructive change in the first half of the republic's life turned into something quite different in the last twenty years. The most visible politicians of the early twenty-first century had all been fixtures in political life for many years and no longer served to truly inspire many voters. Chirac first joined the cabinet in 1963. Jospin had been a leader of the Socialist Party since Mitterrand took it over. Le Pen had first been elected to the parliament in 1956. Mitterrand, first elected to parliament right after World War II, still cast a large shadow over the political life. Obviously, other politicians were important, but most of them paled in comparison with these men, who had been defining French political life for a third of a century or more.

What's more, the image of most party politicians was not helped by a wave of scandals that hit all the major parties other than the Communists. None threatened the existence of the republic as the Dreyfus Affair had a century earlier. But some of them were serious enough to sully the reputations of politicians from every party. Two examples should suffice.

On May 29, 2001, former foreign minister and president of the Constitutional Court Roland Dumas was convicted of influence peddling, sentenced to eighteen months in jail, and fined more than $130,000. The seventy-eight-year-old Dumas was a hero of the World War II Resistance against Germany. He was also a close confidant of former president Mitterrand.

As foreign minister in 1990, he recommended that Prime Minister Edith Cresson (later implicated in a financial scandal in her own right) accept a $2.8 billion agreement to sell six ships to Taiwan. Dumas's recommendation came on the heels of intense lobbying by his mistress, Christine Deviers-Joncour, who was following the orders of Alfred Sirven, a senior executive at the state-owned oil company, Elf-Aquitaine.

Charges of improper use of funds and influence surfaced seven years later when another company went public after it refused to pay "commissions" to Deviers-Joncour. She was then arrested and alleged that she had received about $10 million from Sirven for her "lobbying." The next year she published a "tell all" book, *Whore of the Republic*, in which she detailed her work for Elf and her affair with Dumas. Meanwhile, Sirven mysteriously left France and went into hiding, only to be arrested in the Philippines in 2000.

The inquiry into Dumas and the others continued and uncovered more juicy details. Dumas and Deviers-Joncour had been bribed with millions of dollars, ancient Greek statues, and a luxury Parisian apartment for their rendezvous. Dumas also received a $1,500 pair of luxury boots.

In the end, Dumas was acquitted. Nonetheless, few French men and women who followed the case were convinced of his innocence, or that of anyone else who had been touched by the scandal.

At the same time, an even farther reaching fund-raising scandal hit all the major political parties and seemed to implicate President Jacques Chirac on the eve of his bid for a second term. On September 21, 2000, *Le Monde*, France's most prestigious newspaper, published the transcript of a videotape made by Jean-Claude Méry before his death. In it, the property developer detailed how he had helped gain public works contracts in the Paris region for his company and others by giving money to Chirac's RPR party.

He said he did so on Chirac's orders at a time when the president was mayor of Paris. He also alleged that President Chirac was in the room when he handed nearly $7 million in cash to the president's chief of staff.

The decline in support for the RPR was limited because all the other parties were implicated. The Socialists and Communists got money as well. To make matters worse, Méry's lawyer gave former Socialist finance minister Dominique Strauss-Kahn a copy of the tape, which he held on to for two years. The same lawyer also represented the fashion designer Karl Lagerfeld, who was under pressure from the finance ministry to pay over $10 million in back taxes and by the fact that Strauss-Kahn had been implicated in the Elf-Dumas affair.

The Stakes of 2007

I intentionally left out the results of the 2007 elections because they occurred just as I was finishing the book. In other words, political scientists were just beginning to do more than superficial analyses of why Sarkozy won the presidency and the UMP retained its parliamentary majority. I will use the results of the 2007 elections and their first implications for French politics to conclude this book.

More important, it is worth putting off such a discussion until the end of the book, because in a possibly unusual way, the results of the elections confirm the main thesis of this book. The two elections were a major turning point in the history of the Fifth Republic. There was a changing of the guard in the leadership of almost all of the major political parties, at least some of which may not survive to contest the next election in 2012. Yet, the calm with which the elections were conducted and the ease with which the transitions in both the presidency and parliament occurred, suggested that even major changes come without dramatic consequences or threats for the regime.

As an American deeply involved in the 2008 presidential election here, the similarities between the two countries and the transition in Washington that will follow that in Paris overshadow the differences between them.

Key Concepts

Key People, Entities, and Events

Questions for Discussion

1. France has what political scientists call a multiparty system, in which it is very rare that any single party can win a majority of the seats in the National Assembly. No party or candidate has any real chance of winning a majority of the popular vote in either a parliamentary or presidential election. Why is that the case?

2. Nevertheless, French elections have routinely produced stable majorities since at least 1962. Why is that the case?

3. How would politics in your home country be different if it had an electoral and party system like the one used in France?

7

The State

The very fact that the French use the term "the state" (*l'état*) so much tells us a lot about the way their country is governed. All European languages have an equivalent word, but no people use it in their descriptions of political life as do the French.

And that is no linguistic fluke. The French talk about l'état so much because it is, in fact, at the heart of its politics and has been since before the Revolution.

Indeed, the state is so central to French politics that four chapters are needed to cover it all. This chapter focuses on the formal institutions of French democracy. Subsequent chapters explore its domestic policy, the impact of Europe on policymaking and, finally, France's often controversial foreign policy.

The Constitution

By western European standards, the French Constitution is new. Even though it has now been in force for fifty years it still has another thirty years to go before it sets the French record for longevity.

Constitutions are rarely written during calm political times. Rather, politicians typically decide a new constitution is needed only following a military defeat or some other traumatic event. That has been the case for all the regime changes in France since the Revolution.

Because of the timing of their creation, constitutions tend to share at least three characteristics. First, they often grow out of crisis and thus reflect the issues of the moment and the values of the people that were challenged at that particular historical moment. Second, even when a single individual such as General de Gaulle exerts a tremendous influence over drafting it, the new constitution contains a significant number of compromises that dilute some of the rationality the new system of government might otherwise have had. Finally, constitutions are but one of many building blocks that determine what the new regime will actually be like in practice. That is the case because all constitutions have ambiguous provisions and their authors cannot anticipate all the difficult political situations with which they will have to contend.

All of this was true of the Fifth Republic. With nearly a half century of historical hindsight, it is tempting to look back on its development as one of the best examples of political engineering in any democracy. In fact, at the time, many experts criticized what they took to be its flaws, and a smaller number assumed it could not be made to work, at least not for long.

As noted in Chapters 3 and 4, the constitution was written in the aftermath of the twin revolts in Algeria that destroyed the Fourth Republic and propelled Charles de Gaulle back to power.

The general did not immediately become president or set up his new regime. Rather, the deal he reached with the parliamentary leaders who reluctantly begged him to become the prime minister, gave him extraordinary powers to rule for six months, during which time he would revise the constitution. De Gaulle officially took office on June 1, 1958. Two days later, parliament passed a law creating a commission to revise the Fourth Republic's constitution, and the general named the constitutional lawyer Michel Debré to head it. The law placed few restrictions on the commission, which was given eight weeks to do its work. The commission members quickly realized that they had to write an entirely new document, which may have been de Gaulle's plan from the outset. The deal also called for a **Constitutional Consultative Commission**, which was composed primarily of parliamentary leaders and which had relatively little influence over the work of Debré and his colleagues. Their draft was completed by mid-summer. The proposed constitution was put to a vote in a referendum and passed overwhelmingly on September 28. On October 4, it officially went into effect. The next three months were taken up by other details of the transition from one regime to another, including the election of a new National Assembly and president. The new institutions and personnel were fully in place by early January 1959.

The Presidency

The very structure of the constitution made it clear how different the new republic would be. It starts with a brief preamble, which reconfirms France's commitment to the "rights of man" and offers its colonies the opportunity to become independent or remain a part of France.[1] Article 1 declares France to be a secular and democratic republic and bans discrimination on the basis of national origin, religion, or race. Title I confirms that national sovereignty lies with the people who exercise it through their votes (including in referendum) and through their representatives. It also includes a brief statement affirming that political parties have a role to play in the "exercise of suffrage," one of the few symbolic concessions de Gaulle and Debré made to mainline politicians.

The much longer Title II with its fifteen articles defines the role of the president. That the presidency is the first institution mentioned and discussed at such length made it obvious to everyone that the Gaullists expected it to be far more influential than any other institution. That came as no surprise, since de Gaulle had made it clear from the time of his first speech after returning to France in 1944 that he was convinced that France needed a strong executive separate from the legislature.

> It goes without saying that executive power should not emanate from Parliament or the result will be a confusion of powers which will reduce the Government to a mere conglomeration of delegations. The unity, cohesion, and internal discipline of the French Government must be held sacred if national leadership is not to degenerate rapidly into incompetence and impotency.[2]

As Article 5 put it, "the President of the Republic shall see that the Constitution is observed. He shall ensure, by his arbitration, the proper functioning of the public authorities and the continuity of the State. He shall be the guarantor of national independence, territorial integrity and observance of treaties." This statement is, of course, extremely vague, and the constitution goes on to specify more presidential powers.

Some of these were not new. As in earlier republics, the president named the prime minister and chaired meetings of the cabinet, or Council of Ministers. But this constitution went a bit further and opened the door to some of the actions de Gaulle would subsequently take by giving him the power to appoint the other ministers and to terminate their appointments (Articles 8–10).

The constitution did give the president three new and controversial powers.

First, **Article 11** allowed the president to take certain matters directly to the people in a referendum. These included the organization of public authorities, social and economic reform, treaties, and other subjects that might alter the way the constitution operated. In theory, he could call a referendum only if the government agreed; in practice de Gaulle and later presidents effectively ignored this provision. The use of referenda was extremely controversial because of the way Louis-Napoléon employed it to undermine the Second Republic and make himself emperor. Many politicians accused de Gaulle of having Bonapartist tendencies, which made Article 11 one of the most debated parts of the constitution as long as de Gaulle was in office.

Second, **Article 16** authorized the president to declare a state of emergency "when the independence of the Nation, the integrity of its territory, or the fulfillment of its international commitments are under serious and immediate threat where the proper functioning of the constitutional public authorities is interrupted." As with the referenda, there were some constraints. Before declaring an emergency, the president has to consult with the prime minister, the president of the National Assembly, and the head of the Constitutional Council, and the National Assembly cannot be dissolved as long as Article 16 is in effect. The constraints, however, pale in comparison with this power, which allowed a president to rule by decree for as long as six months. This power, too, was unprecedented in French republican history, and it has never been granted to executives in Anglo-American democracies. That said, it is not without precedent in other countries whose republics were born out of a tragic crisis or military defeat.

Third and perhaps most controversial of all, the president was given the right to dissolve the National Assembly (Article 12). Officially, the prime minister and president had had that authority under the Third and Fourth Republics. However, given President MacMahon's dissolution of parliament at the beginning of the Third Republic, it was a power that existed only on paper, and it was not one that the executive could hope to use. The placement of this article so early in the constitution suggested that this was going to be a real option open to the president. As with the other two new powers, the president could not act arbitrarily. He could dissolve the Assembly only once a year. New elections had to be held within forty days, and the new Assembly had the right to meet for a two-week session once it was elected. But again, as with the other new powers, the constraints only limited what a president could do on the margins.

The president did not get all the powers de Gaulle might have wanted. He does not have the right to veto legislation. He can only refer a bill he disapproves of back to parliament for further consideration. And perhaps most important of all, the original constitution did not call for the direct election of the president.

As noted in Chapter 6, that provision of the Constitution was changed in 1962 and again in 2000. There is some debate about whether or not de Gaulle wanted the **direct election of the president** included in the constitution in 1958. If he did, he did not put up much of a struggle against the mainstream politicians who were dead set against the idea, again out of their concerns about potential "Bonapartism." Still, they allowed the new presidency to have a broader mandate than was the case under the preceding two republics. Under the new republic an electoral college of more than 81,000 members, which included the members of parliament plus a much larger number of local and departmental officials, would choose the president. The one and only time it was used, it gave de Gaulle almost 90 percent of its votes.

It appears that de Gaulle finally decided in mid-1962 that the next president had to be elected when he realized that the electoral college would probably choose one of his rivals were he to leave the scene. His decision was solidified several months later when he barely escaped an assassination attempt.

He invoked Article 11 of the constitution and called for a referendum on the direct election of the president, which itself provoked a constitutional crisis. Despite the cabinet's loss in a vote of confidence and an adverse ruling from the Constitutional Council, de Gaulle pressed ahead and the "yes" side won a resounding victory. In the only major change since then, in 2000, the president's term was reduced to five years both to increase accountability and to make the presidential and parliamentary terms the same under normal circumstances. It was also hoped that the amendment would mean that presidential and legislative elections would occur at the same time and thus reduce the likelihood of the need for cohabitation (see below). The constitution does not specify how the president would be elected. Like many other key provisions, it is left to be determined by an "institutional law" (loi institutionnel).

The Government

By contrast, the Constitution devotes four brief articles to the government and says very little about the ministers' tasks and next to nothing about their relationship with the president. To be fair, many of the provisions about the Parliament do serve to strengthen the power of the government. Nonetheless, the fact that it gets only fourteen sentences and the presidency gets that number of full articles said a lot to observers who were reading constitutional tea leaves in 1958.

In many respects, the Fifth Republic did not change many of the formal powers of the government or the executive team of ministers headed by the president and prime minister. It still "shall determine and conduct the policy of the nation" (Article 20). It runs the civil service and armed forces and coordinates the work of the ministers and their departments. Along with the president, the prime minister makes key administrative, diplomatic, and judicial appointments.

But there were also two changes to the powers of the government in Title III that are worth noting. The first was rather subtle.

Under the Third and Fourth Republics, the prime minister was officially known as the president of the Council of Ministers. Now, he or she (there has been one woman prime minister) was formally given the British title, prime minister, which again seemed to hint at the office's subordination to the presidency.

The other was anything but subtle. **Article 23** declares that the "duties of a member of the Government shall be incompatible with the exercise of any parliamentary office." Any member of the National Assembly or Senate who was named a minister had to resign his or her seat in parliament. That is also the case in the United States, but it is common for individuals to serve in both a cabinet and the parliament at the same time in most parliamentary systems. Indeed, in the United Kingdom, all members of the government *must* be members of Parliament (MPs) as well. This **incompatibility clause** was included to reduce the practice whereby ministers would be willing to

The Presidency

France is one of the few established democracies to have a strong presidency. De Gaulle's model has been adopted by constitution writers in some of the emerging democracies in eastern Europe, often urged on by leaders who wanted to see their personal power maximized.

In the West, however, the head of state is typically a symbolic leader who both epitomizes national unity and largely stays out of political life. France is the one Western country that combines a strong presidency with a parliamentary system that leads to cohabitation and some of the other odd political features to be considered later in the chapter.

Among political scientists who study new democracies, there is considerable debate over whether presidential or parliamentary systems work better.

Here, it is enough to note that at least west of the former Iron Curtain, France is an unusual example indeed.

Pomp and circumstance. François Mitterrand, president of France during the 1980s, sits on a ceremonial throne during an official visit to the region of Lorraine, located in the west of France near the German border.

sabotage the current government they served in knowing that they had a secure seat in parliament to return to following an ensuing cabinet crisis. An institutional law later determined that all candidates for parliament would run with a *suppléant*, who would automatically assume the seat if the individual who won the election was named to the government (or died or resigned). It should be noted that Article 23 applied only to parliament. It did nothing to limit France's notorious *cumul des mandates*, through which individuals often combine membership in a cabinet, the mayoralty of a city or town, membership in a departmental or regional council, and the European Parliament. A later law did reduce the number of offices a person could simultaneously hold to three.

The Parliament

The two longest titles deal with the parliament on its own and its relationship with the government. That might lead you to think that the legislature was to have a lot of power. In fact, most of the articles severely curtailed that power, especially those aspects of it that had hamstrung Fourth Republic cabinets. Indeed, it is a sign of how weak the authors wanted the parliament to be that Title IV deals only with procedural issues, not with the powers granted to either house. The powers (or lack thereof) are addressed only in Title V, which deals with broader legislative-executive relations.

The Constitution called for the creation of a bicameral (two house) Parliament. As is the case in almost every democracy other than the United Sates, the lower house, or National Assembly, is by far the more powerful of the two. However, the Senate has a few more powers than most upper houses, which means it will require more than a passing reference after we finish with the Assembly

The first few articles of the Constitution lay out some of the principles and procedures for the new parliament. Thus, it requires that members of the National Assembly be directly elected, although it leaves the definition of the electoral procedures to an institutional law, the one that the Socialists changed for the 1986 elections.

Members of both houses are given widespread immunity from prosecution for their actions in an official capacity, a right Third Republic deputies did not have, which led to the arrest and trial of many of them. Similarly, members can be tried only for serious crimes committed outside of the parliament and then only if the leadership of the relevant house agrees to proceed. Otherwise, a sitting member cannot be prosecuted until he or she leaves office.

A list of provisions designed to limit the parliament's power and strengthen that of the prime minister and president, however, begins in Article 28. Some of those limits might seem minor. The constitution allows the houses to meet in regular sessions for only 100 days a year and severely restricts the ability of their leaders to convene special sessions and to determine their agendas when they are in session. Government business takes priority over debate on everything else. Although such provisions are common for state legislatures in the United States, they are quite rare for national parliaments.

Limits in other articles are obviously important. Thus, Article 34 delineates the policy areas in which the parliament may pass laws. The list is long and covers taxation, civil liberties, the basic contours of economic and defense policy, and more. However, the very existence of this article and of Article 37, which allows the government to rule in other areas by decree, reflects the authors' intention to limit parliament's potentially disruptive and micromanaging behavior. Article 38 allows parliament to pass laws that let the government issue ordinances (in fact, laws) on a matter for a period of time determined in the initial legislation. Although this provision has not been used often, it has been invoked on some important issues, including maintaining order in Algeria, implementing the Treaty of Rome (which created the Common Market), lowering the retirement age, shortening the workweek, and addressing a host of public policy matters ranging from agriculture to alcoholism.

Other provisions further limit the scope of parliamentary authority. The Assembly cannot vote to raise the expenditures or lower the tax rates proposed in the government's budget. What's more, if the proposed budget isn't passed or rejected within seventy days, it automatically goes into effect.

Similarly, the government may call for a **bloc vote** on a bill, which means that no amendments are allowed and the deputies must vote "up or down" on the proposal submitted by the ministers. It can also determine that a bill is an "urgent matter" and demand an expeditious vote from the Assembly and Senate. Even when there is a clear majority, the government typically resorts to these provisions about one hundred times during the life of a parliament.

Last, an important measure in the constitution limits the ability of the National Assembly to cast and pass a **vote of censure**, or no confidence. New cabinets do not have to win a vote of confidence on taking office as had been the case during the Fourth Republic. A vote to censure the government can occur only if 10 percent of the members sign a petition for one and, if it is rejected, those members may not sign another one during the rest of that session, which could be as long as a year. To pass, a vote of censure has to receive an absolute majority of all members, not just of those voting, a provision that might have saved a number of cabinets under the Third and Fourth Republics.

As already mentioned, the **Senate**, the upper house of the parliament, is far weaker than the National Assembly. It does have somewhat more power than the British House of Lords, but it pales in comparison with the German Bundesrat, let alone the United States Senate.

Its weakness lies, first of all, in its indirect election from what the constitution calls France's "territorial units." As we have already seen, the constitution left many of the details to be determined through "organic" law.

Parliaments

In most parliamentary systems, when a single party or coalition has a working majority the lower house of the parliament exerts a relatively minor role on policymaking.

By the time bills reach the floor of a body like the French National Assembly, the government can normally count on a solid and supportive vote.

There are at least two unusual features in the French system.

First, the upper house, the Senate, has a bit more power than its equivalents in most countries other than Germany. Second, when and if the Assembly and Senate iron out their differences on a bill, the president of the republic does not have to accept it but can send their draft back for further consideration.

Still, it is safe to say that, as in most European countries, the French parliament is little more than a rubber stamp that votes for bills proposed by the government on all major legislation.

Remember, too, that many issues that would be the province of the legislature in other countries are part of the domain of regulation, that is, the government decides, in France.

In a 2006 National Assembly session on corruption and bribe taking, then-interior minister Nicolas Sarkozy confronts Prime Minister Dominique de Villepin over allegations that de Villepin ordered a secret agent to investigate Sarkozy, his chief political rival.

According to the current law the 321 senators are chosen by electoral colleges assembled in each of the departments. The colleges consist of all the deputies, all the general (departmental) and regional counselors, and representatives chosen from the municipal (city and town) councils. Senators serve for nine-year terms, and a third of the seats are up for election every three years. Because the configuration of the departments and their electoral colleges give disproportionate representation to small town, rural, and conservative interests, the Senate has never been representative of the French people nor has it reflected the overall partisan balance of power, realities that have further contributed to its weakness.

The constitution also holds that parliament (that is to say, both the Assembly and the Senate) must pass all legislation. If the two houses pass different versions of a bill, they meet to try to iron out the differences in a procedure not terribly different from an American conference committee. However, if the deadlock cannot be broken, the National Assembly can have its will prevail through an absolute majority vote. The one exception is "institutional" laws that affect the functioning of the Senate, which have to be passed in identical form by the two chambers.

The Senate also lacks the authority to cast a vote of censure against the government. Article 49 requires the government to present its policy proposals only to the Assembly, and the following article gives the Assembly the sole right to introduce and, if the votes are there, pass votes of censure that can force a government to resign.

Amending the Constitution

Finally, Article 89 lays out two main ways of amending the constitution. First, if the two houses of parliament agree on an amendment they instigated themselves, the president must submit it to the people in a referendum. Second, if the president or the cabinet proposes an amendment and it is passed by the two houses of parliament sitting together, it goes into effect without a referendum.

De Gaulle's critics argued that these provisions were honored in the breach. Both the 1962 amendment on the direct election of the presidency and the 1969 proposals on reform of the senate and regional governments were sent to referendum in ways that seemed to violate Article 89.

Since then, amendments have largely fallen into two categories. "Big ticket" items, such as those involving the expansion of the EU, and thus would dramatically affect French sovereignty, were to be submitted to the public for a vote. More limited shifts (changing the president's term to five years and the parity law) were to be handled through the parliament-based process.

In sum, the Fifth Republic's constitution has been amended more than twenty times. But the bottom line is that the constitution has not been amended in any major way for almost fifty years other than the direct election of the presidency. Amending it is easier than in the United States or Canada, but it is not a political tool to which politicians have frequently resorted.

Constitutional Ambiguities

Articles 56 through 88 of the constitution deal with the judiciary, its relations with the European Union, and other topics. They are not covered in this chapter, but they are discussed at various points in the next three chapters.

Before leaving the constitution for now, however, we should consider two major ambiguities in the text itself. Even though both were obvious at the time it was written, it would be more than twenty-five years before the second actually became a political reality.

That there were uncertainties about the constitution should not come as a surprise. Constitutions are building blocks that can go a long way toward determining how a country's political life is shaped. Thus, anyone reading the American or German constitutions would have a reasonably good idea of how the executives and legislatures of those countries operate. Still, there are always key aspects of political life that are not included in constitutions or similar documents, such as the power of committees in the United States House and Senate or the limited impact of the single-member district component of German elections.

Constitutions have ambiguities, too, because they come out of a political process that almost always involves compromises, such as the one that led to the creation of a House of Representatives and Senate of roughly equal power in the United States. That was true even in France in 1958, when the committee drafting the constitution shared a common political point of view and had an unusually firm control over the ratification process. For instance, de Gaulle almost certainly would have preferred to have the president directly elected. However, the mainstream politicians had enough remaining clout to force him to accept the cumbersome electoral college used in 1958.

The first ambiguity, in fact, involved the role of the president in general. The constitution certainly added to the powers of the president under the Third and Fourth Republics. It did not, however, clarify exactly how influential either the president or prime minister would be.

As seen in Chapter 4, de Gaulle quickly resolved any such uncertainty in the president's favor. He did so by personally taking a leadership role on any issue that concerned him, something all subsequent presidents have done except during periods of cohabitation, which is explored next. He also made it clear that the prime minister would be subordinate to the president, first by naming the unpopular Debré to the post, then by firing him four years later, and finally by replacing him with Pompidou, who had never even run for political office before.

The second ambiguity is the one that gave rise to cohabitation for much of the time between 1986 and 2002. The constitutional machinery works quite smoothly when the parliamentary majority comes from the same party or coalition as the president. Under those circumstances, the president routinely appoints a prime minister and cabinet that has the support of the majority in the National Assembly, both on legislation and on votes of confidence.

The constitution, of course, could not guarantee that kind of outcome, especially since presidential and legislative elections did not normally occur at the same time until the reduction in the president's term took effect with the 2002 race. From 1958 until 1986, the voters chose presidents and legislative majorities that were in line with each other. After the economic difficulties of the first years of the Mitterrand presidency, however, the voters returned an overwhelming center-right legislative majority with which Mitterrand had to contend during the last two years of his first term.

As also seen in Chapter 4, the politicians developed rather effective ways of coping with the political imbalance brought on by this French version of divided government, in which the president and prime minister shared power, the former taking the leading role in foreign policy and the latter on domestic issues. What matters here is that few hints to how the president, prime minister, and parliament would get along can be gleaned from the constitution.

The same happened during two periods in the 1990s. Nothing terribly disruptive occurred during any of the cohabitation governments. Instead, potentially warring sides from the Left and the Right handled things quite well, even routinely.

By chance, presidential and legislative elections were both scheduled for spring 2002. That year also marked the first election following the 2000 amendment that reduced the president's term to five years. If the Assembly routinely lasts its full five years and is not dissolved to hold early elections, the two sets of elections should continue to be held in rapid succession, which should, in turn, limit the likelihood of cohabitation occurring as frequently as it has in recent years.

Legislative-Executive Relations in Practice

There have been three main patterns in the way legislative-executive relations have worked in practice. They reflect the three different kinds of results of the nineteen national elections between 1958 and 2002:

- A president confronting a divided and often hostile parliament (1958–1962)

- A president working with a sympathetic parliamentary majority (1962–1986, 1988–1993, 2002–)

- A president confronting a united and hostile majority (1986–1988, 1993–1995, 1997–2002)

One of the peculiar consequences of the emergence of those majorities has been a sharp decline in research on legislative-executive relations by political scientists. It isn't just that party discipline means that most government legislation passes quickly and easily. Because the parliament rarely has intense debates and does not have anything like the dramatic (if largely irrelevant) British prime minister's Question Time, it does not draw much attention, and the work of the National Assembly and the Senate does not attract that much interest from English-language journalists either.

Therefore, the account that follows is not based on the kind of statistical study of voting behavior one finds in research on the United States Congress. Instead, I have tried to illustrate these general trends with a handful of brief case studies of what the parliament has done.

Using All the Constitutional Levers: The Early Years

Michel Debré, the chief architect of the Fifth Republic's constitution, was a long-time admirer of British parliamentary democracy. With its all but guaranteed majority party that voted in a disciplined way in the House of Commons, its cabinets can expect to have their legislative proposals enacted quickly and intact.

Debré wanted the same thing for France. But like almost everyone else, he assumed that there was next to no chance that France would ever produce the kind of parliamentary majority that is the norm on the other side of the Channel. As a result, he included the politically draconian provisions discussed above, which would strengthen the executive's hand when facing the kind of multiparty and ill-disciplined legislature he expected would carry over from the Fourth Republic.

As discussed in Chapter 4, the 1958 elections produced a National Assembly in which the majority of deputies claimed to support de Gaulle and the new republic. That support, however, was quite thin. Many of the politicians who rallied to de Gaulle in 1958 were not particularly enthusiastic about the new president-centered regime, and their opposition to it burst into the open once it became clear that de Gaulle favored granting independence to Algeria. As a result, de Gaulle, Debré, and other leaders had to resort to the powers they had given themselves in the new constitution and then some.

That they could not run roughshod over the Assembly can be seen in an issue of the gravest importance for the new Republic.

One of de Gaulle's first actions after becoming the last prime minister of the Fourth Republic was to pay an official visit to Algeria. There, as noted in Chapter 4, he gave an amazingly ambiguous speech in which his audience thought he pledged them his support, but in fact he did nothing of the kind. By mid-1959, de Gaulle had clearly decided that Algeria would have to be granted self-determination and that that would all but certainly mean independence.

Support from the traditional right-wing politicians began to evaporate. Protests mounted in the streets of Algeria and metropolitan France and came to include attempted coups and assassination attempts by dissident army officers. Knowing that he had no hope of persuading parliament to pass legislation granting Algeria independence, de Gaulle turned to Article 11 and called for referenda.

Clear Majorities and Cohabitation

As suggested in the last chapter, the emergence of clear parliamentary majorities in every election since 1962 has rendered many of the seemingly draconian constitutional provisions unnecessary. Party discipline in the National Assembly has been more or less as unwavering as in Britain or Germany. In other words, governments have rarely had to resort to the bloc vote or other such provisions intended to weaken what the Gaullists assumed would be a divided and independent-minded parliament.

The preceding paragraph actually masks two complicating factors.

The first is that not all of the coalitions that produced those majorities involved commitments to govern together for the life of a parliament, something that is the norm in Germany, for instance. Thus, in 1988 the Socialists fell short of an absolute majority in the National Assembly. They had to rely on the Communists, Greens, and others on the left to maintain their majority on critical votes. It was conceivable that the PS could have lost the support of its partners. However, as Mitterrand's health declined and support for the Left did as well, the other leftist parties stuck with a succession of Socialist prime ministers on the assumption that defecting from the PS on a vote of censure would have disastrous consequences—which is exactly what occurred after the parliamentary term expired in 1993.

Second, and more important, is the role of cohabitation. As noted earlier, it seems as if the architects of the Fifth Republic did not anticipate a time when such a divided government would occur.

In Britain, such a divided government cannot occur, since the parliament and cabinet are inextricably intertwined. In the United States, splits in partisan control of the presidency and at least one house of Congress have been the norm for more than a decade and common for many years before the Republicans gained control of both the House and Senate in 1994 and then when the Democrats gained control of both houses during George W. Bush's final two years in the White House.

It took a quarter century for divided government to occur in Fifth Republic France. But in 1986 the Gaullist coalition gained control of the Assembly even though the Socialist Mitterrand had two years left in his term. As noted above, the 1988 elections returned Mitterrand and the PS to power. But in 1993 the Gaullists regained control of parliament, and cohabitation returned until Chirac won the presidency two years later. Then, when the government called for early parliamentary elections in 1997 and the Socialists won, the two coalitions had to live and govern together until 2002.

Cohabitation has never been easy.

Even though the leadership of both the Left and the Right have more in common than one might think (see the section on the iron triangle below), there is little tradition of political cooperation under any French regime. Nonetheless, the Left and the Right worked out a modus vivendi early in the days of the first period of cohabitation in the 1980s.

Archrivals Mitterrand and Chirac reached an unspoken agreement that there would be few dramatic policy departures as long as they had to govern together. Indeed, Mitterrand's decision to appoint Chirac as prime minister gave a signal that it was important for the top leadership of the Left and the Right to work together; he could, of course, have appointed a less right-wing figure or even a nonpartisan technocrat.

Typically, the prime minister and cabinet have been responsible for the day-to-day operations of domestic politics and policy under cohabitation. Foreign policy has remained largely the province of the presidency. Also typically, both the president and prime minister have represented France at European Union summits and other major international events (see Chapter 9).

The last thing to note here is that "normal politics" has actually continued to operate under cohabitation. The prime minister and cabinet continued to maintain their ironclad parliamentary majority, which they needed to remain in office. The hard part revolved around negotiations between the cabinet and the presidency, which were almost always smoother than analysts of the Fourth Republic—or even the first years of the Fifth Republic—would have predicted.

Decentralization

One of the most intriguing changes that has occurred over the last quarter century has been **decentralization**. Although granting new powers to the regions, departments, and local governments has brought sweeping changes to France, it should be noted that it occurred through normal legislation rather than constitutional amendments.

French centralization has been discussed several times earlier in this book. France's now 22 regions, 96 departments, and 36,679 cities, towns, and villages had very little power. Instead, government below the national level was dominated by the central authorities, in particular through the prefect, who exercised a power known as the *tutelle*, which forced communes and other local authorities to get his prior approval before anything of significance could be done. Prefects occupied a position in their departments that at first glance seemed akin to that of an American governor. However, they were civil servants, not elected officials. And they were rotated every few years so that they would not develop close ties to local officials. Because of the tutelle, the prefect and his staff could determine everything from local budgets to the names of streets and schools.

As France modernized and its cities grew, the tutelle became an anachronism, and the elected leaders of major cities gained more and more de facto power. Thus, when officials in Caen and its suburbs decided that they needed a comprehensive urban plan during the 1960s, they did so largely on their own. If they cooperated with anyone, it was with local business leaders and the development ministries in Paris, not the prefect.

Frustration was particularly intense among the Socialist and Communist mayors who had been elected in most major cities other than Paris. Therefore, when the PS came to power in 1981, the veteran politician and mayor of Marseilles, Gaston Defferre, was put in charge of decentralization, which, in turn, was made the first legislative priority for the new government.

Under his leadership, the Socialist government passed a series of laws during Mitterrand's first term that gave each level of government new powers. Communes, for example, had control over elementary education, welfare, and zoning and other planning issues. Departments had a number of new functions, including managing secondary education. Regions were given authority over higher education, economic planning, and more.

For three reasons, only two of which survive today, these powers were not merely to exist on paper and then honored in the breach. First, the subnational units were given budgetary autonomy, largely through unrestricted bloc grants that the central authorities could not control. These budgetary shifts were solidified in a constitutional amendment in the 1990s. Second, departmental and regional officials are now elected, giving them a broader mandate than any representative of the national administrations. Third, the prefects were initially abolished. However, it soon became clear that the smaller communes (almost 21,000 of them have fewer than 500 residents) could not carry out their new responsibilities, and the prefect-based system was re-created for them.

Decentralization has been particularly important for the larger cities in general and Paris in particular. Following the Communard uprising of 1870–1871, the city was stripped of a mayor and an integrated urban government. Instead, the twenty *arrondissements* (wards) were all but completely independent of each other. Even before the 1982 reforms that reshaped local government nationwide, the government authorized the direct election of a mayor. Chirac was the first to hold the post, which he turned into one of his stepping-stones to the prime ministry and, eventually, the presidency.

The most recent major change was a 2000 law that encouraged the creation of urban regions through which communes would cooperate while maintaining their legal independence. It was an attempt to minimize the impact of having so many small communes and a result of the failure to get small communities to merge.

One of the more intriguing of these urban regions is the Metropolitan Urban Community of Lille in the northeast. The region includes several communities in Belgium, which have not yet been incorporated into the

Capital Cities and Their Mayors

Paris was not the only national capital to be unusually subordinate to national governments.

Washington, D.C., was completely under the jurisdiction of the U.S. Congress until 1971, when it was granted limited home rule and the right to elect its own mayor. It still does not have the right to a representative and two senators as would be the case were it a state. If the Democrats are in power, the District of Columbia delegate to the House of Representatives usually has a vote on the floor. This is not the case under the Republicans. Not surprisingly, the car license plates of many District of Columbia residents include the phrase, "taxation without representation."

London has been something of a political Ping-Pong ball over the last several decades. The Thatcher government abolished the Greater London Council in 1987. The Labour government created a new Greater London Authority and authorized the first direct election of a mayor in 2002. Londoners then elected Ken Livingston, a left-wing socialist who has been a thorn in the side of the Blair government ever since. One of its most creative policy initiatives has been the imposition of a hefty toll that all nonresident drivers must pay to enter the city center.

official governing structure, but negotiations for doing so are currently under way, which might actually make this one of the first locally based international governing bodies in the world. Perhaps most telling of all, the president of the urban community is Pierre Mauroy who was the first prime minister under Mitterrand.

Decentralization is not as wide-ranging as American federalism in at least two respects. First, little of it is enshrined in the constitution and thus could be reversed through an act of parliament. Second, most elections in the bigger cities, departments, and regions are decided more on the basis of national rather than local issues.

Nonetheless, it has changed the face of French politics. If nothing else, it has tempered the centralization that has been an alienating force for centuries.

The Courts

American students are often surprised to discover that few other countries have judicial institutions as powerful as their Supreme Court.

To be sure, the rule of law operates in all democracies. However, few have given their courts the power of judicial review, that is, the authority to determine that certain laws and other governmental actions are unconstitutional.

France had a strong judiciary before 1958 in other respects. Its administrative law system was and still is dominated by some of the country's leading legal scholars and civil servants (see the next section). But judicial bodies such as the Council of State or the Accounting Court had no authority to rule on the constitutionality of governmental acts.

France had long used Napoleonic law, which is very different from anything found in democracies with a tradition of common law. Put simply, Napoleonic law has detailed instructions about what should be done when judges are faced with certain kinds of cases and thus gives them little room to exercise their own discretion.

The founders of the Fifth Republic broke from that tradition somewhat by creating the Constitutional Council. The council has nine members who serve nonrenewable nine-year terms; three of the nine are chosen every three years. At each appointment period, the president of the republic, the president of the National Assembly, and the president of the Senate each appoints one member. Former presidents of the republic can serve for life if they choose to do so, although only Valéry Giscard d'Estaing has chosen to exercise that optional power.

The Constitutional Council was not an important feature in French political life until recently. Indeed, Charles de Gaulle ignored its decision on the 1962 referendum on the direct election of the president.

In the last two decades, however, prominent politicians have been named to the council, and it has come to play a more important role, often in determining disputes that grew out of cohabitation. In early 2007 its members included a former president, a former prime minister, and one of the first women to occupy a senior cabinet ministry.

The council has two main tasks.

It is in charge of making certain that elections are run fairly. It can even go so far as to annul the results of a vote if it determines that a candidate has violated campaign law.

More important for our purposes, it can determine if acts of parliaments or proposed bills are in keeping with the constitution. Like most supreme courts, the council can consider a case only if it is referred to it. However, unlike the United States Supreme Court, the government can refer a bill to it *before* it is presented to the Assembly for a final vote.

In recent years, its most important decision was to rule that the labor law limiting the rights of first-time employees was constitutional (see the next chapter). But, it is not just high-profile issues that get to the council. In 2004 half of the legislation before the Assembly was referred to it by the opposition.

All the signs are that the council will continue to play an important role for the foreseeable future.

The Iron Triangle

What is perhaps the most important component of the French state is not even mentioned in the constitution or any law. As we explore the way this **iron triangle** operates, it is important to recall the idea first laid out in Chapter 1 that the state includes more than just those institutions called for in legal documents.

Critical here is the distinction political scientists draw between the government and the state. The government includes all the official institutions, typically laid out in the constitution or other laws. The state includes them along with other informal bodies and networks that have a significant impact on how public policy is made.

There is no better European country to see how the state is more than the officially prescribed governmental organizations than France. The Fifth Republic has succeeded in large part because of its unusual constitution and the unprecedented parliamentary majorities it produced. Just as important, however, are informal practices operating "behind the scenes" that have provided the country with much of its leadership in both the public and private sectors since the 1960s.

Corporatism

Twenty years ago, **corporatism** was one of the most controversial terms in political science. Colleagues had begun researching collaboration among bureaucrats, politicians, and representatives of "peak associations," or leading interest groups. They acknowledged that off-the-record discussions between the three entities facilitated the making of broadly accepted public policy.

But they also raised doubts about the democratic legitimacy of such practices. If nothing else, the bureaucrats and interest groups were not open to elections or other mechanisms of democratic accountability. Indeed, the very choice of the term "corporatism" reflected scholarly disdain, because it was drawn from the Fascist practice of abandoning elected assemblies for those that supposedly represented "corporations," or social interests, but, in reality, did not.

There is no question that corporatist practices excluded some key players. The most obvious example is the German Concerted Action negotiations, which concentrated on business and labor and left out environmentalists, immigrants, and retirees.

The historical track record of corporatism is neither that dismal nor antidemocratic. In Sweden, in particular, the people who make Royal Commissions and other bodies happen have worked to ensure maximum participation and minimal exclusion.

As we are about to see, France falls somewhere in the middle. It has used corporatist practices to create and implement sweeping economic policies for the last forty years. However, it has also largely frozen out groups that are not committed to economic development.

Grandes Écoles and Power

American political scientists coined the term "iron triangle" to describe the often close relationships between interest groups, members of congressional committees, and civil servants. Most scholars find those relationships worrisome, especially at times such as the early 2000s when lobbyists seem to have traded money for policy "considerations."

Consensus Building

A more positive way of looking at corporatism is what we in the conflict resolution community call consensus building.

I have been fortunate to be involved in projects to bring key interest group leaders together on such issues as the role of faith-based organizations in political life, health care for the uninsured, and the long-term response to terrorism. In each case, policymakers asked my colleagues to bring together all the key actors to meet largely behind closed doors over a period of months.

Each time, the agreements the group reached made further legislative or administrative policymaking possible precisely because unusual political bedfellows were willing and able to work together away from television cameras and the rest of the media (see www.sfcg.org/programmes/us/us_consensus.html).

As I write, the group's leaders decided to focus on expanding health-care coverage for children, and a modified version of the bill that grew out of the consensus-building process is likely to pass in the House and Senate. The president's signature is another issue.

France's iron triangle is far more important than anything we in the United States have dreamed of. American versions are typically quite limited. Members of Congress and their committee staffers meet with their colleagues in the bureaucracy and in the interest groups whose offices surround the Capitol. Thus, members of the House who represent districts with a lot of farmers and sit on the House Committee on Agriculture have regular contact with their colleagues in the Department of Agriculture and such groups as the American Farm Bureau Foundation. Given the overlapping nature of their work, such contact is all but unavoidable. However, especially given the scandals that helped defeat the Republicans in the 2006 election, most Americans do not approve of these kinds of relationships, to the point that former civil servants are not allowed to work with—let alone lobby—their former offices for at least two years following their retirement or resignation.

By contrast, the French iron triangle dominates all of politics as much as any single body does in any democracy. And it is all the more important because it is not discussed in any official document.

The key to the iron triangle lies in the grandes écoles, where most successful political, corporate, and bureaucratic careers begin. France has long had an unusual dual system of higher education. People outside of France tend to think first of the university system, including the Sorbonne, one of the first institutions of higher education in the world. However, the universities are overcrowded and understaffed. Most observers do not think that the universities provide their students with either a quality education or the skills they need to succeed in whatever career they choose to pursue.

In addition to the universities are the grandes écoles, which are smaller, specialized, and highly selective. There are about 250 of them. Some are very old, such as the École des Ponts and Chaussés, founded in 1747 to educate people to design bridges and roads. Napoléon founded the École polytechnique after the revolution to train artillery and other military officers. Others are newer and somewhat less prestigious. Nonetheless, they all are seen as more important and better for a student's career prospects than the conventional universities.

Any student who passes the "bac," or the exam students take, at the end of high school (*lycée*) can go to a university. Admission to a grande école is an entirely different matter. Each one administers its own entrance exam. Students who want to attend one typically spend a few years after high school graduation either at a postgraduate institution (*lycée préparatoire*) or a handful of undergraduate schools outside of the university system, most notably the Institute for Political Studies in Paris.

The grandes écoles are truly the elite of French higher education. Although they enroll only 4 percent of the men and women who study beyond high school, they get about 30 percent of the funding. Moreover, admission to most of them also means membership in a bureaucratic corps or agency that all but ensures lifetime tenure for those who want to stay in the civil service. No tuition is charged; in fact, the students are paid the equivalent of an entry-level salary for the two or three years of their studies.

Many of these schools train students for careers in business or engineering. Typical of these is the École nationale de l'aviation civile, which is located near the headquarters of the Airbus company in the outskirts of Toulouse.

For our purposes, the key is the handful of schools that now produce France's leadership. The top few have transcended their narrow intellectual origins and see their mission as training the future leaders of the country.

The most important is the *École nationale d'administration*, which was created by de Gaulle in 1946 to create a new generation of civil servants who would break the country out of what I called the stalemate society in Chapter 3. Older schools, such as Polytechnique, Hautes études commerciales (HEC) and a handful of others have also become as sought after (and competitive) a place for a young person to attend as the Ivy League colleges in the United States.

Graduates of the ENA and the other top schools join the grands corps of the bureaucracy and are on a fast track to the top of the civil service. However, most only owe the government ten years of service (some less) before they can leave public employment.

And there the politically interesting part begins.

Many ENArques stay in the civil service for their entire careers. Others leave and follow a new career path known as pantouflage, in which they can move on to powerful and lucrative careers in politics or the private sector.

In short, they retire from the civil service, normally long before they turn forty. At that point, they move in one or both of two directions. They can become a manager at a leading public or private sector corporation,

Pantouflage and Amakudari

France is not the only country in which civil servants move on to political careers.

In Japan, the best and brightest bureaucrats stay in government until it becomes clear which ones will reach the top.

At that point, those who will not become permanent secretaries resign and join either the dominant Liberal Democratic Party (LDP) or a corporation.

They normally do so in their fifties, unlike the ENArques, who engage in pantouflage during their thirties.

The Japanese term for this behavior, *amakudari*, is best translated as "descent from heaven."

Enough said.

half of whose CEOs are former grandes écoles students. Or, they can move into politics.

It is hard to pin down the exact number of graduates at these schools who are at the top of French economic or political life. Most leading politicians and, probably, half of the top executives of major corporations are former civil servants and grandes écoles graduates.

In early 2007 most major politicians were graduates of one of these schools, especially the ENA. President Chirac and his erstwhile rival, Lionel Jospin, were two years apart at ENA. The former Socialist prime minister Michel Rocard graduated a year after Chirac. Rumor has it that they engage in their hobby of sailing together.

Among the politicians who are likely to dominate the next decade, Dominique de Villepin graduated from ENA in 1980. One of his classmates was Ségolène Royal, the Socialist presidential candidate in 2007. Her former partner, François Hollande, is a graduate of Sciences Po (the Institute of Political Studies), ENA, and HEC. Among the few current leading politicians, Nicolas Sarkozy did not go to ENA, although he did go to Sciences Po before going to law school.

It's not just any ENA or other grandes écoles graduate who rises to the top. At ENA the 120 students who are part of each class are ranked, and those at the top have the first choice of jobs in the civil service. They typically pick the positions that will either give them the best chance of reaching the top of the civil service or moving on, out, and up through pantouflage.

As Jacques Attali, a former ENArque and chief adviser to President Mitterrand put it: "ENA isn't just a school, it's a selection procedure. If you're ranked in the top 15, your life will be totally different than if you're number 16 or below. The function of ENA is simply to arrive at the final 15."[3]

The iron triangle works because most of the graduates of ENA and similar schools started as part of an intellectual and political elite, saw their status enhanced while studying, and then became plugged into powerful

Figure 7.1 The Iron Triangle

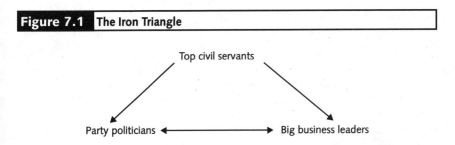

networks of "old boys" (and now a handful of girls) that had a lot to do with their promotion in any important professional community. It has thus been an iron triangle (see Figure 7.1) that has held sway not just on issues such as agricultural subsidies in the United States but at the highest levels of power.

The impact of ENArques and graduates of similar schools is declining. But only by a bit. As revealed in the next chapter, the big public and private companies they run are no longer squarely at the heart of the economy. And their dominance in political life since the mid-1960s has drawn significant criticism at home and abroad.

Nonetheless, the fact that all the serious candidates in 2007 come from the iron triangle tells us a lot about its continuing impact. To see this as bluntly and as clearly as possible, consider two quotes from senior civil servants that Princeton's Ezra Suleiman included in a book on the political clout of the civil service.

> We always consult. It doesn't mean we listen, but we consult. We don't always reveal our intentions. We reveal only as much as we think it is necessary to reveal.
>
> *—Ministry of Education*

> First, we make out a report or draw up a text, then we pass it around discreetly within the administration. Once everyone concerned within the administration is agreed on the final version, then we pass this version around outside the administration. Of course, by then it's a fait accompli *and pressure cannot have any effect.* [Emphasis added.]
>
> *—Ministry of Industry*[4]

Normal Politics in Normal Times

This chapter has covered a lot of ground, some of which is likely to be confusing to readers whose previous work has been focused on American or British politics. Therefore, it is worth returning to the key themes raised so far, before we move on to three others, which complicate the picture even further. France has a strong state that is dominated by the executive for three main reasons. First, there are the provisions of the constitution which favor the president, the prime minister, and government. Second, the results of every election since 1962 have produced a firm parliamentary majority. Finally, informal structures, such as the iron triangles, magnify the power of the executive through cooperation with its allies outside of government.

Key Concepts

bloc vote   120
Constitutional Consultative Commission   114
corporatism   131
decentralization   127
direct election of the president   116
incompatibility clause   117
iron triangle   130
vote of censure   120

Key People, Entities, and Events

Article 11   115
Article 16   115
Article 23   117
Senate   120

Questions for Discussion

1. Political scientists often talk about constitution "engineering" to describe what happened in France in 1958 and, more recently, in the former Soviet bloc. How did constitutional engineering reshape French political life? Why did that happen?

2. Very few other democratic countries have a bureaucratic structure (or culture) to rival that of France. Why is that the case?

3. What if your home country had a civil service and grandes écoles to rival those in France? How would that change politics there?

8

Domestic Public Policy

France is not only a large state but an active one as well. In recent years, state expenditures have accounted for well over 40 percent of the country's GNP, and taxes eat up almost half of the average citizen's pay.

But although the tax rates are at least as high as those in almost any other country, the French get a lot for their money. The state provides an array of social services that are as extensive as any in Europe. For most of the time since World War II, the state also played a major role in sparking an unprecedented rate of economic growth that turned France from an economic backwater into one of the four or five most affluent countries in the world.

The French state certainly has its critics. Many claim that it is bloated and inefficient. It has not, for instance, been able to do much to reduce an unemployment rate that has hovered between 9 and 12 percent for the last twenty years. France has not been able to withstand the "liberal" policy shifts since the Reagan and Thatcher years that have seen the size of most states in the industrial democracies shrink. And there are whole areas of French life that the state cannot address, something ruefully noted by then Prime Minister Raffarin during the heat wave of 2003, when hundreds of Parisians died of weather-induced heart attacks and other diseases.

Yet, on balance, the French state is impressive. Indeed, it does so much that all of its policies cannot be covered in a single chapter. Some of its more unusual (and criticized) functions must, alas, be skipped here, such as the machines that used to pick up dog droppings from Parisian streets or the commission that routinely bans words like "e-mail" from the French language. Instead, the focus here is on the social and economic policies that have made the French state such a central feature in people's daily lives.

Social Services

Politicians throughout Europe and North America refer to the **welfare state** as a "safety net" that protects people who fall on hard times because of unemployment, illness, old age, and other reasons. Nevertheless, no two safety nets are alike in regard to what they cover and how they go about achieving their goals.

The governments in the United States and Japan offer fewer services than their European counterparts. As of this writing, for example, about 45 million Americans lacked basic health care coverage. The United States is also the only country where health insurance is typically tied to one's employment status.

Similarly, tuition at George Mason University (a state institution), where I teach, is about $6,500 a year. Room and board can be more than that, depending on the type of room and meal plan a student chooses. Tuition, room, and board at Oberlin College (a private school I went to as an undergraduate) is more than $43,000.

Furthermore, in legislation passed during the Clinton administration the United States sharply reduced the amount of time people could receive welfare payments. Social Security payments are reasonably high by global standards. However, more and more employees and retirees are finding that the private pension plans they counted on are either being sharply cut or eliminated altogether and Social Security payments will cover only a fraction of their needs in retirement.

Principle No. 1: From Cradle to Grave

By contrast, safety nets in western Europe have far fewer "holes." Of course, you see homeless people selling newspapers on housing issues in Paris and other major cities. And Paris still has some of its (in)famous clochards, who hang out on the banks of the Seine day and night drinking cheap wine. On New Year's Eve, 2006, a group of activists supporting the homeless camped out on Parisian streets to help revelers see just how difficult life was for the down and out.

Although there is little abject poverty among the white population in France, it is still seen among the nonwhites and some older citizens who never benefited from the postwar economic boom. Indeed, there are cracks in the social service system, and some conservative politicians would like to cut back those programs. It is possible, too, that the new president, Nicolas Sarkozy, will try to reduce taxes and thus some of the benefits even more.

Principle No. 2: Not for the Poor Alone

Americans tend to assume that poor people are somehow responsible for their problems and should "pull themselves up by their own bootstraps." Social service programs typically have stiff eligibility requirements. Only people below the poverty line and with less than $3,000 worth of family assets are eligible for the food stamp program (now administered with debit cards). Such programs are seen as a privilege and often require cumbersome application forms. Some recipients think of the help they get through these programs as a sign of failure and worry that they are stigmatized because they have to take assistance from national, state, or local governments.

In France these services are seen in a very different light. The French tend to view poverty in most of its forms not as a sign of an individual's failure but as a failure of the system as a whole. Of course, in addition to deserving French people and lazy Americans there are lazy French people and Americans whose poverty is no fault of their own.

The point here is that, like most Europeans, the French have decided to err on the side of the disadvantaged. Are there people receiving benefits who conceivably could or should be working? Of course. But French governments on the left and right alike have decided to maintain and even expand benefits to protect the "victims" of capitalism's ups and downs even if that means giving some money to people that some Americans would call "welfare cheaters."

In short, the programs are seen as a right, not a privilege. Many of them have no **means testing** and are referred to as "all in" because everyone is eligible to participate.

The Variety of Social Services

Mass Transportation. It is hard to miss France's social services. Tourists see them the minute they arrive at Charles de Gaulle airport, where they will find three different public transit options to get them to the center of Paris.

Paris's mass transit system is among the most extensive and efficient in any of the world's major cities. The Metro covers the entire city and most of the inner suburbs; there were, for instance, five stops within 200 yards of an apartment I used to live in at the heart of the Latin Quarter. No building in the city is more than 500 yards from one of the 368 stations. The system is also one of the most user-friendly in the world. Ticket prices are subsidized and cheaper than those in London or Washington. The sleek modern cars glide on all-but-silent rubber wheels. Seats are reserved for the elderly, mothers with large families, and men who were gravely wounded in war, of which France today has very few. An integrated network of buses serves the entire region and is often preferred by people who would rather ride above ground and avoid changing trains two or three times.

Paris also has a network of high-speed suburban trains. The RER's five lines and their many branches go to the outermost suburbs, which have seen the most growth in recent years. When they get into Paris itself, the RER's lines are completely integrated with the Metro and have stops at all of the city's major train stations. Suburbs not located on an RER line are served by conventional trains.

France pioneered the TGV, or high-speed trains, which go at speeds of more than 200 miles an hour. Those trains now are linked to lines to most major cities in France and similar networks of sophisticated trains in all neighboring countries.

Most smaller cities are served by slower, local trains, which may stop as frequently as every ten to fifteen miles but do run on a regular basis. The smallest towns and cities still have reasonably reliable bus service.

Raising a Family. All children are eligible for day care through the public school system from the age of three (in some cases two) on. Attendance is voluntary. Children are only legally required to start school at age six. However, most parents send their children to an école maternelle because most mothers and fathers these days both have to work. Thus, about a third of two-year-olds attend one, as do 95 percent of three- and four-year-olds and virtually every five-year-old.

The system is not new. Its precursors date from the eighteenth century and served as homes for orphans or children whose parents could not support them. With the beginning of the Industrial Revolution and the rapid growth in the number of urban women who entered the workforce, a succession of French governments decided to create what has turned into the modern system of "mother's schools."

Teachers and teachers' aides all have the same level of training as their colleagues in elementary schools. The curriculum and other programs are determined by the Ministry of Education. Children master French, begin to learn how to read and write, and explore the arts. They also engage in the kinds of activities found in any early education program, including learning to be with others, playing, and napping. The French system is by far the world's best in integrating preschool with elementary school.

Most maternelles are run by the national and local governments, which cover the cost of about $6,000 per student per year. An effort is under way to enroll more two-year-olds from disadvantaged neighborhoods. The program is extremely popular in the population as a whole.

Most parents receive *allocations familiales* (**family allocations**) to help defray the cost of raising their children. Although best known for those payments, the Caisse des Allocations Familiales also provides legal and other social services. The budget is over 50 billion euros (1 euro equaled U.S. $1.31 on June 12, 2007) and the system has more than 10 million clients.

The allocations were begun in 1932 for a simple reason. The French population was growing at a minuscule rate, whereas that of Germany was skyrocketing. Politicians thus decided to enact policies that would encourage parents to have more children, including paying them subsidies to do so.

In other words, the family allocations were not introduced to provide more social justice. But that is how they are seen today. The amounts parents receive do not have a huge impact on upper-middle-class families. They certainly do help families who are dependent on the minimum wage of about

Transportation in London and Washington, D.C.

The quality of the Parisian system can be seen in quick comparisons with two other cities renowned for their mass transit.

London's Underground (the Tube) is the most heavily used subway system in the world and extends farther into the suburbs than the Parisian Metro. It, too, is connected to a network of suburban and national railroads. However, unlike the system in Paris, the equipment is old. Breakdowns are far more common. Leaves on the tracks have been known to shut down suburban rail lines. Many of the stations are dirty.

Washington, D.C., has the second most widely used mass transit system in the United States. Its Metro is fairly new; its first stations opened in 1976. Therefore, it does not have London's problem of an aging infrastructure. However, it only has eighty-six stations; large parts of the city of Washington are not near a station. That means that many people have to take long and slow bus trips to get to the Metro. Five commuter lines actually go farther from the city than in either Paris or London, but as with the Washington Metro, huge areas of the region have no mass transit service of any sort. As a result, traffic is so bad that one of the most popular columns in the *Washington Post* is by "Dr. Gridlock."

Child Care in the United States and the United Kingdom

Child care and preschool policy in the United States is hard to document. One thing is certain. There is no equivalent of the maternelles.

Child care has historically been poorly regulated and not connected to elementary education, but that is changing. For many Americans, child care services are offered by employers. My university has a center. So does the CIA, although children there have name tags that list only their first name.

The one real success of American preschool education is Head Start. More than 900,000 children are enrolled. Until recently, most of them came from underprivileged families, although most children with disabilities are also now eligible. The evidence that Head Start helps get children ready for school, especially children who might otherwise fail, is overwhelming.

The United States is also a leader in developing before- and after-school programs for children in elementary and secondary school.

France lags both on aid to the underprivileged in other areas, especially regarding before- and after-school programs.

The United Kingdom has a similar system to aid parents and their children, known as Child Benefit. It, too, is tied to other family services. It is not quite as generous as France's. Families get about 100 euros a month (the benefit is paid on a weekly basis) for the eldest child and 70 euros for all the others in the household. But as revealed throughout this chapter, the British and French systems have more in common with each other than they do with that in the United States.

$1,500 a month or the other programs designed to provide subsistence-level income for the unemployed (see the section on the workplace).

In 2006 those payments went to all families that had at least two children. Two-child families got just over 100 euros; each additional child brought the family an additional 150 euros; teenagers from eleven to sixteen got another 30 euros; those between sixteen and eighteen got 30 more.

The Caisse des Allocations Familiales has also been expanding its scope in recent years to cope with changes in family status. Now, its Web site and office helps families rent or buy homes. It has supplemental benefits for single parents and for parents who choose to stay at home to raise their children.

Higher Education. French universities are generally open to anyone who passes the *baccalauréat* exam at the end of high school. Seventy years ago, very few students passed the "bac." Universities were small and elitist. Today, about 80 percent of all students pass the bac and are eligible to go to a university. In recent years, students have been able to take versions of the bac in the sciences, social sciences, and arts and literature, which make them eligible for only some university departments.

Entrance to the schools that prepare students for the grandes écoles requires a higher score on the bac. They later have to pass the exams that each school offers on its own and requires of all applicants.

American students are often shocked to hear that tuition at French universities is typically about 300 euros a year. It may be twice as high at engineering or other technical schools and similar departments in traditional universities. Another 180 euros provides a basic health insurance package. Living costs are normally not subsidized, especially in older universities, which do not have a tradition of residential campuses. Private business schools charge as much as 6,000 euros. Otherwise, the state pays the overwhelming majority of the cost of higher education, which it covers by giving each university about 6,000 euros per year per student (by contrast, George Mason University gets a bit more than $2,000 per student from the Commonwealth of Virginia).

The grandes écoles are an even better deal for students. On matriculation, they are considered civil servants in training and are paid as such. ENA is typical. Students who came directly from a university earned 1,300 euros a month in 2006. Those with experience in the private sector or the civil service made 2,000.

However, as the French would say, *fais gaffe.* Don't read too much into these figures.

Higher education also shows us the first major problems in the French cradle-to-grave network. French universities do not provide as good an education as even the largest and most impersonal American ones.

To start with, France dedicates only about 1.1 percent of its GNP to higher education compared with 2.6 percent in the United States. This is easiest to see in deteriorating buildings, poorly stocked libraries, and lecture halls that are too small to allow all students to attend class. Students get very little attention from faculty members, especially from the "turboprofs," who, as mentioned earlier, teach at provincial universities but refuse to move from Paris and therefore show up on campus for a day or two a week to teach all their classes. Perhaps as a result, the drop-out rate tops 40 percent, and students who do graduate have trouble finding jobs.

There is a widespread understanding that higher education is in trouble. The president of the Sorbonne has written a book, *Youth—They Are Lying to You*. A union leader called the universities the "shame of our nation." A Socialist presidential hopeful for the 2007 election said the system should be "dynamited." During the 2007 campaign, the fiscally conservative Nicolas Sarkozy proposed a 50 percent increase in state funding for higher education, although it is far too early to tell how far his government is likely to go on that pledge.

The Adult Years. We will look at three major concerns adults in any country have during their lifetimes.

First, health care is, for all intents and purposes, free of charge in France. Unlike Britain, French doctors are not state employees but in something akin to American private practice. Still, the government plays a major role in health care.

Like family allocations and the maternelles, there is nothing new to government-funded health care in France. The first voluntary insurance programs date from 1893. Health insurance became mandatory for all salaried employees in 1930. It was expanded soon after World War II to cover farmers and, later, small-business owners and salaried managers. As a result, this incrementally designed system can seem bewildering to outsiders because many funds manage it. However, the differences have little effect on the way most people obtain and fund their health care coverage today.

To begin with, the funds reimburses patients for 85 percent of most fees charged by doctors, pharmacists, and hospitals although only 70 percent for visits to one's primary care provider. Eighty percent of the people take out a supplemental policy (*mutuelle*) to cover the rest. Often, employers pay for those policies. The poorest French men and women receive totally free health care.

However, because patients have to pay for their care up front, as many as a quarter of the population used to delay seeking it because of the short-term costs. Now, everyone has a smart card that a health care provider can swipe, generate the needed forms electronically, and get the patient all but immediate reimbursement.

Most hospitals are run either by the government or by universities. About 3 percent of them are managed by for-profit corporations or non-profit-making charities, including the American Hospital in the suburbs of Paris.

Higher Education in the United Kingdom

Many educational experts on the Continent are finally beginning to look favorably on the British system. Until the late 1990s the state covered all tuition costs, although not room and board. In 1998 the Blair government introduced a scheme that allowed universities to charge tuition, which today can be as much as £3,000 ($5,000) a year. Typically, the government loans the money to students, and they begin to pay it back only after their income reaches a certain level.

Although probably necessary, the tuition fees have been extremely unpopular in Britain. They probably would be in France as well.

More so than their present-day British and American counterparts, French students often take to the street in protest over both domestic and international issues. The French students shown here in Lyons in 2005 were demonstrating against government plans to cut teaching staff.

About 60 percent of the cost of health care comes from Social Security taxes. The rest is provided by sales taxes on such "sin" products as alcohol and tobacco.

There are some holes in the system. Individuals have to pay for their hospital beds. Dental coverage is not as extensive as basic medical care. The cost of medications considered "comfort drugs" are not fully reimbursed. Some eighty-four drugs (including Viagra) are not covered at all.

France commits more of its resources to health care than most countries. In 2005, 9.7 percent of its GNP went to health care, compared with 7.7 percent in the United Kingdom. To the surprise of many, the United States devotes 14.6 percent of its GNP to health care, but at least 1 percent of that goes to the costs of filling out all the forms needed for our disorganized system.

The French health care system is quite popular, including the fact that pharmacists can also offer basic medical advice, often for free if clients pick up a prescription. However, there are problems, although not as severe as those we saw for higher education. Hospitals tend to be old and overcrowded. Costs continue to mount as medications become more expensive and the population ages. There are often long waiting lists for nonemergency surgical procedures.

Still, France, like every industrial democracy other than the United States, provides basic health care and then some for all its citizens.

The second concern is how France deals with unemployment. Before the recession brought on by the OPEC oil embargo of 1973–1974, this was not a major issue. Most people had jobs, and those who lost them could realistically expect to find a new one that paid as well or better quite quickly. In short, unemployment compensation in France as in most countries was designed to provide short-term support for people who would soon be back in the workforce.

Over the last thirty years, that situation has changed dramatically. Between 1959 and 1974, the unemployment rate never reached 3 percent. Since then, it has never been that low. In eight of the ten years of the 1990s, it was over 10 percent. In the first five years of this decade, it never reached 10 percent, but it was over 9 percent in all but one of them. Unemployment figures can be deceptive because countries calculate them differently; the United States, for instance, counts as unemployed only those people actively looking for jobs, whereas France includes everyone who has not had a job in the previous six months. Nonetheless, the French rate is high and has been so for a long time.

It isn't just the overall rate that matters. Many of the people who lurk within the statistics have no chance of getting meaningful work; the best they can hope for are poorly paid, insecure jobs. Three groups are particularly badly hurt—the young, relatively poorly educated middle-aged men and women, and immigrants and their children.

We All Ration

Despite the vast amounts of money that are spent today on health care, no country is rich enough to pay for everyone's needs.

In other words, leaders in the public and private sector in every country have to make tough decisions on how much money is going to be made available to cover which people and to focus on which medical problems.

Needless to say, the problems facing France or Britain or the United States are minor compared with those of a country like Botswana, which cannot afford to pay for the "cocktail" of drugs that could keep the third of its population infected with HIV alive.

Nonetheless, all countries have to make choices and have to ration their expenditures, favoring some people or maladies over others.

France and Britain have chosen to cover everyone even if that means not providing the highest quality health care for everyone. The United States has not. What that means is that 15 percent of Americans have no health insurance. But because I can afford expensive health insurance, I have better coverage than my French friends who are as well off as I am but have to rely on the public health system.

The British have long experimented with a separate private health care system through which people buy their own insurance and, when necessary, bypass the National Health Service and the concerns many people have about quality control and waiting times.

But the fact remains that we all ration.

The choices are never easy.

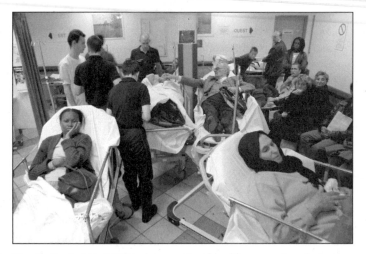

Despite the fact that France has a national health care system that covers everyone, unlike the U.S. health care system, the quality of care can vary greatly according to the socioeconomic status of the patient. Here, immigrant and elderly patients await treatment in the emergency room of a hospital in Creteil, a suburb of Paris with a high immigrant population.

Until the post-OPEC economic crisis hit, France was extremely generous to the unemployed. Depending on why they lost their jobs, laid-off workers could get as much as 90 percent of their previous income in unemployment compensation. That was true only if their employer decided to shut down and move the factory or other workplace. Still, anyone who was unemployed got a generous sum that exceeded the Organization for Economic Cooperation and Development (OECD) norm of 60 percent of either the average or the individual's wage before losing his or her job.

The same authority that supervises the family allocations and pension plans (see below) is responsible for unemployment compensation as well. Its provisions are as complicated for this type of compensation as they are for that of the other plans it administers.

As of 2004, workers contributed 2 percent of their salaries to the unemployment fund; their employers put in a bit more than twice that amount. Not all unemployed workers are eligible for compensation. Essentially one has to have been employed for at least a quarter of the time during the preceding two years and lost the job for reasons other than incompetence or other disciplinary reasons. That means that no more than 60 percent of the unemployed receive benefits, which, alas, is a figure that compares favorably with most other wealthy countries.

If eligible, a worker receives at least 25 euros a day or the equivalent of 75 percent of the going wage rate for his or her job, whichever is lower. Depending on how long the person had worked and other criteria, unemployment benefits are available for between seven months and three years.

The final, most difficult, and potentially most expensive program covers pensions for retirees. As with health care, one of the main problems France and most other industrial countries face is an aging population. As of 2006 a little more than 16 percent of the French population was over sixty-five. That figure was a bit lower in the United States and the United Kingdom, but it now tops 20 percent in Japan and comes very close in Germany. In all these countries, the average life expectancy at birth is close to eighty. Most women live even longer.[1] The burden of an aging population will only grow as the baby boomers retire and new medications and technologies allow them to live long lives, albeit at an ever greater cost to society.

By the 1940s, most industrial democracies had established basic pension programs that would allow retirees to avoid abject poverty. The Germans developed the first comprehensive pension scheme in the late nineteenth century. The United States introduced social security as part of the New Deal reforms during the 1930s. Britain and France enacted all-inclusive programs only after World War II.

The normally accepted goal for pensions is 60 percent of the retiree's annual income. However, few countries achieve that through public pension programs alone.

Therefore, like France and the United States, most have established multitiered systems through which individuals supplement the basic state payment with money they invested through the private sector. Those schemes vary widely from country to country and from industry to industry. Thus, I will have Social Security, a pension through TIAA-CREF (which covers most academics), an IRA, and interest from investments. My wife, who is a retired federal worker, is not eligible for Social Security (until recently federal employees did not pay into the fund) but receives an unusually generous pension, which is about 60 percent of her best three earning years and is adjusted each year for inflation. By contrast, someone in my situation needs a supplemental pension, because Social Security estimates that I will get about $1,500 a month if I retire at sixty-five.

The French system is at least as complicated as that in any other country. About 120 separate pension plans are part of what the French government calls the "general scheme" of social security that now covers almost all private sector workers. Average pensions are somewhat over $20,000 a year, although supplements are available for dependents and other circumstances. The payments individuals and their employers make to the social security system go up with income, and to a lesser degree, so, too, do the size of their pensions. To be fully eligible for a maximum pension, private sector workers have to work for forty years (160 quarters) and be at least sixty-five.

Things are even more complicated in the public sector. There, the various "services" had their own schemes that were often more generous and required less time on the job. The government elected in 2002 to simplify the system and make the benefits in the public and private sectors more similar. The bill incurred the wrath of public sector unions and their workers because it will require them to meet the same criteria in regard to years of service by 2012 and will actually rise to forty-two years on the job by 2020. At that point, public and private sector employees should enjoy the same benefits for the same number of years on the job. Despite protests from railroad and other public transportation workers, the bill did pass, but pensions are not likely to disappear as a political issue.

The one reform that drew almost universal approval but also passed largely below the media radar screen made it easier for workers to set up their own individual retirement funds, much like American 401(k)3 plans. That is especially important in France because private sector firms have very few tax incentives to create their own independent pension schemes, which have been common in the United States—at least until recently.

There are two bottom lines here. First, the French do pretty well on balance. Between publicly and privately funded schemes, the average retiree gets the equivalent of almost 80 percent of his or her salary. Before pensions are taken into account, 40 percent of French retirees would fall below the poverty line. Pensions reduce that figure to 24 percent and other social services to 15 percent. Poverty among the elderly is concentrated in the oldest and least-skilled citizens who did not live under the Sécu for all of their working lives and contributed relatively little to it. Second, the system is so expensive that the 2003 reforms will cut the portion of their former salaries that retirees will get. Nonetheless, the rate of public spending on pensions will rise from 12.1 percent in 2003 to an estimated 16 percent in 2030.[2]

Markets and the Logic of the Interventionist State

For our purposes, French domestic policy is just as important because of the role the state has long played in guiding a basically capitalist economy, something some political scientists and economists call an interventionist state. As a major political force, such a state is a relatively new phenomenon. Prior to the last third of the nineteenth century, few states provided many services of any sort, even police forces or universal elementary education. States became involved because the churches and other bodies that had taken on such responsibilities before were no longer able to shoulder the burden. But in France, the government did not just step in to fill some gaps. Long before the creation of modern capitalism, it had been involved in creating and promoting favored industries. Today, that makes France one of the few countries that still tries to forge cooperative links between the public and private sector, which is yet another version of the interventionist state.

Market Failure

Students who take a course in basic macroeconomic principles learn that the laws of supply and demand should work in a way that minimizes the need for government economic involvement. However, as neoclassical economists have to acknowledge, two major ways in which markets do not always work as the textbooks anticipate have led states to address social and economic problems, sometimes in an aggressive manner.

The first way involves what the economists call public goods. Traditional economists insist that the market is the most efficient way to meet most social needs because the profit motive will reduce costs and maximize benefits to the largest number of people possible. However, there are some public goods that will never be produced if people only pursue their self-interest as economists define that term. The leading neoclassical economist of our time, Milton Friedman, suggested that there were at least two of these—education and defense—which the market would not provide and which therefore became the state's responsibility.[3]

Every country also experiences **market failures,** when something goes wrong with the way the market functions. The most common examples involve corporations or trade unions that have power enough to affect and distort the price-setting operations of the market. Even the most diehard neoclassical economists accept that the state may have to intervene in at least the worst of those instances.

We have already seen a good sample of the kinds of social service programs provided by the French state. On that front, it is very much in the western European mainstream. As seen in the discussion below of macro- and, especially, microeconomic policy, France has long been one of the countries that most used the state to shape economic life.

Before turning to state involvement in the economy, it should be stressed that these programs have lost much of their support since the early 1980s, when the American president Ronald Reagan and the British prime minister Margaret Thatcher spearheaded a trend that reduced, in particular, the number of **nationalized firms** directly owned or controlled by the government. The decline, however, has been less pronounced in France than in most other countries.

Dirigisme and Its Offspring

As capitalism evolved, it developed in two basic but very different ways. In the United States and Great Britain, a market-based version came to dominate in the rhetoric if not always the reality of economic life. In France, Japan, and to a lesser degree Germany, a very different approach took hold, which downplayed the role of the market. Instead, the state would use its influence and legitimacy to actively steer the economy through what the French call dirigisme. Although all but impossible to translate into English, as we saw in Chapter 2, dirigisme refers to a political system in which the government plays a major role in "directing" the economy through a mixture of public ownership, regulation, and informal cooperation between the public and private sectors.

Recall that these are countries in which such cultural norms as the American "the government that governs least governs best" are not strongly held. They also have a long history of state economic involvement that actually antedates the rise of modern market economics, which most observers date with the publication of Adam Smith's *The Wealth of Nations* in 1776.

As we saw in Chapters 3 and 4, dirigisme did not help France develop a modern capitalist economy under the Third and, to some extent, the Fourth Republics. If anything, the state helped prop up a system of fairly small, family-owned, and not very competitive businesses.

What I will try to show here is that under the Gaullists, both during the Liberation and after their return to power with the creation of the Fifth Republic, all that changed. One cannot argue that the state—or any other single factor—produced les trentes glorieuses and the successes France has had since then. However, the transformations either created directly by the state itself or encouraged by it indirectly in the private sector go a long way toward explaining why France is arguably the fourth or fifth leading economic power in the world.

Nationalized Industries

The most controversial aspect of the interventionist state has been the nationalization of what policymakers took to be critical industries. Public takeovers of formerly privately owned companies have their origins in Marxism and social democracy. However, as with the welfare state, many on

What Is Capitalism?

British and American students often have trouble accepting the notion that France can have a capitalist economy *and* have a strong, interventionist state. But that is precisely what this second version of capitalism is built on. The overwhelming majority of the economy is in private hands, and even some of the companies owned by the government are driven by the profit motive every bit as much as any corporation.

the French center right accepted the fact that some enterprises are better run as a public monopoly and have tolerated significant state involvement even in the industries that have been privatized since 1986.

The Left does not have a monopoly on nationalizing industries. Long before there were socialists, the English and French kings promoted public monopolies. In the French case they included such different industries as match and cigarette production and the making of tapestries. However, nationalization became pivotal and controversial when it became a centerpiece for modern socialism. To revolutionary and other orthodox Marxists, virtually nothing would be left of capitalism once they took power. Social democrats, by contrast, were only interested in taking over what the British Labour Party called the "commanding heights" of the economy. In either case, the logic was the same. Privately owned firms would be taken over and run for the public good, not for the profit of a handful of wealthy owners.

France had two waves of nationalization, the first occurring right after World War II and the second following the Socialists' landslide victory in 1981. In practice, the decisions to nationalize what amounted eventually to about a quarter of the economy had three main causes.

Ideology actually was not all that important a factor in the first round of nationalizations. Relatively few manufacturing firms were taken over. Rather, the Gaullist led, but left-of-center, government primarily nationalized public utilities and other firms that provided services the leadership took to be pivotal and thus had to be ensured by the state. These included the railroads, gas and electricity generation, Air France, coal mines, and the like. The government also nationalized a number of companies whose owners had collaborated with the Germans, the most prominent of which was Renault. The only major exceptions to this pragmatic approach were the insurance industry and the "clearing" banks, which were in control of moving money between individual and corporate accounts. Between the late 1940s and 1981, the French nationalized only a few companies, typically those that were in danger of going bankrupt, as was the case with the entire steel industry in the early 1970s. The government also built up many of its assets in petrochemical companies it already partially owned and refused to allow its one computer manufacturer, Bull, to go bankrupt, justifying both in terms of national security needs.

As was the case in Britain, the end of World War II marked the first time that left-of-center parties gained control of the national government, albeit sharing it with de Gaulle. However right wing he was, de Gaulle understood that the state needed to play a major role in rebuilding the economy, which he assumed meant taking over many of the privately owned companies that could not rebuild from wartime damage let alone create a truly modern, industrial economy on their own.

Again as in Britain, the French government took over many public utilities and other firms that seemed to have a natural monopoly in an industrial sector. That included the distribution of electricity and gas, the railroads, the commercial airlines, the three major savings banks, most of the coal mines, and more. The coal mines may have been the most important, because they provided almost all the fuel for both electrical generation and home heating, and the industry was in tatters.

At their peak, the nationalized companies accounted for about 20 percent of total national production. In theory, that was supposed to give the government considerable influence over the way France rebuilt and then re-created a world-class economy.

Until the 1980s, nationalization was not as controversial as it had become in the United Kingdom. There, the government had taken over far more troubled firms (giving rise to the term "lemon socialism"). And generally speaking, French publicly owned firms were run rather well, as evidenced by Renault's position as a European market leader and the introduction of the high-speed TGV trains in the 1970s.

That was not to last. Nationalization was very much an ideological matter for the Socialists in the 1970s and early 1980s. Despite his late conversion to socialism, Mitterrand made nationalizing leading industries a central plank in the Common Program he negotiated with the Communists in 1972 and then in the party's own platform for the 1981 election. One of the Socialists' first acts on taking power was to pass a sweeping nationalization bill that covered five of France's largest multinational firms and thirty-six banks, including the leading commercial and investment firms.

The new Socialist government's program in general was extremely expensive and required heavy borrowing at a time when international interest rates were soaring. The PS had to abandon its radical goals within two years of taking office. Among other things, the nationalizations all but ground to a halt. To make matters worse, many of the newly nationalized companies began to lose money, which undercut support for them.

Nationalized firms, especially those run to enhance grandeur or the power of the state, found it increasingly difficult to compete in what was turning into a global marketplace. Such icons of French industry as Air France and France Telecom were in serious trouble by the late 1980s. Therefore, when Chirac took office as prime minister, he began selling off many of the nationalized firms, but he often did so in a way that maintained a significant state influence over them. That has been the case ever since, although

Gauloises and Gitanes

The two most famous state-owned cigarette brands were Gauloises and Gitanes.[a] The latter were only slightly less foul smelling than the former, and no serious smoker would have considered using a filter before the late 1960s.

The cigarettes were also often considered a sex symbol, especially when smoked by actors such as Humphrey Bogart in films like *Casablanca*.

Bogart's heavy smoking and drinking led to his death at fifty-seven from cancer.

In 2005 the French government and the firm that replaced the nineteenth-century Manufacture Française des Tabacs closed down the last factory in France that made Gauloises and Gitanes, although they are still made in Spain.

Note: Truth in advertising: I have to admit that I smoked Gauloises while living and doing research in France through much of the 1970s.

the slower pace of privatization in the last twenty years has sapped the issue of much of its controversy.

But an understanding of how and why France remained less market oriented than its neighbors and competitors must begin with an examination of the broad evolution of its economic policies in the postwar years.

The Rise of the ENArques

I mentioned tapestries and matches earlier in what might have seemed like a throwaway line. However, the French monarchy subsidized and all but ran the companies that made those large ruglike pieces of art that also served to keep unheated castles a bit warmer. The match industry is a bit newer, perhaps dating only from the 1830s. However, here, too (and later with cigarettes), the French state created a virtual monopoly over manufacture and distribution. In 1843 it did the same for mass-produced cigarettes, which were invented at about that time. The government-owned Manufacture Française des Tabacs gained a monopoly over the domestic market, although it was always possible to get imported cigarettes and other tobacco products.

But the role of the interventionist state came to affect much more than art and smoking products in the years after World War II. As noted in Chapter 4, the Gaullists set out to modernize the country's economy (and much more—see the next two chapters) by changing the kinds of people who ran it in ways eerily reminiscent of late-nineteenth-century Germany and Japan.

As we saw in Chapters 4 and 7, the Gaullists set out to remake the culture of the top civil servants under the Liberation government so that they would make France a more dynamic and modern country. Then, when the Gaullists returned to power, the first generation of ENArques were reaching positions of influence in the bureaucracy, from which the likes of Chirac and Giscard d'Estaing were recruited into the cabinet and then into electoral politics.

In other words, the Gaullist impact on the economy came in two waves. The first occurred in the immediate aftermath of the war. The second stretched from the late 1950s onward, when people in each of the three "points" of the iron triangle reached senior positions in their respective fields.

One cannot claim that the Gaullists were wholly responsible for the thirty years of unparalleled growth between the end of the war and the OPEC oil embargo. They certainly were not, especially in their first period in power.

In fact, economic growth was not a high priority for de Gaulle in and of itself except as it affected France's quest to restore its grandeur. But economics could not be ignored. France had been devastated by the war. Entire cities, especially in the northern half of the country, were in ruins. Its rail, electric, road, and other infrastructural systems were in even worse shape.

The ENA could not help with short-term recovery from either the physical or psychological damage left by six years of war. It was created in 1945, but it was really only in the following year that it was fully up and running. By the time the future president Giscard d'Estaing entered as part of the fourth full class its new kind of academic and practical culture was having ripple effects at other grandes écoles. Giscard was twenty-five years old when he graduated in 1951, which made him one of the first members of the the new elite to finish the two-year program. Nonetheless, because he was only twenty-five he was a full decade away from even thinking about reaching a top-level position either in the civil service or the government.

Instead, along with the Marshall Plan, the key institution during the Fourth Republic was the **General Planning Commission** (*Commissariat Général au Plan*). This should not be confused with Gosplan and other central planning groups that made decisions for all areas of economic life in Soviet-era Communist systems.

Rather, the Plan often did little more than try to predict what was likely to happen if resources were used in one way rather than another. At times—but only at times—governments had the political clout to enact and enforce the Plan's recommendations.

That was definitely the case in its first years. De Gaulle named the remarkable businessman, civil servant, and patriot Jean Monnet to be its first head. His impact on the modernization of France and all of Europe is discussed later, after a consideration of the role he played in creating the first European institutions that paved the way for the EU. Here, it is enough to know that he shared what would come to be common goals among the French economic elite for the next several decades. France had to use its limited resources wisely. That, in turn, required a commitment to transforming the structure and leadership of the economy in ways that entailed more cooperation and risk taking than the country had ever seen before.

The General Planning Commission was an unusual institution by French standards. It was small with no more than 120 staff members in the early years. Of them, no more than 20 percent were civil servants; the rest were hired as what we in twenty-first-century America would class as contractors. Most of the time, the director of the Plan reported directly to the prime minister and thus bypassed the traditional bureaucracy and hierarchy of the dozen or so ministries that had some responsibility for economic policy. Parliament was almost completely frozen out. The best book on the Plan and politics does give the parliament a full chapter, but it is only nine pages long.[4] That's how powerless the legislators were.

By today's standards, the Plan was remarkably simple. The economists created an admittedly large table in which they generated models of what they thought would happen, depending on how key inputs (cement, steel, railroad track, and the like) could be used and how different uses would affect key outputs of the rebuilding industrial economy (factory construction, ending transportation bottlenecks, new housing units, and the like).

The first two directors of the Plan were born in the nineteenth century. The next two were born in the 1920s, had little experience working under the republican synthesis, or stalemate, society; were open to new economic decision-making tools; and went on to prominent careers in the cabinet and the private sector.

By the early 1960s the Plan had begun to outlive its usefulness. Recovery was ensured. France was already being drawn into a more interdependent European and, to some degree, Western-wide economy. There were so many imports and exports that a basic input-output model based on domestic factors alone would not do much good in leading policymakers in promising directions. Perhaps most important, France needed to modernize individual industrial sectors and specific firms. In other words, the economic priorities began to shift from macroeconomic goals for the economy as a whole to microeconomic ones that focused state and private resources in a more intentional way.

It was at this time that the ENArques began to arrive en masse. Giscard was finance minister by 1962. Chirac got his first advisory post in the personal *cabinet* (office) of a minister the following year. The practice of pantouflage (see the preceding chapter) meant that more and more politicians and corporate executives had passed through ENA and the other schools whose curriculum and value system had also changed. Although the numbers have varied from time to time since then, about a third of all cabinet officers and nearly half of all corporate CEOs began their careers as senior civil servants. Not all attended ENA, but most of them have strong family, personal, and professional connections that stretch back to their high school years if not earlier.

Although Giscard was the only president to actually use the term "national champions," the government sought to create firms that would be just that and compete effectively at the European or global levels. Therefore, it used a combination of tax breaks, offers of investment capital, and other incentives to convince corporate leaders that they should merge or relocate to make their companies more efficient and, thus, competitive.

In the most famous example of a merger, France had five different automobile companies in the late 1960s. By the mid-1970s, they had been reduced to two, Renault and Peugeot-Citroen, both of which did very well in European markets (although not in the United States) until well into the 1980s. Similarly, the ENArques in the civil service, their friends in the Gaullist coalition and in the private sector came up with a deal that helped Renault move its aging and inefficient truck factories to the outskirts of Caen.

Overall, during the 1950s, the annual value of firms that merged was about 85 million francs. By 1970 the equivalent figure was 5 billion francs. Companies with more than 1,000 workers accounted for 20 percent of the workforce in the 1950s. Their share of the labor market doubled during the 1960s alone. In the late 1950s, none of the world's most profitable companies was French. In 1972 France had sixteen of them, compared with only five in Germany.

The iron triangles did not operate only at the national level. To see that, return to the city of Caen. Before World War II, Caen was a sleepy provincial town of about 40,000 residents and was all but completely destroyed during the aftermath of the D-Day invasion in 1944. The city was rebuilt quickly and, frankly, in a haphazard manner. Slums abutted middle-class neighborhoods. The neighborhoods near the banks of the Orne River were particularly lugubrious.

So the Gaullist members of the city council of Caen, their friends in real estate and other businesses, and the senior civil servants there and in Paris embarked on an ambitious plan in the 1960s. They knew the population and traffic pressures on Paris were getting out of hand. Caen was only two hours away. So they created a plan to make the city and its surrounding area an attractive place for companies to relocate and thus push the population to the quarter million it is today.

First, they made plans to build a ring road, or beltway, around the city of Caen itself. Industrial facilities were to be moved to the largely unpopulated communes in the suburbs now quickly reached through the new highways. Office-based companies would (re)locate in the center of the city. Rail connections to Paris were improved.

Second, they decided to turn Caen into a *ville verte*, or green city. Over the years, most working-class neighborhoods were razed and gentrified. More park space opened. The riverbank neighborhoods were cleaned up. The downtown shopping district was turned into a pedestrian mall.

Meanwhile, the poor were forced into the suburbs. Typical was the town of Hérouville St-Clair that had about 200 residents in 1960 and has almost 25,000 today, most of whom live in fairly bleak high-rises. The Renault factory is on the edge of town. Things have improved since I started studying the area in the mid-1980s. At the time, however, there were no cafés and few shops in the town. Schools were overcrowded. The iron triangle had won at the cost of the city's working class. Even with a new mall and better mass transit, Hérouville St-Clair is still a bleak place to visit, let alone live in.

The Decline of the ENArques

The title of this subsection is something of a misstatement. There are plenty of ENArques in what is a somewhat enfeebled iron triangle. The school is no longer the only route to power, although it is probably still the best one. For the first time since de Gaulle's presidency, neither the president nor the prime minister is an ENA graduate.

More important than their decline in numbers is their decline in influence. As seen in more detail in the next two chapters, France is less and less master of its financial destiny. No iron triangle can come close to ensuring the creation and nurturing of national champion companies when those companies have to compete globally and not just in France.

Thirty years ago, Air France and other public companies that were part of its group had a virtual monopoly on commercial air traffic. That's gone. France Telecom once had a monopoly on telephone service in France. That's gone, although it has actively invested abroad elsewhere in Europe, most notably in buying Orange, which had been a leading British wireless phone provider. The FNAC is one of the largest retailers of books, music, and electronic equipment. None of the personal computers it sells is French. There is some French software, but mostly the same things are sold as in the United States or any other English-speaking country, except that the package labeling and the instructions are in French.

Phrases such as "national champions" or Mitterrand's "reconquering the domestic market" seem more and more like empty slogans now that purely domestic markets are shrinking. People from the iron triangle have had their share of successes. One of the most notable of them was the public-private partnership formally established in the 1980s to incubate a French Silicon Valley around the small town of Sophia Antipolis just outside of Antibes on the Côte d'Azur. The town, by the way, was named in honor of its founder's wife whose name means "wisdom" in Greek; Antipolis is Greek for Antibes.

The founder, Senator Pierre Lafitte, put together a typical coalition of civil servants, politicians, and business leaders. The first companies moved in by 1988. The campus now has 1,300 employers and 30,000 jobs spread across almost twenty square kilometers, or nearly eight square miles.

But there is a key difference between Sophia Antipolis and the accomplishments of the iron triangle in that most of the companies employing the most people are not French. Of course, Air France, France Telecom, and a number of French university-based research labs are there. But so, too, are Hewlett-Packard, Accenture, Philips, and Cadence. IBM and Texas Instruments have large facilities nearby.

Back to Nationalization and Privatization

In sum, France has not been able to resist the increasingly global pressure to open economies, reduce barriers to trade, and integrate the world's economies and cultures (see the end of Chapter 10 as well). Yet, if we return to the fate of the nationalized industries discussed earlier, France has been at least marginally more effective in maintaining a significant role for the state in an economy in which private ownership increasingly predominates.

As part of the global reaction against big government and nationalized industries, the Gaullists made privatizing companies a central part of their election campaign in 1986. The rhetoric drawn from the policies of Margaret Thatcher in the United Kingdom (prime minister 1979–1990) was not matched by Thatcherite results, however. Although the Gaullists did actually privatize as many firms as Thatcher, they did it in a way that Harvey Feigenbaum calls pragmatic privatization in at least two respects. First, although firms nominally became privately owned because private investors held a majority of their stock, the government often retained enough stock that it de facto continued to dominate it. Second, the government made it impossible for foreigners to buy stock in sensitive companies and made certain that friends of the government held a solid core (*noyau dur*) of shares that went on the market.

The first wave of privatizations was extensive. The major banks, a leading defense firm, a public relations company, and several companies in the petrochemical industry were put on the market. But according to Feigenbaum, Prime Minister Chirac was at least as interested in the revenue the state would get by selling the shares as in the principle of private ownership. Indeed, the top fourteen firms netted the state well in excess of 100 billion francs, or more than $20 billion at the exchange rate at the time.

The privatizations were halted after the 1988 election. Mitterrand's position on the issue during his reelection campaign was summed up in two short words, "ni ni," neither more privatizations nor more nationalizations. His victory, followed by the Socialists' narrow victory in the legislative elections, took privatization off the agenda for the next five years.

Privatizations returned when the Gaullists and their allies won control of the National Assembly again in 1993. More privatizations followed and continued even after Lionel Jospin won the prime ministry in 1997. Some of the leading lights of France's dirigiste past went on the block, including the parts of the telephone system and Air France that could legally be sold (the Constitution has a provision that public utilities must be owned by the state) and Renault.

But again, their pragmatism far outweighed any commitment to free market values. In practice, these companies had become multinationals, operating throughout Europe or even the world, and the logic that owning them could help France, as Mitterrand put it, reconquer the domestic market, had all but disappeared. To survive, they had to operate as profit-maximizing enterprises, whoever owned them.

And up until the day this book was finished, the state was still willing to intervene to "guide" firms in both the public and private sector. In summer 2003, for instance, it loaned billions of dollars to the technology giant Alsthom and the forever struggling Bull in an attempt to keep them from going bankrupt, in the process almost certainly violating European Union policies (see Chapter 9).

France Is Not Dying

France's economy is not in great shape. More important for our purposes, there is little that the government can do to spark major change any more. Its labor market is probably more inflexible than some others; so, too, are some of its firms.

Yet, other G-8 countries, which include the world's seven richest nations and Russia, have troubles of their own. German industry is even more stagnant than the French. Americans are coping with the disappearance of pension plans and manufacturing jobs, and 45 million of them lack any basic health care coverage. The British may be doing a bit better now, but until they resolve their internal debates about the euro, they are likely to be in for a bumpy ride, especially if the pound slips in value.

But the bottom line for these countries is that they are all reasonably prosperous. People who are, say, forty years of age and older can remember a time when they and their families and their neighbors were a lot poorer. And in France most of them realize that the government had a lot to do with what the journalist John Ardagh called the "new French revolution" forty years ago.

Conclusion: Guy de Rothschild and the Passing of a Generation

On June 12, 2007, Guy de Rothschild died at age ninety-eight. He had been the head of the French branch of the famous family of bankers and vintners and racehorse owners. His life is relevant here because the Rothschilds serve as good metaphors for the changing role of the state in the French economy.

The history of the Rothschilds goes back to the middle of the eighteenth century when Mayer Amschel Rothschild established an investment bank in Frankfurt-am-Main in what later would become Germany. The family and the bank were based on Judenstrasse (Jewish Street). That was no coincidence. At the time, most Christians thought that money lending or such activities were beneath them, and Jews filled that and other commercial gaps in much of western Europe. The first Rothschild then used his five sons to expand the bank's influence. One took over the Frankfurt bank. Others went to London, Vienna, Naples, and Paris. Unlike most Jewish bankers or merchants, the Rothschilds made it into the aristocracy in all of the countries in which they established banks. As the *New York Times* put it in his obituary, Baron Guy led "a life that spanned fighting in de Gaulle's French forces to glittering parties."[5]

Guy de Rothschild was controversial as early as the 1930s, when he took over the French wing of the family fortune. He was seen as one of the "two hundred families" whom right-wing critics alleged ruled France. The fact that he was Jewish meant that he also suffered from anti-Semitism. When the leftist Popular Front government took power in 1936, it nationalized some of the family's assets, including its railroad holdings. But mostly the bank continued propping up what I called the stalemate society in Chapter 3. Or, as the *Times* obituary quoted him as saying, his main activity was "gently prolonging the nineteenth century."

When World War II broke out, he was called up to be a cavalry officer, was evacuated at Dunkirk, and won the prestigious Croix de Guerre. After France's defeat, he returned to the small southern town of La Bourboule to which the family had had to move the bank. The German occupiers had decreed that no Jews could run businesses in Paris. Within a year Baron Guy fled and joined the Resistance under de Gaulle.

After the war, he changed the direction the bank followed, just as de Gaulle and the ENArques would change the direction of the economy as a whole. Now the bank invested heavily in industry, providing investment capital for many of the companies that were the "national champions" of les trentes glorieuses. In but another act that symbolized the role that the integrated elite played in the second half of the twentieth century, he brought Georges Pompidou into the bank after de Gaulle went into opposition in 1946. Even though the future president had no banking experience, he soon became the manager.

By the late 1970s, when Guy retired from the day-to-day management, the bank was in decline because its investment strategy was making less and less sense. The overall economic model underlying les trentes glorieuses was running out of steam for the reasons discussed earlier in this chapter and which we will return to in the two chapters that follow.

To complicate matters further, Mitterrand's government nationalized the Rothschild and most other major banks shortly after winning the 1981 election. The baron then moved to New York (where he set up another bank), saying he had been "a Jew under Pétain, a pariah under Mitterrand—for me that is enough."

Once the enthusiasm for nationalized industries ebbed, his sons were allowed to open a new investment bank, now again located at the company's traditional headquarters in the heart of the Parisian financial district. Although no one would confuse these Rothschilds with the risk-happy venture capitalists of Silicon Valley, their emphasis is to provide investment support to the kind of start-up companies that will probably be at the heart of economic growth in France.

In short, Guy de Rothschild's passing reflects the transition France as a whole is going through as far as the state and society are concerned. His family had been part of the creation of the interventionist state in all its guises through the 1960s. Now, his heirs will be part of the gradual transition away from it.

Key Concepts

Questions for Discussion

1. France has one of the world's most generous social service systems, which provides more benefits than does the British government, let alone the United States. Why do you think that happened? How could you explain why few French voters complain about their high taxes, which on average are about twice what an American pays?

2. Many American and British students have a hard time understanding that France can be a capitalist country whose government plays a prominent role in its economic affairs. How can that be the case?

3. President Sarkozy has made it clear that he wants to speed up the transition to a more market-based economy and reduce the tax burden social services impose on businesses. What has happened since these lines were written in the first month of his presidency? Why do you think that has occurred?

9

France and Europe

hen I took my first course on European politics in 1968, France's role in Europe was little more than a footnote in any of the books we read. The **European Economic Community (EEC)** was barely mentioned by my professor, one of the three people to whom this book is dedicated. The same was true two years later in my first seminar on European politics in graduate school. Roy Pierce, one of the book's other dedicatees, did mention European institutions twenty-six times in his textbook published in 1973, but those mentions were hardly central to an analysis that focused all but exclusively on domestic politics.

Thirty-five years later, Europe has to be a central focus of any book on any country on the continent. European institutions have a dramatic impact on what all those countries do, including countries like Switzerland and Norway, which are not members of the EU.

The changes since the late 1960s—and especially since the late 1980s—have been truly spectacular. The end of the Cold War removed tensions that had gripped the continent for almost half a century, all but completely removed the threat of an all-out nuclear war, and allowed the **North Atlantic Treaty Organization (NATO)** to expand eastward to the point that it is likely that almost all the eastern European countries will join sooner rather than later. Less visible but probably more important has been the transformation of the EEC into the far larger and more powerful European Union, which was expanded to twenty-seven members on New Year's Day 2007 and which has broad sway over the economic, judicial, social, and even foreign policies of its member states.

The EU and NATO are not the only European institutions of which France is a part. Its soccer teams participate in the annual Champions League and the quadrennial European Cup. Aspiring French musicians compete in the annual (and very tacky) Eurovision song contest, which is telecast live throughout the continent.

But the EU and NATO so dwarf the others in importance that they are the focus in this book. The next chapter deals with NATO and considers France's role in the wider world, in which NATO's influence is likely to be felt in the foreseeable future.

Here, attention is given only to the EU, because it is by far the most important institution in the daily lives of French citizens. They now buy everything from their food to books in euros, not French francs, which disappeared on January 1, 2002. They drink German beer, eat Belgian chocolates, drive Italian cars, and smoke British cigarettes, all of which are as readily available as products made in their own country. More and more, the policies described in the last chapter are made by the EU, not by the French government. And, perhaps most visible to the majority of French men and women, the EU has dealt a tough blow to French soccer. By creating a free market for European workers, the EU has made it possible for almost all of France's best players to leave the country and sign with teams in Britain, Germany, Italy, and Spain, which can afford the multimillion dollar contracts French teams cannot.

The Question of Sovereignty

This section will be the briefest in the book. But don't be misled, it is also probably the most important.

This chapter is about one of the most important transformations that has happened in the history of world politics over the last six centuries, albeit a transformation that is occurring so gradually not everyone realizes it is happening. The French, like the other members of the EU, are voluntarily giving up some of their **sovereignty** to supranational bodies they do not and cannot control.

International relations scholars look upon the signing of the Treaty of Westphalia, which ended the Thirty Years' War in 1648, as perhaps the most important turning point in global affairs. More than any other single event, it enshrined the notion that a state's rulers were free to determine their domestic policies free of outside intervention. Since then, most observers have been convinced that the nation-state that emerged after Westphalia was the highest level that political organization could take.

The EU suggests otherwise. Although very few European politicians would admit it publicly, they have been giving away more and more of their sovereignty to the EU and its predecessors since they signed the Treaty of Rome in 1957. Today, France has given up control of its borders with its neighbors, the interest rates charged by its central bank, and most visibly, its currency.

As the academic realists are quick to point out, sovereignty has not disappeared. As seen in the preceding chapter, the French government still controls vast areas of public policy. More important to the realists, France and the other member states legally have the right to withdraw from the EU. However, the economic and other costs of doing so are prohibitive.

In short, the EU and the gradual, piecemeal erosion of French sovereignty seem here to stay.

The European Union

As befits an organization that is so important to France, we have to begin considering its impact by describing the EU itself. It is by no means the world's only international governmental organization; several hundred of them are registered with the United Nations. It is, however, by far the most influential and the one that has gone the farthest in limiting the sovereignty of the countries that have joined.

History

European integration is not a new idea. At least since the Roman Empire, leaders have dreamed of uniting all of Europe under their rule. Until the twentieth century all such dreams assumed that military conquest was the only route to unifying a continent whose history has been marked by war after war.

After World War I (dubbed the war to end all wars), some young European intellectuals decided that the only way to prevent another war that took upward of ten million lives was to bring all of Europe together into a single political unit. Their hopes were dashed when World War I proved not to be the war to end all wars after Germany invaded Poland in September 1939 in a conflict that put the extent of the horrors of 1914 to 1918 to shame.

Ironically, the tragedy of World War II only deepened the conviction of the men and women who supported a united Europe. Indeed, many leaders of the Resistance against Nazi and Fascist aggression came from the ranks of the interwar advocates of European integration.

Many of them played an important role in postwar reconstruction, including **Jean Monnet**, the chief architect of the French Planning Commission discussed in Chapter 8. They were not, however, the prime movers behind the first steps toward European integration.

The United States was. In two ways.

First, it decided not to dole out its Marshall Plan funds country by country. Rather, it gave the money to a new multinational agency, the Organization for European Economic Cooperation, the precursor of today's Organisation for Economic Co-operation and Development (OECD), which performed that function. Second, in 1949 it drew most of the European countries together militarily with the formation of NATO. Although not an important direct step on the road to creating the EU, NATO still is important because it was the first institution in which European governments cooperated with each other after the war.

Functionalism

Functionalism is a theory used by many political scientists and by many of the architects of European integration to describe the gradual addition of new members and powers to an international organization. In the case of Europe, scholars speak of *broadening* (adding new members) and *deepening* (adding new powers) the scope of what is now the EU.

The hopes of Monnet, the Belgian Paul-Henri Spaak, and others would not be unmet for long. They reasoned that rebuilding Europe would depend heavily on a few key industries, including coal mining and steel manufacturing. These two products could become the lynchpin in the beginnings of European integration because almost all of continental western Europe's coal lies beneath the surface near the Rhine River, which, in turn, flows through Belgium, France, Germany, Luxembourg, and the Netherlands.

They persuaded the leaders of those five countries and Italy to create the **European Coal and Steel Community** (ECSC) in 1951. The ECSC abolished all tariffs on coal and steel products between the member states and erected a common one levied against materials imported from outside the community. The agreement also created four institutions—a council representing the national governments, a permanent secretariat or administration, a representative assembly, and a court to adjudicate disputes—which remain at the heart of the EU today in only slightly different form.

At this stage, rebuilding Europe by starting to integrate its political life was seen primarily as a way to avoid future wars that would ravage the continent. Over time, as peace within Western Europe (see the next chapter) grew firmer and firmer, that goal gave way to viewing European union as a way to forge an ever more prosperous Europe and a politically united one.

That national security would give way to economic growth was clear within a matter of a few years. The ECSC succeeded beyond its creators' wildest expectations. As a result, they were able to get the leaders of the same six countries to draft and sign the Treaty of Rome, which extended the provisions regarding tariffs to all goods produced in what was now the European Economic Community (EEC), or Common Market for short. They also created Euratom to coordinate their programs for the peaceful use of nuclear energy.

For the next decade, little went well for the EEC, largely due to President de Gaulle, as discussed in the analytical part of this chapter. Finally, after de Gaulle resigned in 1969, the door opened for expanding the number of members to nine when Denmark, Great Britain, and Ireland joined in 1972, twelve when Greece, Portugal, and Spain entered in the 1980s, and fifteen with the admission of Austria, Finland, and Sweden in 1993. Cyprus, the Czech Republic, Estonia, Hungary, Latvia, Lithuania, Malta, Poland, Slovakia, and Slovenia swelled the EU's ranks to twenty-five states in 2004 (Table 9.1).

Table 9.1	The History of the European Union
Year	Event
1951	Creation of the ECSC
1957	Treaty of Rome
1972	Accession of Denmark, Great Britain, Ireland
	EEC becomes European Community
1980s	Accession of Greece, Portugal, Spain
1986	Passage of SEA
1992	Treaty of Maastricht
1995	Accession of Austria, Finland, Sweden
2002	Formal launch of the euro
2004	Expansion to 25 member states
2007	Expansion to 27 countries

The powers of the EU also grew from the 1980s onward. In 1985 the European Communities (as it was then known) adopted the **Single European Act (SEA)**, which swept away the many remaining barriers to trade that still existed despite the abolition of all internal tariffs. It created a set of common European standards so that any product that could be legally sold in one country would pass muster in all of them. The same would now be the case for professionals as well. Meeting the legal criteria for being a hairdresser or professor made one eligible to work in all member states. There are a few exceptions to the rule. The British still use their awkward three-pronged electric plugs (it was deemed not worth the $70 billion estimated cost of changing them to the continental standard of two rounded prongs), and lawyers have to be accredited nationally because the legal systems in the member states are still quite different. However, on balance, the SEA created a single market for almost all goods and services, which in time will make the European economy as integrated as that of the United States.

That means that, among other things, governments now have to purchase services and supplies from the entire community, not just their own country's companies. Such purchases routinely amount to 10 percent or so of GNP.

Just as the officials in Brussels finished implementing the SEA, the member states adopted the **Treaty of Maastricht** in 1992. The treaty formally created the European Union, laid the groundwork for the creation of the euro, and expanded the community's scope to include three **pillars**—the traditional economic issues of the common market, a variety of judicial issues, and plans to create a common foreign and security policy.

During the 1990s, the EU had its share of problems, including its inability to settle the fighting in Bosnia. However, it proceeded in a number of other areas, including removing many border controls within the EU, which means you can travel from, say, Paris to Amsterdam just as easily as you can from New York to Washington. Maastricht also set monetary union in motion, which led to the creation of a European central bank in 1999 and the launch of the euro in 2002.

As of this writing, the prospects for further European integration are not very bright. There is, for instance, little likelihood that the British will adopt the euro during the life of the Parliament elected in 2005. It is also difficult to see a quick recovery from the bitterness provoked by the divisions over the 2003 war in Iraq. Finally, the EU was dealt a telling blow when the French joined several other countries in rejecting the draft European constitution in summer 2005.

Nonetheless, it is hard not to agree with the words that Yale's David Cameron wrote more than a decade ago.

> Over the longer term, the institutions and powers of the [Union] will continue to expand and certain policy-making powers heretofore vested in the member states will be delegated or transferred to or pooled or shared with [Union] institutions. As a result, the sovereignty of the member states will increasingly and inevitably be eroded.[1]

The European Union Today: Institutions and Influence

On May 9, 2003, T. R. Reid of the *Washington Post* was interviewed on National Public Radio's *Morning Edition* about the book he was writing, *The United States of Europe*. It was not a coincidence that Reid was interviewed that day. It is Europe Day, the equivalent of July 4 or Bastille Day. Reid made the case that the EU was close to being a state, something reflected in the title of the book he was writing at the time. It had a capital city (actually three, since EU offices are scattered in Brussels, Luxembourg, and Strasbourg), a flag, and the music to an anthem (the theme from the choral movement of Beethoven's Ninth Symphony).[2] Reid reported that MTV played only European rock music that day. There were the same kinds of parades and fireworks you find on most country's national days. As Reid put it, "they're beginning to look a lot like a country."

The uniting Europe is based on four main institutions, each of which affects French politics. Although versions of the four are found in most international organizations, the EU's institutions are far more powerful than any of their equivalents in other such entities. That is the case, because the EU makes policy in three areas known as pillars, mentioned above.

- Broad areas of economic policy

- Justice and Home Affairs

- Common Foreign and Security Policy

It has by far the most sway over the first pillar with states retaining most of their control over the other two.

Council of the European Union

The **Council of the European Union** (sometimes called the Council of Ministers) is often the most important and usually the European decision-making body least supportive of expanding the powers of the EU. It must approve all new major initiatives, including major new legislation, treaties, and other binding agreements, and the addition of new members.

The Council actually meets in two different versions. Every six months the heads of state meet for a summit where the boldest new initiatives are agreed upon. When the Council has to deal with a specific policy issue, it meets as needed and is made up of the relevant cabinet minister from each country. Thus, during the often acrimonious debate over what to do about mad cow disease, the Council meetings included the agriculture ministers, including Britain's appropriately named Quentin Hogg.

The presidency of the EU rotates every six months. The country that occupies the presidency hosts the summit during that period and issues most of the formal statements made on behalf of the union. The current, past, and next country to control presidency make up the "troika" that coordinates meetings and other activities.

The Council also votes in two different ways. On some aspects of pillar one and almost all of the other two as well as admitting new members, it must vote unanimously for an initiative to pass. Indeed, until the 1970s, all Council votes had to be unanimous; as discussed later, this allowed France, under de Gaulle, to come close to destroying the EEC.

Now, most votes are held under a complicated system of **Qualified Majority Voting**. As Table 9.2 shows, each country is given a certain number of votes in rough proportion to its share of the EU population. It then casts those votes as a bloc. It is called a qualified majority vote because passage of a measure requires a supermajority, calculated in such a way that neither the big countries nor the smaller ones alone can determine the outcome of a vote.

To constitute a qualified majority, 232 votes are needed. That means that a coalition of large and small countries is necessary to pass any legislation. Table 9.2 depicts how the system worked in 2006, after the defeat of the new constitution at the polls in France, the Netherlands, and beyond.

The Commission

If the Council is the European institution that most reflects the interests of national governments, the **European Commission** is the one that is most likely to promote the expansion of the EU's power. It has been responsible for most of the major initiatives of the last generation, including the Single European Act and the Treaty of Maastricht.

Until the 2004 expansion, the Commission had twenty members. The ten smaller countries had one member each; the five larger ones (France, Germany, Italy, Spain, and the United Kingdom) had two commissioners. Now, there are twenty-seven commissioners, one per country. The draft constitution would have reduced the number back to twenty. The five large countries would always have had a commissioner; the remaining fifteen seats would have gone to the other countries on a rotating basis.

Table 9.2	Qualified Majority Voting in the European Union: 1995–2007	
Countries		Votes allocated
France, Germany, Italy, the UK		29
Poland, Spain		27
Netherlands		13
Belgium, Czech Republic, Greece, Hungary, Portugal		12
Austria, Sweden		10
Denmark, Finland, Ireland, Lithuania, Slovakia		7
Cyprus, Estonia, Latvia, Luxembourg, Slovenia		4
Malta		3
	Total	**321**

Commissioners are nominated by their home governments for a five-year term and can be reappointed once. One of their members is designated the president of the Commission and also serves as an ex-officio member of the Council at its semiannual summits. When they take office, the commissioners swear an oath of allegiance to the EU and (supposedly) take no instructions from their home governments.

Today, most commissioners have had prominent careers as politicians in their own country. The current president, José Manuel Barroso, is a former prime minister of Portugal. France's commissioner, Jacques Barrot, has long been a prominent UDF politician who has held a number of ministerial posts in Gaullist governments.

The commissioners have two main functions.

First, they oversee the everyday operations of the EU. Each commissioner supervises the work of one or two of the twenty-three directorates, which are akin to departments in a national government. In that guise, they and the roughly 12,000 senior civil servants who work for the EU are responsible for implementing its policies. But because so few people are directly employed by the EU in senior positions, much of the administrative burden falls on the bureaucracies of the member states.

Second, the Commission has an important policymaking role. It has the authority to issue binding regulations on the details of directives (as the EU's laws are known) approved by the Council and the **European Parliament**. Thus, between 1985 and 1992, the Commission drafted more than 300 regulations needed to implement the Single European Act, which is why seven years passed between its passage and its full implementation. Even more important, as noted earlier, the Commission is normally the source of major new programs like the SEA, although these do have to be approved by the Council and, normally, the parliament before they go into effect.

In other words, the Commission is the closest equivalent in the EU to a national cabinet. That analogy should not be taken too far, however, since ultimate decision-making authority lies with the Council. Its role may change when and if a constitution or new treaty is adopted following the European summit of June 2007.

The European Parliament

For most of its history, the European Parliament has been the weakest of the EU institutions. From 1957 until 1979 its members were appointed by the national legislatures. What's more, the parliament was denied the two most important powers exercised by national governments. It had no control over the budget, and it could not hold the Commission accountable through a vote of confidence, which is a central feature of all parliamentary systems.

The parliament is a large body. Before the 2004 wave of enlargements, it had 540 members. Each country has a delegation proportionate to its population. Thus, for example, 99 of the members are German, 87 French, and 6 Luxembourgeois. Members, or MEPs, as they are known, will be added on a similar basis as each country joins until the 2009 election, when the size of delegations will be recalibrated for a total of 732 seats.

The influence of the parliament has grown dramatically in the last quarter century. Members are now directly elected. Although most politicians would still rather serve in their national legislatures, the parliament is beginning to attract a number of prominent figures, including—for good or ill—Jean-Marie Le Pen.

It now has to approve the budget proposed by the Commission each year. And, following a series of scandals toward the end of Jacques Santer's term as president of the Commission in 2000, the parliament gained the de facto right to vote no confidence in the Commission.

Most important of all, it is now deeply involved in the legislative process through a complicated "codecision procedure," which occurs in two stages. First, the parliament must be consulted after the Commission makes a proposal for a new directive (as bills before the parliament are officially known) and before the Council votes on it. Second, once the Council votes, the parliament is normally brought into the picture again when it can approve or reject the directive or propose amendments to it. Amendments must be considered by the Commission within a month, and if the parliament rejects the bill out of hand, the Council can pass it only if it votes unanimously to do so.

The European Court of Justice

Many international organizations have courts. Few of them have the sweeping powers exercised by the **European Court of Justice (ECJ)**. The court has fifteen judges, one appointed by each member state. The number of justices will grow to twenty-seven after enlargement, but the entire court will rarely meet as a whole, working instead in smaller "chambers."

Like members of the Commission, the justices swear an oath to the EU and no longer take instructions from their home governments. What's more, the court decided shortly after it was created that it was empowered to conduct constitutional law and rule on the legality of actions taken by the EU, its member states, corporations, and individuals, because the governments had signed the legally binding **Treaty of Rome**.

And the court has done so on numerous occasions. Indeed, two seemingly minor decisions have set the stage for some of the most sweeping changes in European life in the last generation.

In 1979 the court ruled that the German law that banned the import of cassis was illegal. Cassis is a liqueur made near Dijon and used to make a sweet but potent drink, *kir,* when mixed with white wine. The German authorities held that cassis was too strong to be classified as a wine and too weak to be considered a liqueur by German standards, hence the ban. The court ruled for the French exporter, arguing that if a good met the standards of one country it should meet that of all others. This principle of mutual recognition led to the passage of the Single European Act seven years later.

In 1995 a mediocre Belgian soccer player, Jean-Marc Bosman, sued his national federation when his contract expired, demanding the right to become what Americans call a free agent. Not only did the court side with Bosman in that case, it overturned the rules that limited teams to having no more than three foreign players on the field at the same time. It held that the SEA had created a single market for workers as well as for goods and that any EU national could play for a team in any EU country. That immediately set off a frenzy of activity by the richest clubs in England, Germany, Italy, and Spain, which transformed the face of European soccer. In one 2001 Champions League game, for instance, Atalanta of Rome played Chelsea of London. Chelsea had no players from the United Kingdom but had more Italian players than the supposedly Italian team!

The European Constitution?

The future of Europe is very much up in the air. In part because of a "no" vote from France in 2005, the plans for a European constitution are on hold. The length of the draft—nearly 500 pages—was a good sign that it did not have widespread popular support. Nonetheless, its rejection strongly suggests that the EU will remain roughly as it is for the foreseeable future.

How France Has Dealt with Europe

France's relationship with Europe has gone through three distinct phases. Under the guidance of Monnet, Robert Schuman, the French foreign minister at the time, and others, it was one of the leaders of the effort to create the ECSC and EEC. However, de Gaulle (who returned to power the year after the Treaty of Rome was signed) was at most a reluctant supporter of European integration in any form and, as mentioned above, almost destroyed the EEC. Since then—and especially since the presidency of Valéry Giscard d'Estaing—France has again become one of the champions of both broadening and deepening the EU. Because the earlier part of the chapter covered the formation of the EU, here the focus will be on the latter two stages.

The Gaullist Years

As the next chapter shows in more detail, Charles de Gaulle's primary goal was to restore what he called France's grandeur. That made him first and foremost a French nationalist, which meant that he had doubts about European integration and anything else that he feared might undermine France's national interests.

De Gaulle was by no means hostile to Europe. Indeed, aspects of European integration were central to his goals. Among other things, he thought French and German reconciliation was vital for the continent's future. He accepted the tariff and other provisions of the Treaty of Rome without reservation. And he was convinced that a stronger Europe would help France carve out a meaningful place for itself in the Cold War rivalry between East and West.

Early in his presidency, de Gaulle actually seemed a strong supporter of European integration and even talked fleetingly about political union of the six member states. The hallmark of his European policy, however, did not deal with the EEC, per se, but with the rapprochement with West Germany. This work, carried out through his personal relationship with his fellow aging leader, Chancellor Konrad Adenauer, culminated in the 1963 signing of a formal Treaty of Friendship between the two countries.

His view of Europe, however, was that of a Europe des patries (Europe of nations). To that end, he came to oppose any deepening of the EC's powers or expansion of its membership.

The most important issue regarding Europe during his presidency was the possibility of British membership in the Common Market. The United Kingdom was not one of the original six members of the EEC. During the 1950s almost all members of the British Labour Party and many in the ruling Conservative Party were opposed to joining, preferring to maintain what they saw as a special relationship with the United States.

However, by 1961, the Conservative government led by Harold Macmillan decided that the costs of staying out of Europe were too great. The British filed a formal application to join that summer, and negotiations began between the UK and the Common Market shortly thereafter. The following year de Gaulle used the unanimity rule to block the British application and did so at a press conference without having informed the leaders of the other member states beforehand. He vetoed British membership again in 1965.

That same year, de Gaulle provoked another crisis that almost destroyed the EEC. By then, the Treaty of Rome's provisions that abolished tariffs among the member states of the EEC were well in place, and a number of other proposals to deepen its powers and its control over its revenues were put forward. The last straw for de Gaulle was the failure of the other countries to accept an agricultural policy that would provide financial support to France's relatively inefficient small farmers.

In fact, de Gaulle was more concerned about the threat that the EEC would erode French sovereignty than he was about any specific initiative or policy. The immediate threat was a provision of the Treaty of Rome that would have provided for majority voting rather than requiring unanimity in 1966. As he put it at a 1965 press conference:

We know—and heaven knows how well we know it—that there is a different conception of European federation in which, according to the dreams of those who have conceived it, the member countries would lose their national identities, and which would be ruled by some sort of technocratic body of elders, stateless and irresponsible. However big the glass which is proffered from the outside, we prefer to drink from our own glass, while at the same time clinking glasses with those around us.[3]

De Gaulle followed his statements by provoking what came to be known as the "empty chairs crisis." France refused to participate in meetings of the Council of Ministers at which key decisions were made until its demands were met, which essentially paralyzed the EEC. For seven months, the other members of the EEC refused to give in. Finally, in early 1966, the member states agreed to the Luxembourg Compromise, which, for all intents and purposes, kept the unanimity rule and limited the Commission's activist stance. It would be another generation before the effects of the Gaullist policies were eroded, and then, ironically, under the leadership of French politicians.

After de Gaulle

French policy toward Europe changed almost as soon as de Gaulle resigned from the presidency in 1969. His successor, Georges Pompidou, was a far stronger supporter of the EEC. In fact, he had been part of the group of young intellectuals who first seriously discussed European integration during the years between the two world wars. Although Pompidou retained much of de Gaulle's rhetoric, he made one extremely significant policy shift during his brief tenure in office, when he agreed to allow Britain, Denmark, Ireland, and Norway to join the EEC in 1972 (the Norwegian voters rejected membership in a referendum, as they would do again in the 1990s).

In the early 1970s, there was some opposition to Europe on the left. The then active Unified Socialist Party and its popular leader, Michel Rocard, viewed the EEC as an institute that primarily served the interests of large corporations that were able to take advantage of the ever-integrating market.

All subsequent presidents and prime ministers have strongly supported European integration, but none of them did so out of the visionary and ideological commitment of Jean Monnet's generation. All at least accepted some aspects of de Gaulle's idea of a Europe des patries. More important, all supported the broadening and deepening of the EU for such largely pragmatic reasons as enhancing French prosperity or countering the growing influence of Germany.

Central here have been the Mitterrand and Chirac presidencies. The EU made its most important advances in their terms, and the two men were essential to their achievement.

In Mitterrand's case, it was not just his own impact that was significant but his appointment of Jacques Delors to be president of the Commission in 1985. Delors had been finance minister and was a rising star in French politics. Some think that Mitterrand cynically exiled him to Brussels so he would not become a threat to Mitterrand's own popularity.

Whatever the real motivation, Delors breathed new life into the presidency and the Commission as a whole. More than any other individual, he was responsible for the Single European Act and the Maastricht Treaty. Indeed, he was the rare politician whose stature and popularity rose as a result of his work at the EU to the extent that he could well have won the 1995 French presidential election had he chosen to run against Chirac.

Mitterrand's personal contribution lay primarily in his ability to work with the Christian Democratic chancellor of Germany Helmut Kohl, who was in office throughout the French president's two terms. Their relationship proved most important in steering Europe through the collapse of communism and the unification of Germany. Although the European Community (EC) as the EEC was then known, was not a major actor in any of those events, there is little doubt that their positive relationship had a profoundly positive, if indirect, impact on the EU.

As for the EU itself, the most important and most revealing issue about France and European integration is France's consistent—although not unwavering—support for monetary union from Giscard's presidency onward. As David Howarth has shown in his excellent book on the subject, the last three presidents steered France toward the creation of the euro and all that goes with it as a response to pressures from average citizens as well as elites.[4] Thus, Giscard and some of the other more liberal leaders used the growth of monetary union as a lever to push for making the market a more powerful force in the domestic economy. All the presidents saw a common currency as a way of countering Germany's macroeconomic clout and the role of the dollar as the world's reserve currency.

This kind of pragmatic commitment to Europe continues to this day. When Chirac came to office, there were significant doubts about his commitment to Europe. It was frequently reported that he opposed adding many, if any, new members and that he balked at the full integration of French troops into NATO.

But he proved to be a strong supporter of those policies and of monetary union as well. His commitment to making the fiscal sacrifices needed to qualify for European Monetary Union membership by 1999 led him to call for the early elections that led to the defeat of Juppé and the election of Jospin in 1997.

Jacques Delors and the Evolution of the European Union

Jacques Delors is generally considered the second most important person in the evolution of the EU, trailing only Jean Monnet. Born in 1925 in a working-class neighborhood of Paris, Delors was unable to attend university because of both World War II and his father's demand that he go to work. He thus started his career as a clerical worker in a Parisian bank and came to politics through his Catholicism and the trade union movement.

From the 1950s on, he was involved in attempts to redefine what it meant to be on the left. This led him at times to work with groups to the left of the Communists and at others to serve as an adviser to Gaullist ministers. In 1981 President Mitterrand appointed him minister of finance, from which position he was largely responsible for the U-turn of 1983 that ended the Socialists' radical reforms. Two years later, he went to Brussels as president of the Commission. He retired after two terms and resisted attempts to draft him as the Socialist candidate for president of France. He remains an avid soccer fan. His daughter, Martine Aubry, was slated to be the next leader of the French Socialist Party until her surprise defeat in the 2002 legislative elections.

The Impact of the European Union on France

A visit to any French supermarket provides clear, if unquantifiable, evidence that the impact of the EU on France has been immense. In addition to the culinary delights that have made French cuisine famous, you will see products from all over the EU, including wines and cheeses on which so much of France's gastronomic reputation has been based.

The Economy

Still, as with the domestic policies discussed in the last chapter, it is difficult to determine just how much of an impact European policy has had either on the overall French economic success of the last fifty years or on its difficulties in the last twenty. Nonetheless, almost every observer thinks that Europe's impact has been substantial. If nothing else, the French civil service and judiciary have become much more effective in translating European directives into decrees and regulations for implementation in France.

At this point it is safe to say that more of the key policies that shape the evolution of the French policy are made by the EU than by the French government. There are, of course, areas in which the French government still makes its own policies, some of which run counter to European trends, such as the relative resistance to privatization and other market mechanisms discussed in the last chapter. However, the most critical macroeconomic policies in particular, such as interest rates or the heavy reliance on the value-added tax, lie outside French control.

And the statistics suggest that the quick and unscientific conclusions one reaches at the supermarket are correct. In 2005 France both exported and imported about 300 billion euros worth of goods and services. About two-thirds of that trade was with other European states. By contrast less than 10 percent of it was with the United States. One complicated econometric study estimated that the creation of a single market had led to a 2 percent increase in French trade with the rest of the EU and a slight drop in its dealings with other economies.

The impact of Europe can be seen in most sectors of the economy. Pressures from Brussels have made it harder and harder to maintain Giscard's policy of actively using the state to create and promote companies that could be "national champions." The Commission has frequently taken France to court for subsidies it paid to nationalized companies or over the way it limited the ability of foreigners to buy shares in them when they were privatized. And, in perhaps Europe's least successful endeavor, the Common Agricultural Policy has allowed far more inefficient French farmers to stay in business than there could have been under a free market.

The People

Public opinion polls give us a reasonable idea of how the French people view the EU. We are especially fortunate to have the Eurobarometer survey, conducted by the EU itself in all member countries every six months.

Data from the interviewing done in late winter 2002 suggest that 19 percent of the French population pay a lot of attention to European news, 1 percent less than that of the EU as a whole.[5] When asked how much they know about the EU on a ten-point scale, where ten signifies a lot, the French average 4.27, whereas the European mean is 4.35. Fifty-six percent of them are at least nominally aware of the ten leading European institutions, which is slightly more than the European population as a whole. Overall support for the EU and the degree to which the people feel that their country has benefited from the EU are both slightly lower in France than in eight of the other countries. However, supporters vastly outnumber critics even though the French electorate endorsed the Maastricht Treaty by the narrowest of margins and voters have given significant support to politicians like Le Pen who are hostile to further European integration. What's more, there has been surprisingly little change in support levels for the EU, which were almost exactly as high in 2002 as they had been in 1981. As is the case with most European populations, the French are most likely to express trust in the parliament, Commission, and Court of Justice. Even though this poll was conducted a few weeks after the euro was launched, the overwhelming majority of the French public thought that it was a good thing and that it made them think of themselves more as Europeans.

But it should not be concluded that the French are enthusiastic about every aspect of the EU. At least two-thirds of them worry that the EU will bring more unemployment, crime, and drugs and will lead to the erosion of the social service programs discussed in Chapter 8. Only 4 percent claim to think of themselves as Europeans rather than as French, but that figure is topped only by the Germans, Belgians, and Luxembourgeois. France was the only country in which more people voiced opposition to than support of the enlargement that was still being negotiated when this poll was conducted.

And some clear—and worrisome—patterns have emerged, both in support of and in opposition to the EU. Unlike the situation in the United Kingdom, qualms about Europe have always been found on both the left and the right. In France, opposition is concentrated in two areas. First are the more extremist politicians. These include not only parties like the PCF and FN, which are usually seen as outside the political mainstream, but also a number of prominent politicians on the center left (such as Jean-Pierre Chevènement) and on the right (Charles Pasqua). At the grassroots level, the decades of Eurobarometer research have shown that opposition is clustered among the most disadvantaged segments of the population, who feel they have the most to lose if there is more integration, and that such opposition rises and falls in sync with the evolution of the French economy.

Globalization

The hot topic of globalization is considered in more detail in the remaining two chapters of this book. For now, it is enough to see that many in France, including many strong opponents of the EU a decade or so ago at the time of the referendum on Maastricht, view European integration as the one possible protection against the negative effects of rampant globalization.

As discussed in the next chapter, the French have been among the most vocal critics of globalization. That runs the gamut from former foreign ministers who argued that it would undermine French sovereignty to protesters who have damaged McDonald's restaurants, which they take to be the archetypical symbol of globalization's social and gastronomical evils.

But the EU has been important in making policy on issues as different as trade with countries the United States disapproves of, a ban on the import of genetically modified food, and the strength of the euro against the dollar. The creation of the Common Foreign and Security Policy, with its plans for a rapid deployment force, is beginning to give all the European states a vehicle to counter the overwhelming military might of the United States, something they have become especially eager to do since the election of George W. Bush and the invasion of Iraq (see Chapters 10 and 11).

Conclusion: A Fact of Life

The bottom line is that the EU has become a fact of life for almost everyone in France. This may not be obvious to British readers, who still use pounds and have to go through border formalities when they go to the Continent. It may be unfathomable to readers in North America or the antipodes, where regional institutions are not even at the same stage Europe was in the years between the creation of the ECSC and the EEC.

But for the French and the other long-term continental members of the EU, it is a different matter. "Europe" may not evoke much passion on the part of most citizens. Nonetheless, most citizens also understand that what happens in Brussels, Frankfort, Luxembourg, and Strasbourg shapes their lives in numerous and important ways.

What's more, the French have adopted a more "normal" or pragmatic approach to Europe, in keeping with the thesis of this book. To be sure, there are politicians like Le Pen and de Villieres who rant and rave about the evils of European integration. To be sure, too, there are still a few politicians and business executives scattered across the political spectrum who share the fervor of Monnet, Schuman, and others in their generation of visionaries.

More generally, most people at all levels of the political and economic hierarchy undoubtedly share the conclusion reached by David Howarth, who is probably the best young scholar of France's relationship with the EU in the English-speaking world:

> From the creation of the European Coal and Steel Community, European integration—and the loss, restriction, and sharing of state powers—has been supported to the extent that it serves French economic interests, promotes French leadership in the European Community, and reinforces European power in relation to the United States. These preoccupations reflect long-standing French Realpolitik, discourse, and identity on European matters.[6]

Key Concepts

Key People, Entities, and Events

Questions for Discussion

1. France has a long history of nationalism. Why would it have agreed to join the EEC and then endorse its later expansion? Consider your answer in light of de Gaulle's commitment to grandeur.

2. The EU today probably has more power over economic decision making than the French government itself. What difference does that make in the way France is governed? What would happen if the same were true of your home country?

3. For all of its successes, the EU has not been able to create a common foreign and security policy. Why do you think that's the case? You might want to reconsider this question after reading the next chapter.

10

Foreign Policy

As important as Europe is to France, most people do not think of Franco-European relations as "foreign policy" in the way it is taught in international relations courses. As we saw in the preceding chapter, France's relations with Europe are as much about domestic politics as international relations.

The government's interactions with its European partners are not always easy. But they are normal, as I've used the term throughout this book, in the sense that disagreements with other European states are handled more or less as easily and more or less in the same way that we Virginians work out our problems with Maryland.

France is also now what international relations scholars call a second-tier power. It has a large and powerful military, including nuclear weapons. Nonetheless, its might pales in comparison with that of the United States, the world's only superpower.

But we cannot forget that France was one of the world's major—and sometimes most aggressive—countries as recently as the 1930s. Although the Cold War and events since it ended have pushed France off center stage, it is still one of the four or five most influential countries on the planet, however one chooses to define the term.

French foreign policy has been controversial throughout its history. And it remains controversial today.

Indeed, that's another way of saying that this chapter will be the most controversial one in the book in regard both to French politics and to my argument about normal politics. That argument remains largely the case today, despite French opposition to the American invasion and occupation of Iraq beginning in 2003.

It is tempting to go straight to the current differences between Washington and London on the one hand and Paris and other capitals on the other. However, in order to understand why France opposed the United States in 2003 (but not 2001), it is also important to see how French foreign policy evolved throughout the history of the Fifth Republic toward normal politics.

A short intellectual and fictional detour might clarify what I am driving at. In 1997 the *Washington Post* columnist David Ignatius published a novel, *A Firing Offense*.[1] In it, a dashing young journalist investigates an alleged link between the French and Chinese intelligence services that threatens a lucrative contract for the American telecommunications industry.

It is no coincidence that the French are the "bad guys" in Ignatius's book, not the British or the Germans or the Canadians. Ignatius is no Francophobe. He has lived and reported from France for much of his career. However, French policy has been at odds with that of the United States often enough during the history of the Fifth Republic that the French-American rivalry made for the only plausible plot line.

For today's readers, there is no better example of the flare-ups that have occurred between Paris and Washington than the war in Iraq that was begun in 2003. Although France had been critical of Saddam Hussein's regime and had participated in the first Gulf War and supported the American invasion of Afghanistan in the weeks after the 2001 terrorist attacks, France led the global opposition to the George W. Bush administration's plan to invade Iraq.

As late as Chirac's New Year's address to the nation in 2003, it seemed possible that France might join what he would call the "coalition of the willing." But that was not to be. From Washington's perspective, France was way too close economically to the regime in Baghdad, and that view only solidified the perception that France lacked an ethically based foreign policy. The French, in turn, felt demeaned by what they thought were arrogant American neoconservatives, especially the then secretary of defense, Donald Rumsfeld. The antagonism between the conservative French administration and its equivalent in the United States was probably as visible and virulent as any in the Western world since the end of World War II (see Box 10.3 on French fries and French toast later in the chapter).

But the frequent critiques coming from Paris and Washington miss two important trends. First, the two countries are as close as they have been since the start of the Fifth Republic. Second, Chirac might have been right to stress French national interests and other factors in opposing the war.

The Historical Context

As we saw in Chapters 3 and 4, France has existed for a millennium or more. Borders came and went. The powers of monarchs and other rulers came and went as well.

Nonetheless, France was one of Europe's most powerful countries long before the Treaty of Westphalia (1648) set the stage for the modern state. At that time France was one of the main rivals of England, the Habsburg Empire, Prussia, and other European powers. It also had its share of colonies elsewhere, most notably, part of today's Canada as far west as Montreal. Later, it would establish Louisiana (for Louis et Anne) from its base in New Orleans (Nouvelle Orléans) from which it nominally controlled the western half of what is now the United States.

Although historians argue about this, France was probably the single most important power during most of the past millennium until the nineteenth century. Under Napoléon, it created the first draft of young men into the military (the *levée en masse*) to bolster the emperor's designs for controlling all of Europe.

For good or ill, Napoléon and his forces were defeated at Waterloo in 1815, which dashed all such hopes. For the next century and a half, France suffered defeat after defeat at the hands of its continental enemies, most notably Germany. Its defeat by the newly unified Germany destroyed Napoléon III's Second Empire. World War I was nominally a victory for France, but the costs of the war in human and economic terms made it all but a defeated power. France lost its struggle with Germany in World War II in a matter of weeks. In a powerful symbolic move, Hitler forced French officials to sign documents of surrender in the same railroad car German generals had had to do the same thing barely a generation earlier.

Still, France remained a power to be reckoned with. That was easiest to see in the colonial empire it acquired in Africa, Asia, the Caribbean, and the Middle East. But its defeats in Indochina and North Africa suggested that it was losing control of its overseas possessions, as were the other European imperial powers.

As was seen earlier in the book, France's declining power on the world stage contributed to the collapse of the Third and Fourth Republics. And for a nationalist like Charles de Gaulle, the desire to restore France's clout and prestige was an obvious issue to raise with the French people when he returned to power.

The Gaullist Legacy

Charles de Gaulle entered political life reluctantly. He was a military officer and assumed he would always be one, until his beloved country's inability to stop the German invasion in 1940 thrust him onto the political stage. In the early 1930s no one would have assumed de Gaulle would have any kind of meaningful political career. He was a maverick military thinker who advocated building an aggressive armed force based on tanks and airplanes rather than relying on a defensive strategy dependent on a cluster of forts known as the Maginot Line. In addition, de Gaulle called for a career military rather than one based heavily on draftees, a notion that also offended many traditionalists in national security circles.

In the dying days of the Third Republic, de Gaulle's maverick status served him well. On June 6, 1940, Prime Minister Reynaud appointed him a deputy minister of defense responsible for relations with Britain. Ten days later he was sent to London to meet with his British counterparts. While he was on his way, the French government made Marshal Pétain head of what would become the Vichy government. By the time de Gaulle arrived in London two days later he represented a government that no longer existed.

As a result, he was the obvious person for the British to call on to make a statement to the French people on the BBC World Service shortly after the surrender on June 18. Although few people in France probably heard the short speech, de Gaulle's words helped inspire the Resistance to Nazi Occupation and Vichy collaboration and, in turn, his own vision of what French foreign policy should be.

> The leaders that have been at the head of the French armies for many years have established a government. This government has put forward the defeat of our armies and has contacted the enemy to end the combat. It is true that we have been—and continue being—overtaken by the enemy's mechanical power, both land-based and aeronautical. Much more so than their numbers, it is their tanks, their airplanes and German tactics that have made us retreat. It is the tanks, the airplanes, the tactics of the Germans that have surprised our leaders to the point of leading them to where they are today.

> But has the final word been spoken? Must hope disappear? Is the defeat final? No! Believe me, I who speak to you with full knowledge of the facts, and tell you that nothing's lost for France.[2]

Although de Gaulle did not use the term **"grandeur"** in this or most of his other major foreign policy speeches, it became the central principle not only of his foreign policy agenda but in his goals for the country's government as a whole. As he saw it, France had been and should still be one of the world's great powers. The kind of poor political leadership discussed in the historical section of the book and only the kind of state discussed in the last three chapters could re-create it.

As we also saw earlier, de Gaulle's disdain for traditional republican politics only grew during the twelve years of the Fourth Republic when he was out of power. The defeats in Indochina and North Africa convinced him all the more of the need for strong leadership, something he found lacking in the crisis-and-compromise style of government France had had for seventy-five years.

De Gaulle: Myth and Reality

Not surprisingly, then, de Gaulle made foreign policy a high priority in his decade as the first president of the Fifth Republic.

In part, that reflected his motivation for seeking political office. In part, it reflected the realities he faced the day he returned to power.

The immediate crisis was the Algerian fight for independence and its implications for all of France's colonial possessions. Contrary to most people's expectations, de Gaulle and his colleagues dealt with Algeria and the rest of the colonies by shedding them.

Through the referenda discussed earlier and intense negotiations with the National Liberation Front, Algeria gained its independence. A series of decisions also led to independence for almost all of France's remaining colonies, but in a way that continued to tie them to Paris politically, culturally, and economically.

Although these decisions came to haunt de Gaulle domestically, they were widely appreciated in the new countries of what came to be known as the third world.[3] De Gaulle always gave third world issues a lot of importance, most notably through one of his most trusted deputies, **Jacques Foccart**. Foccart held a variety of offices under all Gaullist presidents until his death in 1997; it was rumored later that he was making phone calls to African leaders on France's behalf until a week before he died.

Less universally appreciated were acts de Gaulle took to separate France from the superpower rivalry and, especially, from American dominance. It should be noted that not all of what he did was purely symbolic. He caused tremendous disruption to NATO during an important turning point in the Cold War. And although he and his colleagues thought they were acting in France's national interest, their critics in the United States and other countries viewed France's actions as dangerous threats.

The most important symbolic and least important substantive position he took came on June 24, 1967, when de Gaulle was visiting the French-speaking center of Canada, Montréal. He was driven with great pomp and ceremony to the city hall, where he was not expected to give a speech. However, the crowd insisted that he say something.

These were the early days of modern French-Canadian nationalism. Increasingly, French-speaking Canadians were upset at what they took to be their second-class citizenship. He had been invited by Québec's provincial premier, Richard Johnson. Despite his name, Johnson had had a Francophone mother, was educated exclusively in French, and spoke that language better than his father's English. Although by no means a nationalist, he was part of a generation of Québecers who opened the door to the protests and legislation that made French and English both official languages for the country and prioritized French in the province of Québec. Indeed, Johnson had run for office in 1966 advocating equality or independence, making him the first prominent politician to raise the possibility that the province could secede from the Canadian federation.

De Gaulle apparently told Montréal's mayor, Jean Drapeau, that he had to speak to the crowd that he claimed was clamoring for him. He uttered the unrehearsed words, *"Vive le Québec libre! Vive le Canada Français! Et vive la France!"* (Long live free Quebec! Long live French Canada! And long live France!)

This was a huge diplomatic gaffe, because de Gaulle was interfering in the domestic politics of another country without having been asked to do so by his Francophone, let alone his Anglophone, hosts. It confirmed his growing reputation as something of a political loose cannon, which was already well established given other—less symbolic—actions of his first years as president.

In 1960 France joined the nuclear club by detonating its first, primitive atomic bomb. Going at least as far back as Pierre and Marie Curie, France had been a leader in nuclear science. And under the Fourth Republic it made some tentative steps to develop its own weapons.

However, given the risk avoidance of politicians at the time, as discussed in Chapters 3 and 4, no premier or defense minister was willing to commit to a wholehearted program to develop these weapons of mass destruction.

De Gaulle showed no such reluctance. Even before he assumed the presidency, he was briefed about France's scientific progress and all but immediately authorized the rapid development of nuclear weapons, which he labeled the *force de frappe* (usually translated as the "striking force").

De Gaulle had few illusions. He knew that France would never rival the superpowers. By the time the first weapon was tested in Algeria, the United States and the Soviet Union each had more than 1,000 strategic and tactical warheads.

But de Gaulle assumed that the force de frappe was important for two reasons. First, because he never fully trusted the "security blanket" supposedly offered by the United States–led NATO, he felt France needed its own nuclear deterrent to protect itself against the Soviet Union. He may have been right. After all, the United Kingdom had already built its own arsenal. Even more important, having nuclear weapons was a symbolic sign of France's reemergence as one of the world's great powers; in other words, it was a sign of its renewed grandeur.

None of his successors has wavered in his commitment to maintaining the arsenal. Even the Socialist Mitterrand worked to maintain and modernize it. And France was the last country to conduct nuclear tests before India, North Korea, and Pakistan did so in recent years.

The arsenal is not big. One recent estimate put its size at about 480 weapons, which could be delivered from submarines or airplanes. That makes it noticeably larger than that of Britain, India, Israel, North Korea, and Pakistan. However, the total number of weapons pales in comparison with that of the United States and Russia, which still have about 10,000 each.

Probably more important and (to many) more annoying yet was France's decision to withdraw from NATO's integrated command in 1966. De Gaulle's Fourth Republic predecessors had all been loyal supporters of the United States during the first years of the **Cold War**. There was a strong feeling of gratitude to the country that helped liberate France and which many saw as the one force that could guarantee French security against what was still believed to be a threat from an apparently expansionist Communist bloc. In other words, the same politicians who had enthusiastically supported the first steps in European integration supported the Western alliance as it emerged during the first tense years of the Cold War. In fact, NATO headquarters were located in France, and hundreds of thousands of non-French NATO troops were based on its soil.

In 1966 de Gaulle surprised the allies by announcing that France was pulling its own forces out of NATO and insisted that the alliance remove all of its bases and foreign troops from its soil (NATO headquarters subsequently moved to Brussels). This should not have come as a complete surprise. Four years earlier, he had removed France's navy and air force from NATO control. Still, he made it clear that France remained a part of the Western alliance; it never formally left NATO as a whole. Nevertheless, the 1966 decision was both a further sign that he wanted France to pursue a more independent foreign policy, and it served as a major irritant for NATO at a time when superpower détente was progressing but the war in Vietnam was also escalating.

The final and most applauded of de Gaulle's foreign policy initiatives was his desire to play a kind of intermediary role between the two superpowers. De Gaulle's anticommunist credentials were beyond critique. Nonetheless, he saw an important opportunity for France to help the superpowers find a degree of common ground.

The key to this was his brokering of the first formal peace talks between the United States and the Vietnamese Communists, which began in Paris in 1968. The talks could not have begun had it not been for the growing opposition to the war in the United States and beyond. Nonetheless, the fact that the talks were held in Paris reflected both France's own tragic history in Indochina and de Gaulle's willingness to work with all sides.

De Gaulle would not live to see the final accord, which was signed in 1973. Still, his role in getting the talks started is seen as one of his great foreign policy accomplishments by almost all commentators.

Change amid Continuity

The four men who succeeded de Gaulle from 1969 until 2007 pursued far more pragmatic and supportive policies toward Europe, as discussed in Chapter 9. The same can be said about most of their foreign policies in general.

None of the four was anywhere near as nationalistic. The word "grandeur" has almost never found its way into major presidential addresses since de Gaulle's retirement.

Still, France has always been something of the "odd country out" in the Western alliance. Whether in its policies toward Africa or its attitudes toward the United States, it has usually been the member of the alliance most willing to go off on its own. Nevertheless, in keeping the overall argument of this book, like its domestic policy, French international relations have become more normal.

For many American readers there is one glaring exception to that rule: France's behavior regarding Iraq. That topic is dealt with in depth at the end of this chapter, but even there I argue that President Chirac's opposition to the 2003 American invasion had more to do with his definition of French national interests and the overall geopolitical situation after 9/11 than it had to do with what many in the Bush administration saw as French chauvinism.[4]

Pompidou

Georges Pompidou's foreign policy is the most difficult to reach firm conclusions about because he held the presidency for only four years and was too ill to do much in the year before he died. Almost certainly, his most notable accomplishment came in opening the door to broadening and deepening the EEC, something he had strongly believed in since his student days in the 1920s.

In other areas Pompidou continued most of de Gaulle's policies, although he always did so without the general's ideological fervor. In particular, he continued to help in the negotiations to end the war in Vietnam and worked with the new Socialist chancellor of West Germany to build closer ties to the Soviet bloc.

Pompidou also did not share de Gaulle's degree of skepticism about the United States, which dated at least to World War II, when de Gaulle frequently felt snubbed by the U.S. government in general and President Franklin D. Roosevelt in particular. The Soviet invasion of Czechoslovakia in 1968 had been a stunning blow to de Gaulle's hopes of deepening the rapprochement between the superpowers. It is hard to tell how de Gaulle would have reacted to the heightened cold-war related tensions in Europe, because he had barely a year left in office.

However, Pompidou realized that France needed to improve its relations with the entire Western alliance. And, unlike de Gaulle, who had mediocre—at best—relations with Presidents Eisenhower, Kennedy, and Johnson, Pompidou got along rather well with Richard Nixon and his team.

France's ties with its supposed allies did improve. There was never any possibility that Pompidou would question the three basic tenets of Gaullist grandeur. The force de frappe was sacrosanct. He apparently never considered reintegrating French forces into NATO. He also tried to maintain

European and U.S. Foreign Policy during the Cold War

It was during de Gaulle's presidency that French foreign policy was the most different from that of any of the members of the Western alliance.

Because of its position in the Cold War, Germany had little choice but to support the United States on almost every critical issue. Most British politicians could have been more critical, for instance, of Vietnam, but chose not to be. Everyone understood that the United States provided a nuclear safety blanket and hundreds of thousands of ground troops to help protect Western Europe from the Soviets.

Although de Gaulle's France was more independent—as the French had often been in the past—we should not make too much of the general's rebellious streak. France never left NATO altogether. De Gaulle always made it clear that when push came to shove, France would line up with the American-led alliance.

As seen in the rest of the chapter, France's cantankerous tendency has reappeared from time to time since de Gaulle's departure. However, it has done so less frequently and less divisively, despite what critics in Washington seem to think.

A French machine gun crew aims at a Hanoi street during a 1947 uprising in the French colony of Indochina. The failed French colonial policy in that region led to the 1954 debacle of Dien Bien Phu and the subsequent American involvement in the country later known as Vietnam.

France's hoped-for role as an intermediary, this time shifting his attention to the Middle East.

Finally, he continued de Gaulle's efforts to build ties in the third world, especially to former French colonies and other Francophone countries. By the time of his death, most of France's former colonies had been independent for at least a decade. Under Foccart's leadership, France continued to strengthen its cultural and economic—and, hence, political—relations in Africa. During Pompidou's presidency, his government even helped establish a number of semigovernmental agencies dedicated to promoting French language and culture in Louisiana. He went so far as to authorize the deployment of *coopérants* (France's equivalent of the peace corps) to the state.[5]

Giscard d'Estaing

The most significant change to "normal" foreign policy occurred during Giscard's one seven-year term.

In part, that reflected Giscard's background, which was very different from that of most Gaullists. To be sure, he cast his lot with them at the ballot box very early, in 1962. But his own political background was in the centrist politics of the Third and Fourth Republics. His father had been a civil servant who was serving in Germany in 1926 when the future president was born. Several ancestors on his mother's side had served as cabinet members. In short, his family combined the skills needed to compete in a political system in which small towns and rural areas dominated and the sophistication that came from being part of the intellectual and economic elite.

In part, the shift during his presidency reflected the international realities he had to cope with.

The **Organization of Petroleum Exporting Countries oil embargo** actually began on October 17, 1973, or about six months before Pompidou died. Its member countries refused to ship oil to any country that supported Israel in what is known as both the Yom Kippur and the October War, depending on which side you supported. The price of gasoline and related products skyrocketed by as much as 400 percent in countries that were most dependent on oil from the Middle East. In the United States, it went up by about half, to an average of $0.58 a gallon in spring 1974, a price most readers of this book could only dream of paying.

However, it took some time before the overarching impact of the crisis took hold, by which time Pompidou was dead, Giscard had won the presidency, and the first serious postwar recession in France and many other industrial countries was well under way. The "thirty glorious years" discussed in the chapter on domestic public policy were over. Overall growth rates were cut in half during Giscard's presidency. In some years the economy actually shrank. Unemployment and inflation both routinely topped 10 percent at a time when conventional economic wisdom held that they could not both increase at the same time.

We have already seen the policy consequences of the sharp and surprisingly long-lasting economic downturn. Despite his own desire for a more liberal and market-driven economic policy, Giscard understood that creating one or two firms that could be national champions in a given sector was the best route to guaranteeing French recovery and the competitiveness of those firms in an increasingly global economy. At times, the French government seemed desperate to find quick fixes for its problems, including an inane swindle in which it invested money in avions renifleurs, "sniffing" airplanes that could purportedly find underground oil deposits. Sometimes, Giscard and his second prime minister, Raymond Barre, referred to their actions as *piloter à vue,* which can best be translated as flying by the seat of one's pants.

Although it is impossible to be positive about Giscard's and Barre's leadership (especially since they were both economists), their difficulties reflected what has probably been the government's highest foreign policy priority ever since: its standing in the global economy. We political scientists do not have the statistical or other research tools to rank foreign policy issues according to their importance in any country. But given the difficulties in the economy covered in Chapter 8, there is no escaping the dramatic growth in importance economic issues have at home and abroad.

Superpower relations also took a turn for the worse during Giscard's presidency. The United States and the Soviet Union signed their most important agreements limiting the spread of nuclear weapons during the 1970s, and the Vietnam War finally came to an end, with France mostly on the political sidelines.

But a lot also went wrong. Israel and its Arab neighbors fought their fourth war in thirty years. With the rise of terrorism in Palestine and elsewhere, the region seemed to become an intractable hotspot. Things were only made worse in 1979 when what became the Islamic Republic overthrew the shah of Iran and the Soviets invaded Afghanistan. Further, the election of Margaret Thatcher and Ronald Reagan in 1979 and 1980, respectively, brought intransigent conservatives to power in Great Britain and the United States.

In short, the events of Giscard's seven years made France into an increasingly marginal player as far as the major questions of international relations were concerned.

That should not obscure two important characteristics of his policy and style, which built on Pompidou's approach to the world. First, Giscard was a pragmatist who did not rule out working with people with whom he disagreed. Thus, he held regular meetings, routinely in English, with the German Socialist chancellor Helmut Schmidt. Second, he was more of an "Atlanticist" than either of his predecessors.

He met regularly and worked smoothly with Presidents Nixon, Gerald Ford, and Jimmy Carter. It helped that he was the first president of the Fifth

Republic to speak English well and that he seemed to enjoy spending time in the United States.

At the same time, he did not challenge most of the key foreign policy tenets he inherited from de Gaulle and Pompidou.

Mitterrand

Perhaps the most important presidential transition as far as foreign policy is concerned was that from Valéry Giscard d'Estaing to François Mitterrand in 1981. Its importance lies as much in how much continuity there was from Gaullist foreign policy under the leadership of a man who had been one of the regime's and the general's fiercest critics in the 1950s and 1960s.

It is also important because the shift in leadership from one party or coalition to the opposition is vital for the future of any new democracy. Even though the Fifth Republic was almost a quarter century old when Mitterrand won, his election marked the first time someone from outside the Gaullist majority had occupied the Elysée Palace. The Socialists' sweeping victory in the subsequent legislative elections marked the first time that anyone other than the Gaullists and their allies controlled the National Assembly.

There were important changes in French foreign policy under Mitterrand, changes that were largely the result of a world that was turned upside down during his fourteen years in office. But the key thing to see first is that, in many ways, his overarching goals were closer to de Gaulle's than to those of either Pompidou or Giscard.

To that end, consider the words of one of France's leading foreign policy experts, Dominique Moïsi, written in the first months after Mitterrand's election:

> If we can speak of continuity in Mitterrand's foreign policy, it is a continuity that has more in common with de Gaulle's policies than with Georges Pompidou's or Valéry Giscard d'Estaing's. For Pompidou, France was to become a major industrial power. For Giscard d'Estaing, she was to hold her place among the advanced countries in the world. Rejecting these legitimate but highly unromantic ambitions, Mitterrand shares de Gaulle's faith in France's special mission in the world.[6]

Of course, Mitterrand would approach strengthening French grandeur in a different way from de Gaulle. In particular, he strengthened ties in Europe (see Chapter 9) as well as the United States. His Western tilt made sense, given his history as one of the leaders of the anticommunist Left, which made any relations with the Soviet Union difficult at best. One indication of France's tilt toward the United States was its acceptance of placing intermediate range nuclear weapons in Europe, although none would be on French soil.

For Mitterrand, Moïsi's phrase "France's special mission in the world" certainly meant keeping its nuclear arsenal and strengthening its military in general. At a time when most of the then five acknowledged nuclear powers were looking for ways to end testing of nuclear weapons, Mitterrand and his government were open about what they were convinced was the need to continue them.

That commitment led to one of the most embarrassing scandals of Mitterrand's presidency. In 1985 the government announced that it would conduct tests at Moruroa, an atoll in the overseas territory of French Polynesia. Greenpeace members snuck into the forbidden zone to protest the test. Their boat was escorted out. Several weeks later, French secret service officers blew up the Greenpeace ship *Rainbow Warrior*, docked in New Zealand, killing one member of its crew.

Mitterrand also maintained and, to some degree, expanded on France's commitments to the third world. Rhetorically, he gave support to insurgent left-wing movements, drawing heavily on the work of the activist Régis Debray, who became a member of the presidential staff. To cite but one concrete example, he condemned American support for the Contras in Nicaragua and even provided limited military aid to that country's left-wing government.

He also continued France's involvement in the Middle East, although he did have a more nuanced approach than some of the Gaullist governments. Thus, although he criticized Israel when it invaded Lebanon (which had close ties to France) in 1982, he also made it clear that the international community had to recognize Israel and help guarantee its survival.

But the most important change in foreign policy under Mitterrand came as a result of shifts in the international environment that could not have been anticipated even in the middle of his first term. When **Mikhail Sergeyevich Gorbachev** was chosen general secretary of the Communist Party of the Soviet Union, almost every analyst assumed that the Cold War would remain the defining feature of global international relations.

We were all wrong.

For the next six years, Gorbachev and his colleagues unleashed a wave of reforms that both transformed the world and destroyed his own country. The specifics of glasnost, perestroika, and other reforms take us beyond the scope of this book.

What matters for our purposes is how the end of the Cold War transformed French foreign policy. During the first year of his rule, Gorbachev tried incremental reforms to reinvigorate the Soviet economy, for instance, by sharply reducing the hours liquor stores were open on the assumption that that would lead people to work harder. By late 1986, however, it had become clear that more profound reforms were needed, which opened the door to unprecedented political openness and protest in the Soviet Union.

By 1988 the thirst for political change had spread to what we in the West called the Soviet satellites in Eastern Europe. That year and, especially, the next saw massive demonstrations in every member of the Warsaw Pact.

The Significance of 11/9 and 9/11

Thomas Friedman of the *New York Times* frequently reminds us that the Berlin Wall fell on 11/9 and the terrorist attacks in New York and Washington occurred on 9/11. The numerical parallels are obviously a coincidence.

The trends they represent are not. Both changed politics in France and in the rest of the world forever.

For all intents and purposes, 11/9 ended the Cold War and with it the division of Europe and the threat of a major nuclear war.

The events of 9/11 made terrorism a major issue for Americans as it had already been for most Europeans, a theme returned to at the end of the chapter.

The most important of these to France occurred in Germany, culminating in the symbolic destruction of the **Berlin Wall** on November 9, 1989. East Germans crossed the previously forbidden boundary to visit the West. Their western compatriots (and often relatives) went in the other direction.

Within days, it was clear that the German Democratic Republic, the official name of East Germany, could not survive. What was to happen next was obviously going to be a massive challenge for everyone with an interest in European politics.

The leaders faced many questions. They ranged from how they would merge the very different Germanys to how a united Germany would fit into Europe as it was evolving in the West.

Mitterrand does not deserve the most credit for the surprisingly easy unification of the two Germanys. That goes to his conservative counterpart, the German chancellor **Helmut Kohl.**

Nonetheless, Mitterrand's role in German unification cannot be understated. The French faced a difficult challenge.

France and Germany had already emerged as the two most powerful countries in what was then the European Community. Their populations were about the same size. Germany was a little bit wealthier. France's military was a lot more powerful.

But adding the roughly seventeen million people of East Germany to the West was going to make Germany the largest EC member. And the newly united Germany was going to be the most powerful economic force in Europe, once the two commercial and monetary systems were fully integrated. To complicate matters even further, it was not clear how—even if, given the opposition of the Soviets—the new Germany would become part of NATO.

Like many of his colleagues in other countries, Mitterrand was initially caught politically flat-footed. Initially, he had hoped to slow down, if not end, any discussion of German unification. Nonetheless, he soon realized that it was inevitable and that his best approach was to strengthen European institutions and Germany's role within them.

By early in 1990 an agreement was reached to start what came to be known as the **two by four negotiations** involving the two Germanys and the four countries that had occupied the country after World War II—Britain, France, the Soviet Union, and the United States. France's most important formal accomplishment was a German agreement that the postwar boundaries of the two Germanys would be those of the newly unified country as well. Then, largely off the record, Mitterrand helped convince Kohl and the other negotiators that Germany should be in both the EC and NATO, despite the initial resistance of the Soviets. East Germany was successfully integrated into the West in October 1990, and Mitterrand was seen as one of the key architects of the transition.

For the remaining five years of Mitterrand's presidency, France was as closely integrated into the Western alliance as it had been before the creation of the Fifth Republic. After Iraq occupied Kuwait in 1990 France quickly joined the international coalition assembled by the United States under the auspices of the United Nations. In all, it sent 18,000 troops, 60 combat aircraft, 120 helicopters, 40 tanks, 100 armored vehicles, 1 missile cruiser, 3 destroyers, and 4 frigates. Of countries outside of the Middle East, only the United States and the United Kingdom made a larger commitment.

In 1993, two years after the Gulf War, France brought its key military forces under NATO command.

In short, the man who came to power as the most nationalistic president since de Gaulle became the most pragmatic and pro-Western leader since 1958. Because he wanted to? Probably not. Probably because events made him so.

In sum, the same two factors that have been put forth since Chapter 5 have made French foreign policy less nationalistic and less idiosyncratic over the last fifty years. First, the men who succeeded de Gaulle all lacked his unusual views and his charisma, which left an indelible imprint on French politics, domestic and international. Second, France's room for maneuvering on the international stage declined as trends as different as European integration, the end of the Cold War, and globalization left it less and less master of its own destiny.

Now to a discussion of the Chirac presidency and the politically and intellectually difficult case of Iraq, where the argument about "normal" politics is most open to scrutiny, if not objection.

Chirac and the Case of Iraq

Any analysis of French foreign policy that ended with the Mitterrand era would be received with derision, especially by people in the United States or the United Kingdom who have supported the Bush or Blair governments. For many of them, France has returned to its old, anti-American ways out of a combination of nationalistic vitriol and national interest.

As already seen, France has been the most independent of the Western democracies for a century or more. And the French clearly have a significant dislike of things American, ranging from the culture of Coca-Cola and Big Macs to what many see as overly aggressive foreign policy in which the views of the French and other allies are too often given short shrift.

To some degree, the jury is still out, especially on the most vexing case of the Chirac years—his government's refusal to support the American-led invasion and occupation of Iraq. However, as noted at the beginning of the chapter, I will argue that, on balance, French positions on most security-related issues have been based more on their assessment of what France's national interests were than on any sort of Gaullist nationalism. In short, normal politics.

Jacques Chirac became president in 1995 as the last of the leaders who rose to prominence under de Gaulle to reach any top office. Even more than Mitterrand, Chirac came from the tradition that equated proper foreign policy with the pursuit of grandeur.

Like all of his predecessors, Chirac had a number of trouble spots he had to address, including relations with the Western alliance, Europe (see the previous chapter), the third world, the Middle East, and the international political economy. Only three of them are dealt with here: nuclear weapons, globalization, and Iraq.

Again, I do not want to downplay the tensions between the French approach to international relations and those of many other Western countries. Indeed, they have existed whether the Left or the Right is in power in Paris. However, again, the point here is that France has moved more into the mainstream of the international community. And, at the times when it has not, it has done so out of its leadership's understanding of the country's self-interest, which is also the sine qua non of most theories of international relations.

Strategic Policy

Chirac's first term began amid controversy. He made it clear that he would lead France in a reasonably independent direction when he announced that it would conduct a final series of nuclear tests on June 13, 1995, and then ratify the Comprehensive Nuclear Test Ban Treaty (CTBT). After France held its final test in late January 1996, Chirac kept his promise, making the country the last acknowledged nuclear power at the time to ratify the treaty.

Chirac's decision to resume testing was not that dramatic a break with the past. For the first fourteen years of his term, Mitterrand's government continued to carry out tests under French-controlled islands in the South Pacific.

The controversy over the tests died down shortly after France acceded to the CTBT regime.

Chirac's decision produced outrage from most of the rest of the world. By that time, most nuclear experts—including those who favored developing new weapons—had become convinced that tests added little to any government's capacity to improve its stockpile. You could just as well simulate explosions on a supercomputer.

Nonetheless, the Chirac government continued with plans to shut down production of all new nuclear weapons and even of weapons-grade fissile materials, something neither the United States nor the United Kingdom has done to this day.

French policy changed somewhat in early 2006 once it became clear that Iran had no intention of ending its projects to develop sophisticated forms of plutonium that could be used in nuclear weapons (but could also be used for the generation of electricity). In a surprise announcement a few months later, Chirac had said that the number of warheads per missile in its submarines would be reduced. This was, he made clear, not a step toward disarmament but an initiative to make the weapons more accurate so that they could reach any potential enemy.

In a speech a few weeks later, the defense minister, Michèle Alliot-Marie, added to the president's remarks:

> These evolutions are aimed at better taking into account the psychology of the enemy. A potential enemy may think that France, given its principles, might hesitate to use the entire force of its nuclear arsenal against civilian populations. Our country has modified its capacity for action and from now on has the possibility to target the control centers of an eventual enemy.[7]

In practice, the real changes under Chirac were not those early tests or the rhetoric (and reality) of modernizing its arsenal. Instead, they were the same as in all the major Western powers. Their own nuclear weapons are no longer a major source of dispute in international relations, at least among themselves. The question now is what those powers can do about the proliferation of nuclear weapons, which has reached India, North Korea, Pakistan, and might possibly reach Iran in the not-so-distant future. On this, the Western powers are in agreement: there is no obvious way to move forward.

Globalization

No issue is grabbing more worldwide attention than **globalization**, or the supposed shrinking of the planet's economic, environmental, cultural, and political systems. Everywhere it has its supporters as well as its critics. Thus, in the United States, many observers, such as the acclaimed *New York Times* writer Thomas Friedman, think globalization has literally brought us a world of good and little else. Yet, every time the World Bank or the International Monetary Fund holds meetings at their headquarters in Washington, D.C., I have to find an alternative Metro route to my office because protesters are likely to be rampaging at the station I normally use.

Among the Western democracies, France has seen the most controversy over globalization. This controversy includes the often black-clad and occasionally violent protesters who turn up whenever the world's economic and political leaders meet. In part it includes José Bové and other colorful activists who see the likes of McDonald's restaurants eroding France's cultural (and culinary) identity. But unlike in other countries, it also includes public intellectuals and senior politicians on both the left and the right, including many who were close to the Chirac government.

In fact, according to one count, candidates voicing concerns about globalization won almost half the votes in the 2002 presidential election. Since then, antiglobalization forces have quieted somewhat both in the streets and in the media.

Nonetheless, opposition to globalization is still there. That anger also misses important facts about French politics that reinforce my argument about more normal politics. As globalization became a prominent issue during the Chirac years, there was a broadly based consensus among leading Gaullists and Socialists that it was a fact of life and that France had to adapt.

In practice, much of the criticism of globalization addressed cultural rather than political or economic issues. And for someone who loves French cuisine, film, and soccer, many of the critiques are on target. Young people drink Coke more and wine less. Fast food is rapidly replacing the long lunch or even the home-cooked dinner. After decades of controversy, foreign (read American) films far outnumber French ones at the multiplex cinemas (often accused of being part of an American invasion) that now are becoming almost as common as they are in the United States. And, among young people, the National Basketball Association (NBA) has become almost as popular as France's domestic soccer league, which admittedly is not one of the best in Europe.

More high-browed, intellectual critics point to other problems in addition to the war in Iraq, which is considered later in the chapter. For them, globalization is a code word for what they see as the growing American hegemony over all areas of everyone's lives. As they see it, French companies are losing out to the likes of Microsoft and Boeing.

Digging a bit below the rhetorical surface during the Chirac years, one finds three common denominators that suggest that French antiglobalization sentiments are less important than either their domestic supporters or American critics would suggest.

First, the emerging global culture is increasingly popular among the French, especially younger people. I wrote this section the day after the final episode of *The Sopranos*, which played on HBO in the United States. HBO is not available in France (yet), but *The Sopranos* is watched by millions on the cable-satellite network Jimmy. The issue is not whether *The Sopranos*, the NBA, or rap music are inherently good or bad, French or foreign. The fact is that they are becoming an inescapable part of French culture, just as players such as France's Tony Parker take over the NBA and reality TV (primarily a British and Dutch invasion) takes a growing share of the American television market.

Second, despite all the rhetoric, France is going through what Philip Gordon and Sophie Meunier called "globalization by stealth" at the start of this decade.[8] As seen in the last chapter, France's membership in the EU is part and parcel of its growing insertion into an increasingly global market. By the turn of this century, about a fourth of France's GNP was accounted for by imports and a fourth by exports, about twice the comparable figures for the United States or Japan. And, as discussed in Chapter 8, that means that France can no longer even try to control its domestic economy, whether that desire comes from the government or the private sector.

To be sure, as also seen in Chapter 8, Chirac's governments were more successful than others in Europe in protecting to some degree French control over the armaments, banking, and other industries deemed to be in the national interest. Those efforts, however, cannot mask the new economic realities alluded to in that chapter.

Some of it is easy to see by any tourist. Your rental car is as likely to be a Toyota as a Renault. The clerk at the check-in counter is probably using a Dell or a Toshiba computer. If you left something at home by mistake, FedEx or UPS (with their totally French workforce) will get it to you the next morning. You can buy books through the Amazon Web site or check out your favorite videos on the French MTV site.

One trade association estimated that direct foreign investment brought more than a trillion dollars into France in 2006 and created about 40,000 jobs for French men and women that year alone, including 300 at FedEx.[9] And contrary to much of the antiglobalization rhetoric, the majority of the investment and job creation came from European firms, not ones in the United States.

According to that same report, almost two million French workers, or 16 percent of all private sector workers, are employed by foreign-based companies. Almost half of the capital trading monitored by the CAC 40 (France's equivalent of the Dow Jones 500) is owned by foreign individuals and corporations.

French companies are just as active in foreign markets. France, Germany, Japan, and the Netherlands all compete for second place after Great Britain as the largest foreign investor in the United States, with $143 billion in assets in 2006. The French are active in almost all sectors of the American economy, ranging from airplane sales to public opinion polling and marketing. Food and wine make up less than 10 percent of the French involvement in the American economy, although it should be pointed out that the French firm Evian owns Poland Springs and other popular bottled water brands.

Still, the concern here is not who owns whom. Rather, it is that both the Chirac government and the opposition endorsed these initiatives. And they did so in ways that were not terribly different from those practiced by their counterparts elsewhere in Europe and North America.

The third common denominator is a point missing from most of the French debate (and that in other Western countries) on globalization. The French arguments on the subject have revolved around the degree to which the country has been victimized by globalization.

What many of the activists (including those I criticized above) properly call attention to is that the rich countries in the "north" are all the beneficiaries of globalization, whoever comes out on top in their internal competition. France has been duly criticized for its role in the "south," or third world, ever since the days when Jacques Foccart all but controlled policy toward its former colonies.

To begin with, France does not do as much to help third world development as most of its counterparts. According to the 2004 United Nations *Human Development Report* it ranked eighth among the world's wealthiest countries, contributing the equivalent of $137 per person per year. France was not all that much of a laggard. It came in slightly ahead of the United Kingdom, and its giving was just about double that of the American government.

Perhaps this is a statement about how little *all* Western governments are doing to help development for the poorest billion people on the planet, most of whom live on the equivalent of about a dollar a day. In the 1960s the twenty-four members of the OECD committed themselves to spending at least 0.7 percent of their GNP per year on foreign aid. In 2004 only five countries—Denmark, Luxembourg, the Netherlands, Norway, and Sweden—reached that level. France was in seventh place, spending 0.42 percent of its overall income to help the less-developed world, admittedly far better than the 0.16 percent spent by the United States.

The other concern often missed in the French debate over globalization is the role it has often played in exacerbating rather than resolving conflict in the developing world, especially in the former French and Belgian colonies. French policy did begin to change after the 1994 overthrow of the government of Rwanda (which it had supported) and the resulting genocide. In the first decade of the new century, French troops have been involved in peace imposition and peacekeeping missions in the Democratic Republic of Congo, the Ivory Coast, and Liberia, although many people doubt the commitment and effectiveness of the troops sent by Paris.

Overall, the point of this section is not to castigate France. If there is criticism to be handed out, it should go to all Western countries. France is very much in the mainstream.

Normal politics.

Iraq

President Chirac's decision not only to oppose the American-led invasion of Iraq in 2003 but to cast France's veto in the United Nations Security Council doomed any hope that the international community would intervene as a

French Fries and French Toast

Even supporters of the war have to admit that there was a lot of silliness in the American reaction to French policy.

In classic French fashion, the silliest of them involved food.

Conservative members of Congress wanted to make their cafeterias and other restaurants rename French toast and French fries as Freedom Toast and Freedom Fries.

There was one problem. Neither dish had anything to do with France.

In France, French fries are called simply *frites* (fries). In England, they are chips (American tourists also have to learn that potato chips are crisps). Everything we know suggests that the "French" fry was actually a Belgian invention.

The uproar about French toast was even more absurd. The historical record has two stories. First (and less likely), it was named for an eighteenth-century innkeeper near Albany New York, named French. More likely, it has culinary origins in many places in Europe. It was widely known as German toast when World War I broke out, leading Americans to start calling it French toast instead.[1] All I know for sure is that when I tried to serve it to French friends when I was doing my Ph.D. research in Paris, I could not find maple syrup anywhere, and my friends looked at the dish in disbelief. Later I learned that there is a related dish, *pain perdu*, made with stale bread, but I've never seen it served.

---

1. American authorities also tried to rename the frankfurter and hamburger when the United States entered World War I. "Hot dog" stuck. "Salisbury steak" did not.

---

whole, as it had during the first Gulf War, and produced a firestorm of protest among the war's supporters.

In retrospect, some of it seems silly. Boycotts of French products were organized in the United States. Angry restaurant owners poured bottles of French wine into the sinks in their kitchens—in front of television cameras, of course.

Serious pundits saw the French opposition to Bush and Blair as yet another example of the long history of French nationalism and anti-Americanism.

To be sure, there was some of that.

However, my reading of the evidence is that the president and other members of the French government operated largely out of what they perceived to be France's own national interest. And, as I've hinted earlier in the chapter, they, and not George Bush or Tony Blair, may well have been right.

What's more, France was not the only country to object to the invasion. Russia and China used their veto powers as well. Germany, then a nonpermanent member of the Security Council, voted against authorizing military force as well.

Yet the French got the bulk of the criticism. Indeed, one American critic (who actually lives in France) called it the "French betrayal of America."

My goal here is not to rehash the still ongoing debate over whether the war and occupation made sense, then or now. Rather, it is to examine French decision-making processes during the run-up to the war and consider the argument that it was acting out of a combination of nationalism and national interest, with the latter prevailing.

On one level, the critics were right. France had closer commercial and cultural ties with Saddam Hussein's regime than most Western governments. Along with the United Kingdom, it had been responsible for carving up the Arab parts of the Ottoman Empire during and after World War I. Truth be told, however, the British had more of an impact on the creation of the troubled, modern state of Iraq, because they got control of it and its transition to nominal independence in the years thereafter.

Still, France almost certainly had closer ties to Saddam's regime than any other NATO member. If the American conservatives are to be believed (and they are probably right here), French firms did end runs around the post–Gulf War embargos to sell arms to and buy other goods from Iraq. Certainly, those ties had existed for a long time, including French technical and financial support for the Osirak nuclear reactor, which the Israeli Air Force destroyed in the late 1960s.

And there was more than a bit of pique in France's reaction to the United States—and Washington's to France. Press reports have long speculated that Chirac felt personally insulted by what he took to be the demeaning way that he was treated by Bush administration officials, especially by the then secretary of defense, Donald Rumsfeld. Yet there is no doubt that the seemingly arrogant foreign minister, Dominique de Villepin, ruffled many political feathers in the much more informal American diplomatic community at the United Nations.

At the same time, we should remember three other things.

First, like many skeptical members of the international community, France actually wavered regarding its own policy at least until the end of 2002. Chirac's statements were always ambiguous. Nonetheless, he consistently supported actions at the United Nations that could potentially compel Iraq to disarm. Where he differed from the United States was on the question of whether Iraq had weapons of mass destruction and how much of a threat it actually posed to its neighbors and the overall region, at least in the short term.

Along these lines, it is important to note that France was a willing participant in the American-led alliance during the first Gulf War, which followed the Iraqi invasion of Kuwait in August 1991. France deployed almost 15,000 troops for what Americans call Operation Desert Shield and then Desert Storm (Opération Daguet to the French). Of the European countries, only the British sent more.

France also was a strong supporter of the intervention in Afghanistan after the terrorist attacks in the United States on September 11, 2001. Chirac was one of the first leaders to express his sympathy with and support for the victims of the attacks and the United States as a whole. French troops were among the first to be deployed to Afghanistan. In mid-2007, it still had 1,000 troops on the ground even though most voters did not approve of their continued presence.

Second, as with globalization, the apparent nationalism of French leaders and pundits was almost certainly overestimated by their foreign critics. As discussed earlier, there is some resentment toward the United States among French politicians—left and right alike—who feel that it has usurped France's own proper role as one of the world's great powers. But no one of any significance in France had any support for the Iraqi regime or for terrorism. In fact, France had been a victim of terrorism far more than the United States, dating back to the aftermath of the Algerian war of the 1950s.

Finally, most mainstream analysts in France and the rest of the world have argued that Chirac, de Villepin, and their colleagues simply reached a different conclusion about the most realistic strategy to use regarding what, again, everyone acknowledged was an unacceptable regime in Baghdad. Discussions inside the French government remain reasonably secret. Nonetheless, leaks have indicated that policymakers there decided that Bush, Rumsfeld, and the neoconservatives in the United States grossly underestimated how difficult it would be to occupy and govern the country once Saddam was toppled, something everyone realized would happen quickly and easily. And it seems that they told emissaries from Washington and London that France had better intelligence about the real situation on the ground in Iraq and was less dependent on what turned out to be less-than-reliable exile groups such as the Iraqi National Congress.

In short, the French government based its decision on what it thought to be its own national interest. Isn't that what normal politics in international relations is all about?

Conclusion: We're Number Thirty-Four

To get a glimpse from another perspective of how much French foreign policy has become more normal, consider a very different example.

As I was finishing this book, the world's first global peace index was published by a team of Australian business leaders and the Economist Intelligence Unit.[10] It was the first attempt to systematically document how peaceful a country is and to include indicators that might help us understand why some countries fared better in this regard than others did.

As the first attempt to do so, the index can—and will—be improved on. Whatever its faults, the index uses twenty-four different indicators of peacefulness. Some are part of the traditional core of international relations, including involvement in war, possession of weapons of mass destruction, commitment to peacekeeping missions, and so on. Some are part of the new world of international security, including the country's commitment to the environment and economic development. Some, finally, tap peacefulness inside the country with indicators ranging from the amount of domestic violence to the number of people in prison.

Not surprisingly, most of the countries at the top of the index are relatively wealthy democracies that have been able to avoid international disputes because of their location or as a result of relatively easy policy decisions their governments have made over the last decade or two.

Norway is number one. New Zealand is number two. Denmark, Ireland, Japan, Sweden, Finland, Canada, Portugal, and Austria round out the top ten, in that order. No surprises.

France is number thirty-four. That rank is also no surprise. France has more global responsibilities than any of the top ten. It has—and probably has to have—a larger military, although maybe it doesn't need its nuclear arsenal. Even though Canada and the Nordic countries have developed militaries that specialize in peace building, the French forces are much larger and, therefore, more likely to be deployed. Perhaps because of the diversity of its population, France has also had to deal with more violence within its borders than most of the members of the top ten.

So number thirty-four wasn't so bad. It reflects the fact that France is both a powerful and, normally, responsible member of the international community. The country does "well" on some key indicators, including the number of deaths associated with its involvement in international conflicts abroad. It does not do as well on others, such as the size of its arsenal or its arms sales. Overall, it is ranked one place lower than Italy.

The United Kingdom is number forty-nine.

The United States comes in ninety-sixth place, just ahead of Iran.

Key Concepts

force de frappe   185
globalization   196
grandeur   183

Key People, Entities, and Events

Berlin Wall   193
Cold War   186
Foccart, Jacques   184
Gorbachev, Mikhail Sergeyevich   192
Kohl, Helmut   193
Organization of Petroleum Exporting Countries oil embargo   189
two by four negotiations   194

Questions for Discussion

1. How can you explain why French foreign policy has evoked so much controversy throughout the life of the Fifth Republic, if not longer?

2. This book is based on the argument that French politics has become more "normal" since de Gaulle returned to power in 1958. What counter-evidence can you find?

3. Especially if you supported the American policy in Iraq since 2003, how would you respond to the argument made here about French foreign policy?

4. This chapter was finished just before the 2007 presidential election, which brought a new generation and new team of leaders to power. How do you think French foreign policy has changed since then? Why?

11

Conclusion
Sarkoland

The Fifth Republic held its eighth presidential election just as I was finishing this book. Like many before it, the 2007 presidential election marked a major transition in French political life. In the past, most elections involved a leader with a new set of ideas replacing someone whose views had lost most of their popularity.

This time, the election and the legislative ones that followed marked a generational changing of the guard. Jacques Chirac was leaving office at age seventy-four. Chirac had been a fixture in conservative circles since he first became a cabinet adviser in the early 1960s. His main left-wing opponent in his two presidential victories, Lionel Jospin, was only five years younger.

Both also represented the intellectual, political, and bureaucratic elite that have been featured so prominently in this book. Both were ENA graduates; both started their careers in the civil service; both were political insiders in ways that most of us Washington "inside the Beltway" policy wonks can only dream of.

The 2007 election drew more interest from English-speaking pundits than any other in recent memory because it was going to change so much in French political life. And given the controversies surrounding French policy on Iraq, almost any change would be welcome in London or Washington.

The drama was magnified by the fact that Ségolène Royal was the first woman candidate with a serious chance to win the presidency. Although women had served as prime ministers of Canada, Germany, and Great Britain, she would have been the first woman directly elected to govern a major democracy. To make things even more interesting, Senator Hillary Clinton was leading the race for the Democratic nomination in the United States.

Neither Royal nor the eventual winner, Nicolas Sarkozy, would have made a successful candidate in either the United States or Britain. Sarkozy was the child of immigrants and had a complicated family life that included multiple divorces and an uncertain relationship with his current wife, who almost never appeared with him in public. Royal was estranged from her father's military family and had never married her partner, Socialist Party president François Hollande, who actually considered running for the presidential nomination against her and with whom she has had four children.

The two leading candidates were also polar opposites.

Sarkozy's fiery temper and inflammatory rhetoric were legendary, including his calling North African immigrant rioters "scum." He was also not part of the traditional elite. He had been a mediocre student in high school and thus "had" to go to law school rather than one of the grandes écoles. But he rose quickly in politics. Before he turned thirty, he was defeated by a Gaullist stalwart, Charles Pasqua, to be elected mayor of the posh Parisian suburb of Neuilly. President Chirac named him to the cabinet, where he held a number of critical positions, including that of interior minister. Thus he was in charge of law and order when many of the poor suburbs erupted in violence in 2005. He also had a falling out with Chirac, which left the outgoing president, at most, cool to his most likely successor.

Royal was born in Africa, where her father was serving in the French colonial army. She did graduate from ENA and embarked on the kind of career typical of France's bureaucratic and political elite. Her lack of a marriage contract with the father of her four children would have been political suicide in the United States or the United Kingdom. To the degree that Sarkozy was seen as a firebrand, she was seen by many as an overly slick fashion plate as well as a politician.

The differences between the two candidates were so clear that just before the election, the cover of one of the newsweeklies appeared without any words, just a picture of a bundled stick of dynamite and a pair of stiletto heels.

France being France, there were plenty of other candidates, including a kindly Trotskyite mailman who won almost 5 percent of the vote (see Table 11.1). Only two of them, however warrant any attention here. At one point, François Bayrou, a centrist and former classics teacher and farmer, seemed to be a challenger for one of the top two spots. And the seventy-eight-year-old Jean-Marie Le Pen was running as a potentially major candidate in an unprecedented fifth consecutive presidential campaign.

As the first round of balloting approached, the drama around the election had largely disappeared. As has been the case with centrist candidates since the 1960s, Bayrou's support began to evaporate. Sarkozy was gaining support among voters whose anti-immigrant concerns might have led them to vote for Le Pen. In short, 2007 was not going to be a rerun of 2002, when only Chirac topped 20 percent of the vote on the first ballot and Le Pen squeezed ahead of Jospin and kept the Left off the second ballot.

Table 11.1	The Presidential Election, 2007		
Candidate	Party	First ballot (percentage)	Second ballot (percentage)
Sarkozy, Nicolas	UPM	31.2	53.1
Royal, Ségolène	PS	25.9	46.9
Bayrou, François	UDF	18.6	—
Le Pen, Jean-Marie	National Front	10.4	—
Others		15.0	—

Note: Dashes = not applicable.

Perhaps the most notable feature of the election was the turnout, which reached record levels at about 85 percent in both rounds of voting. This came at a time when voter participation had been declining for many years in most Western democracies.

Between them, Royal and Sarkozy won almost 60 percent of the first ballot vote. The election also marked the end of any real hope for the Communists and UDF as discussed in Chapter 6, at least for now. The high turnout ended more than a decade in which increasing numbers of voters chose not to show up at the polls. Only one election, the first presidential election in 1965, had had a higher turnout rate. What's more, most voters returned to one of the three main parties, which had seen their share of the vote drop. If one includes Bayrou as a major candidate, the "big" parties won three-quarters of the vote. Le Pen did worse than he had at any election since the 1980s. The PCF candidate did not win even 2 percent of the vote.

Center and right-wing candidates won a strong majority of the vote. That meant that unless the vast majority of Bayrou's voters chose to support Royal, Sarkozy would have an easy route to the Elysée Palace. In the end, that's exactly what happened. Royal did win a slight majority among Bayrou's first-ballot voters but won barely a quarter of Le Pen's. Sarkozy won easily with more than 53 percent of the second-ballot vote.

It will be some time before political scientists reach a definitive explanation for why Sarkozy won and Royal lost. Part of her loss has to be due to the gaffes she made, especially on foreign policy. Part of it has to be due to the failure of the Socialists to update their vision of the Left along the lines of Tony Blair in Britain or Bill Clinton in the United States. Part of it has to be due to the voters' greater concern about immigration and the other issues that Sarkozy stressed rather than the bread-and-butter questions that Royal stressed. And part of it has to be because many voters in France—including a majority of its women—were not ready to vote for a female candidate.

Indeed, as shown in Table 11.2, the two candidates split the male vote, but Sarkozy actually outpolled Royal by 8 percent among women. Royal won a majority only among young voters, but even the nearly three million newly enrolled voters were not enough to take her to victory.

Table 11.2	Who Voted for Whom, Second Round, 2007	
	Royal (percentage)	Sarkozy (percentage)
Men	50	50
Women	46	54
Under 30	65	38
Between 30 and 49	47	53
50 or over	43	57

Source: www.csa-fr.com (accessed June 1, 2007).

Changes continued in the legislative elections held on June 10 and 17, 2007. Given the presidential results, most pundits, pollsters, and politicians expected a massive victory for the new president and his party.

That is not quite what happened. The UMP and its allies did win a resounding victory with 345 of 577 seats (see Table 11.3). However, they actually lost about 40 seats from their 2002 total. This was written in the weeks after the vote, so observers were still trying to figure out why this happened. First, turnout was much lower than in the presidential election. Perhaps many overly confident UMP voters decided to stay home. Second, one of Sarkozy's first initiatives was a proposal to raise the value-added tax (a kind of sales tax built into the purchase price of a good or service, not added at the cash register) from 19.5 percent to as much as 24.5 percent. To say the least, this trial balloon did not go over well with the public. Former prime minister Raffarin estimated that the proposal cost the majority as many as 60 seats, although there is no way of determining how accurate he was at this point.

Sarkoland

When I finished writing this book, less than a month after the election, it was still far too early to tell just how much change Sarkozy will introduce. The Gaullists' sweeping victory in the legislative elections in June 2007 should allow Sarkozy and his team to govern more or less at will until the next elections in 2012.

However, as seen in earlier chapters, Chirac and the UMP were elected by large majorities five years earlier. But a combination of Chirac's age, an economic downturn, and unexpected issues, including Iraq, Europe, and immigration, all but immobilized the governments led by prime ministers Raffarin and de Villepin.

Indeed, Sarkozy won by the largest majority of any center-right president other than de Gaulle himself. And his election was the first one since 1974 in which a retiring (or deceased) president's party won the next contest. The incumbents Mitterrand and Chirac had won reelection, but their likely successor had hitherto been beaten by a candidate from the other end of the political spectrum.

Table 11.3	Legislative Elections, 2007	
Party	First ballot vote (percentage)	Seats in the National Assembly (numbers)
UMP and allies	45.58	345
PS and allies	35.55	227
Modern Democrats (UDF)	7.61	3
National Front	4.29	0
Others	6.97	2

Things are going to be different because Sarkozy is a different kind of politician. He is the most openly pro-American president in the history of the Fifth Republic, even though he continues to make the case that the invasion of Iraq was a mistake. He ran the first American-style campaign, in which he published a campaign biography and allowed himself to be called "Sarko" at public rallies.[1]

He also made it clear that he was going to govern differently. Even before his inauguration, he announced that his cabinet would be smaller than normal and would contain some surprises. His choice of his long-time ally **François Fillon** as prime minister shocked no one. But seven of the cabinet's fifteen members were women, by far the highest percentage in any Western government ever. One of them was forty-one-year-old Rachida Dati, who became the highest-ranking person of North African origin in French political history. Dati grew up in one of the roughest suburbs in the Paris area. Even more surprising was that Sarkozy named two Socialists to his cabinet. The more prominent of them was Bernard Kouchner, who had been one of the founders of Médecins Sans Frontières (Doctors without Borders), one of the world's leading humanitarian nongovernmental organizations. Kouchner had held a number of positions in Socialist governments and was the first administrator of post-Communist and postwar Kosovo.

Sarkozy's legislative agenda will largely be set as the results of the parliamentary elections sink in. But if the first month of his presidency is an indication, both the French government and the French Right will never be the same again.

Despite the complaints of many commentators, including Sarkozy himself, about France's economic and other problems, he inherited a country in better shape than most of its European counterparts. Its economy had been growing at almost twice the rate of Germany's for more than a decade. Its aerospace and other defense-related industries were among the strongest in the world. What had aged—and what was the leading cause of the malaise that showed up so obviously in the polls—was its political leadership.

If there is a recent parallel among the world's leaders, it might well be Britain's Tony Blair, whose decade in power ended just after Sarkozy took office. Blair won a landslide victory in 1997 and set out on an ambitious program of reforms that gave rise to rave praises of his leadership of what many called "cool Britannia." Blair resigned the prime ministry in 2007 as one of the least popular politicians in recent history, in part because of domestic concerns but mostly because of his support for American policy in Iraq.

It remains to be seen whether Sarkozy will leave office as the kind of popular and innovative leader Blair was a decade ago or as unloved an official as Blair had become.

And the Left?

The future is less clear for the Left. Most of the aging Socialist leadership was either cool or hostile to Royal's candidacy. The likes of Laurent Fabius and Dominique Strauss-Kahn had come of political age as part of the generation of 1968. They saw the 2007 election as their last shot at the presidency and were clearly disappointed to be outmaneuvered by Royal, who was more than a decade their junior.

In practice, Royal proved to be a weak candidate. Despite her credentials and experience, she made many serious mistakes during the campaign. In particular, her views on foreign policy and domestic security issues, Sarkozy's strong points, were shown not to have been well thought out. According to one poll, conducted on the eve of the first round, barely 40 percent of the voters believed that she had the right stuff to be president of the Republic, compared with 69 percent who thought Sarkozy did. As a result, she did worse than all but one Socialist presidential candidate who made it to the second ballot; only Mitterrand, in his uphill and unlikely campaign against de Gaulle in 1965, had done worse.

Although she pointed out that 2007 was almost forty years after 1968, the French Left was not as close to shedding the legacy of the 1960s as its fellow leftists in Europe and North America. It is unlikely that Royal will be able to retain her position in the leadership following the expected legislative defeat. Hollande announced his decision to step down from the leadership of the Socialist Party no later than its next conference.

In the aftermath of the election, most pundits argued that the Left really did have to modernize and at long last follow the model of the German Social Democratic Party, British Labour, or the American Democrats. That will be easier said than done. Many party activist and union officials remain as committed as ever to such policies as the thirty-five-hour workweek and the rules that allow government employees to retire earlier and with more generous pensions than their colleagues in the private sector. The same holds for the health and other benefits that remain extremely popular even as they cost taxpayers and employers ever more money.

The one obvious shift would be some sort of center-left coalition that combines the PS with most of the people who supported Bayrou on the first ballot. That would be a coalition that could win a popular majority under a more attractive candidate than Royal. But the PS and Bayrou's UDF have totally different traditions and bases of support.

On the night of the second ballot of the legislative elections, France was hit by a not unexpected bombshell. Rumors had been circulating for months that Royal and Hollande no longer had much of a relationship. Then it was announced that a book was to be published the following week alleging that he had been having an affair. Three hours after the results of the elections were announced, Royal had an announcement of her own. She and Hollande had separated.

Only in France.

Normal Politics

The underlying argument of this book is that France has become more like other democracies since de Gaulle created the Fifth Republic half a century ago. That may seem an odd case to make, given the changing of the guard to what William Pfaff calls "Sarkoland," itself the most un-Gaullist of terms.

France does remain France. Where else in western Europe or North America could a Trotskyite mailman win 5 percent of the vote?

But Sarkozy and Royal were also quintessential early-twenty-first century politicians. Slick and telegenic, they both led catch-all parties that were shadows of their ideological selves. Both seemed committed to loosening the hold the iron triangle has held on French politics since the likes of Chirac, Giscard d'Estaing, and Jospin took center stage in the 1970s.

As we saw in Chapter 10, France may be something of a maverick in foreign policy for years to come; but only something of a maverick. It is, as we have seen, a major player in European integration. Indeed, before his first day as president was over, Sarkozy had flown to Berlin to meet with Chancellor Angela Merkel, whose government held the presidency of the EU and was hoping that an agreement on a European constitution could be reached before the post rotated to another country in the middle of the summer.

And given the way events in Iraq have turned out, it may be that President Chirac pursued a policy that meshed with French and international values better than the one championed by the Bush and Blair governments.

None of this is to argue that "normal politics" is any better or any worse than what we saw for Third or Fourth Republic France even if it is less dramatic, or traumatic. That is a decision that the present generation of political science students will have to make. Not to mention the present generation of French citizens.

Key People, Entities, and Events

Questions for Discussion

1. Does the argument made throughout this book still hold, given the results of the 2007 elections? Why or why not?

2. This chapter was written within weeks of the presidential election. Obviously, much has changed since then. What have been the most important shifts in French politics since June 2007? How can you account for them?

3. Royal's defeat was widely seen as a blow to the chances of other women politicians, including Senator Hillary Clinton in the United States. Do you think that is likely to prove to be the case, or was her defeat largely a fault of problems within her own campaign or French political culture, or both?

Notes

Chapter 1 Notes

1. Words in bold can be found in the lists of key terms at the end of each chapter and in the glossary at the end of the book.
2. Max Singer and Aaron Wildavsky, *The Real New World Order: Zones of Peace/Zones of Turmoil* (Chatham, N.J.: Chatham House Publishers, 1996).

Chapter 2 Notes

1. Hans Koning, "A French Mirror," *Atlantic Monthly* 276 (December 1995), 95–106.
2. John Ardagh, *The New French Revolution* (New York: Harper and Row, 1968). This book has been revised and expanded under different titles several times, the most recent of which is *France in the New Century* (London: Penguin, 1999).
3. The MTV France Web site: www.mtv.fr.
4. Philip H. Gordon and Sophie Meunier, "Globalization and French Cultural Identity," *French Politics, Culture, and Society* 19 (Spring 2001).
5. Richard Bernstein, *Fragile Glory: A Portrait of France and the French* (New York: Penguin, 1990), 110ff.

Chapter 3 Notes

1. Seymour Martin Lipset and Stein Rokkan, "Party Systems and Vote Alignments," in *Party Systems and Voter Alignments,* ed. Lipset and Rokkan (New York: Free Press, 1967), chap. 1.
2. See the Web site www.europeanhistory.about.com/od/france/.
3. The rest of this chapter draws heavily on Charles Hauss, *Politics in Gaullist France: Coping with Chaos* (New York: Praeger, 1991), chap. 2.
4. Philip M. Williams, *Crisis and Compromise* (London: Longman, Green, 1964), 36.
5. Stanley Hoffmann, *In Search of France* (Cambridge: Harvard University Press, 1963).
6. See Michel Crozier, *The Stalled Society* (New York: Viking Press, 1973); and Michel Crozier, *The Bureaucratic Phenomenon* (Chicago: University of Chicago Press, 1964).
7. Philip Converse and Georges Dupeux, "Politicization of the Electorate in France and the United States," in *Elections and the Political Order,* ed. Angus Campbell, Philip Converse, Warren Miller, and Donald Stokes (New York: Wiley, 1966), 269–291.
8. William Schonfeld, *Obedience and Revolt* (Beverly Hills, Calif.: Sage, 1976), 30–31.

Chapter 4 Notes

1. This version of the famous quote is from Bernard Brown, *Comparative Politics: Notes and Readings,* 9th ed. (Belmont, Calif.: ITP Learning, 2000), 147.
2. John Ambler, "Trust in Political and Non-Political Authorities in France," *Comparative Politics* 8 (1975): 31–58.
3. Giscard is the true family name. The "d'Estaing" was added in the nineteenth century when one of his ancestors bought a noble title.

Chapter 5 Notes

1. Philip Converse and Georges Dupeux, "Politicization of the Electorate in France and the United States," in *Elections and the Political Order,* ed. Angus Campbell, Philip Converse, Warren Miller, and Donald Stokes (New York: Wiley, 1966).
2. Russell Dalton. *Citizen Politics: Public Opinion and Political Parties in Advanced Industrialized Democracies* (New York: Chatham House/Seven Locks Press, 2001).

Chapter 6 Notes

1. Otto Kirchheimer, "The Transformation of the West European Party Systems," in *Political Parties and Political Development,* ed. Joseph LaPalombara and Myron Weiner (Princeton: Princeton University Press, 1966), 177–200.

2. Wilson, Frank L., "When Parties Refuse to Fail," in *Political Parties and Linkages,* ed. Kay Lawson (New Haven: Yale University Press, 1980).

3. Jean Charlot, *The Gaullist Phenomenon* (London: George Allen and Unwin, 1971), 14.

4. It is also a statement about the importance of anticlericalism on the French left that the SFIO was actually meeting on Christmas.

5. Jonathan Marcus, "The Long March of Bruno Mégret," *New Statesman,* February 14, 1997, 26.

6. This material is drawn from a poll by CSA-TMO conducted in April 2002, www.csa-tmo.fr/fra/dataset/data2002/opi20020404b.htm (accessed October 28, 2002).

7. The data that follow are drawn from www.tns-sofres.com/etudes/pol//12072_elections_r.htm (accessed December 20, 2006).

8. The one exception came in 1986, when a modified version of proportional representation was used. The fact that the Front won thirty-five seats was one of the main reasons the Gaullist-led National Assembly voted to return to the two-ballot system for the 1988 election.

Chapter 7 Notes

1. The full text of the constitution is included at the end of this book as Appendix A. The official version of the constitution, of course, is in French, and there are some minor differences in the available translations. The one in the appendix was published by the National Assembly at www.assemblee-nationale.fr/english (accessed November 12, 2002).

2. Charles de Gaulle, quoted in Vincent Wright, *The Government and Politics of France,* 3d ed. (New York: Holmes and Meier, 1989), 134.

3. See www.time.com/time/europe/magazine/2002/0422/cover/ ena3.html (accessed January 3, 2007).

4. Quotations in this paragraph come from, Ezra Suleiman, *Politics, Power, and Bureaucracy in France* (Princeton: Princeton University Press, 1974), 329–334.

Chapter 8 Notes

1. See "Life Expectancy of 14 Nations in Europe," *Medical News Today,* July 9, 2006, www.medicalnewstoday.com/articles/46767.php. For more related data, see www.cia.gov/cia/publications/factbook/.

2. These data are drawn from David Natali, "La méethode ouverte de coordination (MOC) en matièere des pensions et de l'intégration européenne," http://www.ose.be/natali/default.htm (accessed March 17, 2007).

3. Milton Friedman, *Capitalism and Freedom* (Chicago: University of Chicago Press, 1962).

4. Stephen S. Cohen, *Modern Capitalist Planning: The French Model,* 2d ed. (Berkeley and Los Angeles: University of California Press, 1977), 229–237.

5. *New York Times,* June 14, 2007, A25.

Chapter 9 Notes

1. David Cameron, "The 1992 Initiative: Causes and Consequences," in *Euro-Politics,* ed. Alberta Sbragia (Washington, D.C.: Brookings Institution, 1992), 73.

2. http://discover.npr.org/rundowns/rundown.jhtml?prgId=3&prgDate=May/9/2003.

3. Cited in Derek W. Urwin, *The Community of Europe,* 2d ed. (Harlow, UK: Longman, 1995), 111–112.

4. David Howarth, *The French Road to European Monetary Union* (Basingstoke, UK: Palgrave, 2001).

5. The data in this section are all taken from the European Commission, *Eurobarometer 57,* (Spring 2002). Some of the data are also available at the Eurobarometer Web site: http://europa.eu.int/comm/public_opinion.

6. David Howarth, "The French State in the Euro-Zone: 'Modernization' and Legitimizing *Dirigisme,*" in *European States and the Euro,* ed. Kenneth Dyson (Oxford: Oxford University Press, 2002), 152–153.

Chapter 10 Notes

1. David Ignatius, *A Firing Offense* (New York: Ballantine Books, 1997). Truth in advertising: I have worked with Ignatius on a number of projects involving American foreign policy.

2. www.64-baker-street.org/organisations/orgs_the_bbc_de_gaulle.html. The 64 Baker Street Site was created by several women who worked in the Secret Service during World War II.

3. The very term, "third world" (*tiers monde*) is French in origin. It was coined in a 1952 article in L'Observateur by the economist and demographer Alfred Sauvy, who used it to designate the parts of the planet not part of the first (democratic) and second (Communist) worlds. In 1956, a group of social scientists associated with Sauvy's National Institute of Demographic Studies in Paris published a book entitled *Le Tiers-Monde*.

4. It should be pointed out that the term "chauvinist" has distinctly French and nationalist origins. It seems (much of this is clouded in uncertainty) that a certain Nicolas Chauvin was born in France about 1780. He was drafted into the French army during the Revolution, probably in 1793. He served with distinction and later became one of Napoléon's most devout supporters. Toward the end of the Napoleonic wars, he was gravely wounded and received a sword and a pension from the emperor to honor his service. Later, his intense loyalty became a source of derision (some of the first vaudeville plays were critiques of him), and the word that bears his name came to be political shorthand for extreme nationalism and, today, more generally, prejudice, as in "male chauvinist pig."

5. France's interest in Louisiana resurfaced in the aftermath of Hurricane Katrina in August 2005. It was the first country to send condolences to the United States people and their government. It made its initial offer of aid two days later on August 31. The Bush administration initially turned France down but changed its mind on September 3. France already had humanitarian supplies pre-positioned in its remaining Caribbean islands and cargo planes ready to leave from metropolitan France. The U.S. government took two more days before providing France with landing information. But then, on September 5, relief supplies donated by the French military, some of its nongovernmental organizations, and its multinational corporations with operations in the United States began to arrive.

6. Dominique Moisi, "Mitterrand's Foreign Policy: The Limits to Continuity," *Foreign Affairs*, Winter 1981–1982, www.foreignaffairs.org/19811201faessay8274/dominique-moisi/mitterrand-s-foreign-policy-the-limits-of-continuity.html (accessed January 16, 2007).

7. Cited in *Guardian* (London), February 10, 2006.

8. Philip Gordon and Sophie Meunier, *The French Challenge: Adapting to Globalization* (Washington, D.C.: Brookings Institution Press, 2001).

9. See the 2006 Report on Foreign Direct Investment, put out by the Invest in France Agency. A copy of the report can be found at "Foreign Direct Investments in France Rises in 2006," 2/28/2007, Reuters press release, http://www.investinfrance.org/north-america/en/in-the-press.html?page=5.

10. See "The Global Peace Index," http://www.visionofhumanity.com. Truth in advertising again: I was heavily involved in publicizing this project, "The Global Peace Index,"among both policy wonks and the conflict resolution community in the United States. The GPI, a ranking of 121 nations according to their peacefulness was developed by an international team of academics and peace experts.

Chapter 11 Notes

1. Nicolas, Sarkozy, *Testimony: France in the Twenty-First Century* (New York: Pantheon, 2007).

Constitution of 4 October 1958

This text incorporates the constitutional statutes of 1 March 2005, which modify Title XV of the Constitution and pertain to the Charter for the Environment.

This English translation was prepared under the joint responsibility of the Press, Information and Communication Directorate of the Ministry of Foreign Affairs, and the European Affairs Department of the National Assembly. The French original is the sole authentic text.

CONTENTS

PREAMBLE

PREAMBLE

The French people solemnly proclaim their attachment to the Rights of Man and the principles of national sovereignty as defined by the Declaration of 1789, confirmed and complemented by the Preamble to the Constitution of 1946, and to the rights and duties as defined in the Charter for the Environment of 2004.

By virtue of these principles and that of the self-determination of peoples, the Republic offers to the overseas territories that express the will to adhere to them new institutions founded on the common ideal of liberty, equality and fraternity and conceived with a view to their democratic development.

Article 1

France shall be an indivisible, secular, democratic and social Republic. It shall ensure the equality of all citizens before the law, without distinction of origin, race or religion. It shall respect all beliefs. It shall be organised on a decentralised basis.

TITLE I - on sovereignty

Article 2

The language of the Republic shall be French.

The national emblem shall be the blue, white and red tricolour flag.

The national anthem shall be La Marseillaise.

The motto of the Republic shall be "Liberty, Equality, Fraternity".

Its principle shall be: government of the people, by the people and for the people.

Article 3

National sovereignty shall belong to the people, who shall exercise it through their representatives and by means of referendum.

No section of the people nor any individual may arrogate to itself, or to himself, the exercise thereof.

Suffrage may be direct or indirect as provided by the Constitution. It shall always be universal, equal and secret.

All French citizens of either sex who have reached their majority and are in possession of their civil and political rights may vote as provided by statute.

Article 4

Political parties and groups shall contribute to the exercise of suffrage. They shall be formed and carry on their activities freely. They must respect the principles of national sovereignty and democracy.

TITLE II - the President of the Republic

Article 5

The President of the Republic shall see that the Constitution is observed. He shall ensure, by his arbitration, the proper functioning of the public authorities and the continuity of the State.

He shall be the guarantor of national independence, territorial integrity and observance of treaties.

Article 6

The President of the Republic shall be elected for five years by direct universal suffrage.

The manner of implementation of this article shall be determined by an institutional Act.

Article 7

The President of the Republic shall be elected by an absolute majority of the votes cast. If such a majority is not obtained on the first ballot, a second ballot shall take place on the fourteenth day thereafter. Only the two candidates who received the greatest number of votes in the first ballot, account being taken of any withdrawal of candidates with more votes, may stand in the second ballot.

Balloting shall be begun by a writ of election issued by the Government.

The election of the new President shall be held not less than twenty days and not more than thirty-five days before the expiry of the term of the President in office.

Should the Presidency of the Republic fall vacant for any reason whatsoever, or should the Constitutional Council on a reference from the Government rule by an absolute majority of its members that the President of the Republic is incapacitated, the duties of the President of the Republic, with the exception of those specified in articles 11 and 12, shall be temporarily exercised by the President of the Senate or, if the latter is in turn incapacitated, by the Government.

In the case of a vacancy, or where the incapacity of the President is declared permanent by the Constitutional Council, the ballot for the election of the new President shall, except in the event of a finding by the Constitutional Council of force majeure, be held not less than twenty days and not more than thirty-five days after the beginning of the vacancy or the declaration that the incapacity is permanent. If, in the seven days preceding the last day for lodging presentations of candidature, any of the persons who, less than thirty days prior to that day, have publicly announced their decision to be a candidate dies or becomes incapacitated, the Constitutional Council may decide to postpone the election.

If, before the first ballot, any of the candidates dies or becomes incapacitated, the Constitutional Council shall declare the election postponed.

In the event of the death or incapacitation of either of the two candidates in the lead in the first ballot before any withdrawals, the Constitutional Council shall declare that the electoral procedure must be repeated in full; the same shall apply in the event of the death or incapacitation of either of the two candidates remaining standing for the second ballot.

All cases shall be referred to the Constitutional Council in the manner laid down in the second paragraph of article 61 or in that manner laid down for the presentation of candidates in the institutional Act provided for in article 6.

The Constitutional Council may extend the time limits set in the third and fifth paragraphs, provided that polling takes place no later than thirty-five days after the decision of the Constitutional Council. If the implementation of the provisions of this paragraph results in the postponement of the election beyond the expiry of the term of the President in office, the latter shall remain in office until his successor is proclaimed.

Neither articles 49 and 50 nor article 89 of the Constitution shall be implemented during the vacancy of the Presidency of the Republic or during the period between the declaration that the incapacity of the President of the Republic is permanent and the election of his successor.

Article 8

The President of the Republic shall appoint the Prime Minister. He shall terminate the appointment of the Prime Minister when the latter tenders the resignation of the Government. On the proposal of the Prime Minister, he shall appoint the other Members of the Government and terminate their appointments.

Article 9

The President of the Republic shall preside over the Council of Ministers.

Article 10

The President of the Republic shall promulgate Acts of Parliament within fifteen days following the final adoption of an Act and its transmission to the Government.

He may, before the expiry of this time limit, ask Parliament to reconsider the Act or sections of the Act. Reconsideration shall not be refused.

Article 11

The President of the Republic may, on a proposal from the Government when Parliament is in session or on a joint motion of the two assemblies, published in either case in the Journal officiel, submit to a referendum any government bill which deals with the organization of the public authorities, or with reforms relating to the economic or social policy of the Nation and to the public services contributing thereto, or which provides for authorization to ratify a treaty that, although not contrary to the Constitution, would affect the functioning of the institutions.

Where the referendum is held in response to a proposal by the Government, the latter shall make a statement before each assembly which shall be followed by a debate.

Where the referendum decides in favour of the government bill, the President of the Republic shall promulgate it within fifteen days following the proclamation of the results of the vote.

Article 12

The President of the Republic may, after consulting the Prime Minister and the Presidents of the assemblies, declare the National Assembly dissolved.

A general election shall take place not less than twenty days and not more than forty days after the dissolution.

The National Assembly shall convene as of right on the second Thursday following its election. Should it so convene outside the period prescribed for the ordinary session, a session shall be called by right for a fifteen-day period.

No further dissolution shall take place within a year following this election.

Article 13

The President of the Republic shall sign the ordinances and decrees deliberated upon in the Council of Ministers.

He shall make appointments to the civil and military posts of the State.

Conseillers d'État, the grand chancelier de la Légion d'Honneur, ambassadors and envoys extraordinary, senior members of the Audit Court, prefects, State representatives in the overseas territories to which article 74 applies and in New Caledonia, general officers, recteurs des académies and heads of central government services shall be appointed in the Council of Ministers.

An institutional Act shall determine the other posts to be filled in the Council of Ministers and the manner in which the power of the President of the Republic to make appointments may be delegated by him to be exercised on his behalf.

Article 14

The President of the Republic shall accredit ambassadors and envoys extraordinary to foreign powers; foreign ambassadors and envoys extraordinary shall be accredited to him.

Article 15

The President of the Republic shall be commander-in-chief of the armed forces. He shall preside over the higher national defence councils and committees.

Article 16

Where the institutions of the Republic, the independence of the Nation, the integrity of its territory or the fulfilment of its international commitments are under serious and immediate threat, and where the proper functioning of the constitutional public authorities is interrupted, the President of the Republic shall take the measures required by these circumstances, after formally consulting the Prime Minister, the Presidents of the assemblies and the Constitutional Council.

He shall inform the Nation of these measures in a message.

The measures must stem from the desire to provide the constitutional public authorities, in the shortest possible time, with the means to carry out their duties. The Constitutional Council shall be consulted with regard to such measures. Parliament shall convene as of right.

The National Assembly shall not be dissolved during the exercise of the emergency powers.

Article 17

The President of the Republic has the right to grant pardon.

Article 18

The President of the Republic shall communicate with the two assemblies of Parliament by means of messages, which he shall cause to be read and which shall not be the occasion for any debate.

Outside sessions, Parliament shall be convened especially for this purpose.

Article 19

Acts of the President of the Republic, other than those provided for under articles 8 (first paragraph), 11, 12, 16, 18, 54, 56 and 61, shall be countersigned by the Prime Minister and, where required, by the appropriate ministers.

TITLE III - the Government

Article 20

The Government shall determine and conduct the policy of the Nation.

It shall have at its disposal the civil service and the armed forces.

It shall be responsible to Parliament in accordance with the terms and procedures set out in articles 49 and 50.

Article 21

The Prime Minister shall direct the operation of the Government. He shall be responsible for national defence. He shall ensure the implementation of legislation. Subject to article 13, he shall have power to make regulations and shall make appointments to civil and military posts.

He may delegate certain of his powers to ministers.

He shall deputize, if the case arises, for the President of the Republic as chairman of the councils and committees referred to in article 15.

He may, in exceptional cases, deputize for him as chairman of a meeting of the Council of Ministers by virtue of an express delegation of powers for a specific agenda.

Article 22

Acts of the Prime Minister shall be countersigned, where required, by the ministers responsible for their implementation.

Article 23

The duties of a Member of the Government shall be incompatible with the exercise of any parliamentary office, any position of occupational representation at national level, any public employment or any occupational activity.

An institutional Act shall determine the manner in which the holders of such offices, positions or employment shall be replaced.

The replacement of Members of Parliament shall take place in accordance with the provisions of article 25.

TITLE IV - Parliament

Article 24

Parliament shall comprise the National Assembly and the Senate.

The deputies to the National Assembly shall be elected by direct suffrage.

The Senate shall be elected by indirect suffrage. The representation of the territorial units of the Republic shall be ensured in the Senate. French nationals settled outside France shall be represented in the Senate.

Article 25

An institutional Act shall determine the term for which each assembly is elected, the number of its members, their allowances, the conditions of eligibility and the terms of disqualification and of incompatibility with membership.

It shall likewise determine the manner of election of those persons who, in the event of a vacancy, are to replace deputies or senators whose seats have become vacant, until the general or partial renewal by election of the assembly to which they belonged.

Article 26

No Member of Parliament shall be prosecuted, investigated, arrested, detained or tried in respect of opinions expressed or votes cast in the exercise of his duties.

No Member of Parliament shall be arrested for a serious crime or other major offence, nor shall he be subjected to any other custodial or semi-custodial measure, without the authorization of the Bureau of the assembly of which he is a member. Such authorization shall not be required in the case of a serious crime or other major offence committed *flagrante delicto* or a final sentence.

The detention, subjection to custodial or semi-custodial measures, or prosecution of a Member of Parliament shall be suspended for the duration of the session if the assembly of which he is a member so requires.

The assembly concerned shall convene as of right for additional sittings in order to permit the preceding paragraph to be applied should circumstances so require.

Article 27

Any binding instruction shall be void.

The right to vote of Members of Parliament shall be personal.

An institutional Act may, in exceptional cases, authorize voting by proxy. In that event, no member shall be given more than one proxy.

Article 28

Parliament shall convene as of right in one ordinary session which shall start on the first working day of October and shall end on the last working day of June.

The number of days for which each assembly may sit during the ordinary session shall not exceed one hundred and twenty. The sitting weeks shall be determined by each assembly.

The Prime Minister, after consulting the President of the assembly concerned, or the majority of the members of each assembly may decide to meet for additional sitting days.

The days and hours of sittings shall be determined by the rules of procedure of each assembly.

Article 29

Parliament shall convene in extraordinary session, at the request of the Prime Minister or of the majority of the members of the National Assembly, to consider a specific agenda.

Where an extraordinary session is held at the request of members of the National Assembly, the decree closing it shall take effect once Parliament has dealt with the agenda for which it was convened, or twelve days after its first sitting, whichever shall be the earlier.

Only the Prime Minister may request a new session before the end of the month following the decree closing an extraordinary session.

Article 30

Except where Parliament convenes as of right, extraordinary sessions shall be opened and closed by decree of the President of the Republic.

Article 31

Members of the Government shall have access to the two assemblies. They shall address either assembly whenever they so request. They may be assisted by government commissioners.

Article 32

The President of the National Assembly shall be elected for the duration of the term for which the Assembly is elected. The President of the Senate shall be elected after each partial renewal by election.

Article 33

The sittings of the two assemblies shall be public. A verbatim report of the debates shall be published in the Journal officiel.

Each assembly may sit in camera at the request of the Prime Minister or of one tenth of its members.

TITLE V - on relations between Parliament and the Government

Article 34

Statutes shall be passed by Parliament.

Statutes shall determine the rules concerning:

- civic rights and the fundamental guarantees granted to citizens for the exercise of their public liberties; the obligations imposed for the purposes of national defence upon citizens in respect of their persons and their property;

- nationality, the status and legal capacity of persons, matrimonial regimes, inheritance and gifts;

- the determination of serious crimes and other major offences and the penalties applicable to them; criminal procedure; amnesty; the establishment of new classes of courts and tribunals and the regulations governing the members of the judiciary;

- the base, rates and methods of collection of taxes of all types; the issue of currency.

Statutes shall likewise determine the rules concerning:

- the electoral systems of parliamentary assemblies and local assemblies;

- the creation of categories of public establishments;

- the fundamental guarantees granted to civil and military personnel employed by the State;

- the nationalization of enterprises and transfers of ownership in enterprises from the public to the private sector.

Statutes shall determine the fundamental principles of:

- the general organization of national defence;

- the self-government of territorial units, their powers and their resources;

- the preservation of the environment;

- education;

- the regime governing ownership, rights *in rem* and civil and commercial obligations;

- law, trade-union law, and social security.

Finance Acts shall determine the resources and obligations of the State in the manner and with the reservations specified in an institutional Act.

Social security finance Acts shall determine the general conditions for the financial balance of social security and, in the light of their revenue forecasts, shall determine expenditure targets in the manner and with the reservations specified in an institutional Act.

Programme Acts shall determine the objectives of the economic and social action of the State.

The provisions of this article may be enlarged upon and complemented by an institutional Act.

Article 35

A declaration of war shall be authorized by Parliament.

Article 36

Martial law shall be decreed in the Council of Ministers.

Its extension beyond twelve days may be authorized only by Parliament.

Article 37

Matters other than those that fall within the ambit of statute shall be matters for regulation.

Acts of Parliament passed concerning these matters may be amended by decree issued after consultation with the Conseil d'État. Any such Acts which are passed after this Constitution has entered into force shall be amended by decree only if the Constitutional Council has declared that they are matters for regulation as defined in the preceding paragraph.

Article 37-1

Statutes and regulations may contain provisions enacted on an experimental basis for limited purposes and duration.

Article 38

In order to carry out its programme, the Government may ask Parliament for authorization, for a limited period, to take measures by ordinance that are normally a matter for statute.

Ordinances shall be issued in the Council of Ministers, after consultation with the Conseil d'État. They shall come into force upon publication, but shall lapse if the bill to ratify them is not laid before Parliament before the date set by the enabling Act.

At the end of the period referred to in the first paragraph of this article, ordinances may be amended only by an Act of Parliament in those areas which are matters for statute.

Article 39

The Prime Minister and Members of Parliament alike shall have the right to initiate statutes. Government bills shall be discussed in the Council of Ministers after consultation with the Conseil d'État and shall be introduced in one of the two assemblies.

Finance bills and social security finance bills shall be presented first to the National Assembly. Without prejudice to the first paragraph of article 44, bills having the primary purpose of organising territorial units and bills relating to bodies representing French nationals settled outside France shall be presented first to the Senate.

Article 40

Bills and amendments introduced by Members of Parliament shall not be admissible where their adoption would have as a consequence either a diminution of public resources or the creation or increase of an item of public expenditure.

Article 41

Should it be found in the course of the legislative process that a Member's bill or amendment is not a matter for statute or is contrary to a delegation granted by virtue of article 38, the Government may object that it is inadmissible.

In the event of disagreement between the Government and the President of the assembly concerned, the Constitutional Council, at the request of one or the other, shall rule within eight days.

Article 42

The discussion of government bills shall pertain, in the assembly which first has the bill before it, to the text introduced by the Government.

An assembly which has before it a text passed by the other assembly shall deliberate upon that text.

Article 43

Government and Members' bills shall, at the request of the Government or of the assembly having the bill before it, be referred for consideration to committees specially set up for this purpose.

Government and Members' bills concerning which such a request has not been made shall be referred to one of the standing committees, the number of which shall be limited to six in each assembly.

Article 44

Members of Parliament and the Government shall have the right of amendment.

Once the debate has begun, the Government may object to the consideration of any amendment which has not previously been referred to committee.

If the Government so requests, the assembly having the bill before it shall decide by a single vote on all or part of the text under discussion, on the sole basis of the amendments proposed or accepted by the Government.

Article 45

Every Government or Member's bill shall be considered successively in the two assemblies of Parliament with a view to the adoption of an identical text.

If, as a result of a disagreement between the two assemblies, it has proved impossible to adopt a Government or Member's bill after two readings by each assembly or, if the Government has declared the matter urgent, after a single reading by each of them, the Prime Minister may convene a joint committee, composed of an equal number of members from each assembly, to propose a text on the provisions still under discussion.

The text drafted by the joint committee may be submitted by the Government to both assemblies for approval. No amendment shall be admissible without the consent of the Government.

If the joint committee does not succeed in adopting a common text, or if the text is not adopted as provided in the preceding paragraph, the Government may, after a further reading by the National Assembly and by the Senate, ask the National Assembly to make a final decision. In that event, the National Assembly may reconsider either the text drafted by the joint committee, or the last text passed by itself, as modified, if such is the case, by any amendment or amendments adopted by the Senate.

Article 46

Acts of Parliament that the Constitution characterizes as institutional shall be passed and amended as provided in this article.

A Government or Member's bill shall not be debated and put to the vote in the assembly in which it was first introduced until fifteen days have elapsed since its introduction.

The procedure set out in article 45 shall apply. Nevertheless, in the absence of agreement between the two assemblies, the text may be adopted by the National Assembly on final reading only by an absolute majority of its members.

Institutional Acts relating to the Senate must be passed in identical terms by the two assemblies.

Institutional Acts shall not be promulgated until the Constitutional Council has declared their conformity with the Constitution.

Article 47

Parliament shall pass finance bills in the manner provided by an institutional Act.

Should the National Assembly fail to reach a decision on first reading within forty days following the introduction of a bill, the Government shall refer the bill to the Senate, which must rule within fifteen days. The procedure set out in article 45 shall then apply.

Should Parliament fail to reach a decision within seventy days, the provisions of the bill may be brought into force by ordinance.

Should the finance bill establishing the resources and expenditures for a financial year not be introduced in time for promulgation before the beginning of that year, the Government shall as a matter of urgency ask

Parliament for authorization to collect taxes and shall make available by decree the funds needed to meet the commitments already voted for.

The time limits set by this article shall be suspended when Parliament is not in session.

The Audit Court shall assist Parliament and the Government in monitoring the implementation of finance Acts.

Article 47-1

Parliament shall pass social security finance bills in the manner provided by an institutional Act.

Should the National Assembly fail to reach a decision on first reading within twenty days following the introduction of a bill, the Government shall refer the bill to the Senate, which must rule within fifteen days. The procedure set out in article 45 shall then apply.

Should Parliament fail to reach a decision within fifty days, the provisions of the bill may be implemented by ordinance.

The time limits set by this article shall be suspended when Parliament is not in session and, as regards each assembly, during the weeks when it has decided not to sit in accordance with the second paragraph of article 28.

The Audit Court shall assist Parliament and the Government in monitoring the implementation of social security finance Acts.

Article 48

Without prejudice to the application of the last three paragraphs of article 28, precedence shall be given on the agendas of the assemblies, and in the order determined by the Government, to the discussion of Government bills and of Members' bills accepted by the Government. At one sitting a week at least precedence shall be given to questions from Members of Parliament and to answers by the Government. At one sitting a month precedence shall be given to the agenda determined by each assembly.

Article 49

The Prime Minister, after deliberation by the Council of Ministers, may make the Government's programme or possibly a statement of its general policy an issue of its responsibility before the National Assembly.

The National Assembly may raise an issue of the Government's responsibility by passing a motion of censure. Such a motion shall not be admissible unless it is signed by at least one tenth of the members of the National Assembly. Voting may not take place within forty-eight hours after the motion has been introduced. Only the votes in favour of the motion of censure shall be counted; the motion of censure shall not be adopted unless it is voted for by the majority of the members of the Assembly. Except as provided in the following paragraph, a deputy shall not sign more than three motions of censure during a single ordinary session and more than one during a single extraordinary session.

The Prime Minister may, after deliberation by the Council of Ministers, make the passing of a bill an issue of the Government's responsibility before the National Assembly. In that event, the bill shall be considered adopted unless a motion of censure, introduced within the subsequent twenty-four hours, is carried as provided in the preceding paragraph.

The Prime Minister may ask the Senate to approve a statement of general policy.

Article 50

Where the National Assembly carries a motion of censure, or where it fails to endorse the programme or a statement of general policy of the Government, the Prime Minister must tender the resignation of the Government to the President of the Republic.

Article 51

The closing of ordinary or extraordinary sessions shall be postponed by right in order to permit the application of article 49, if the case arises. Additional sittings shall be held by right for the same purpose.

Treaties or agreements duly ratified or approved shall, upon publication, prevail over Acts of Parliament, subject, in regard to each agreement or treaty, to its application by the other party.

TITLE VI - on treaties and international agreements

Article 52

The President of the Republic shall negotiate and ratify treaties.

He shall be informed of any negotiations for the conclusion of an international agreement not subject to ratification.

Article 53

Peace treaties, commercial treaties, treaties or agreements relating to international organizations, those that commit the finances of the State, those that modify provisions which are matters for statute, those relating to the status of persons, and those that involve the cession, exchange or addition of territory, may be ratified or approved only by virtue of an Act of Parliament.

They shall not take effect until they have been ratified or approved.

No cession, exchange or addition of territory shall be valid without the consent of the population concerned.

Article 53-1

The Republic may conclude, with European States that are bound by commitments identical with its own in the matter of asylum and the protection of human rights and fundamental freedoms, agreements determining their respective jurisdictions in regard to the consideration of requests for asylum submitted to them.

However, even if the request does not fall within their jurisdiction under the terms of these agreements, the authorities of the Republic shall remain empowered to grant asylum to any foreigner who is persecuted for his action in pursuit of freedom or who seeks the protection of France for some other reason.

Article 53-2

The Republic may recognize the jurisdiction of the International Criminal Court as provided by the treaty signed on 18 July 1998.

Article 54

If the Constitutional Council, on a reference from the President of the Republic, from the Prime Minister, from the President of one or the other assembly, or from sixty deputies or sixty senators, has declared that an international commitment contains a clause contrary to the Constitution, authorization to ratify or approve the international commitment in question may be given only after amendment of the Constitution.

Article 55

Treaties or agreements duly ratified or approved shall, upon publication, prevail over Acts of Parliament, subject, in regard to each agreement or treaty, to its application by the other party.

TITLE VII - the Constitutional Council

Article 56

The Constitutional Council shall consist of nine members, whose term of office shall be nine years and shall not be renewable. One third of the membership of the Constitutional Council shall be renewed every three years. Three of its members shall be appointed by the President of the Republic, three by the President of the National Assembly and three by the President of the Senate.

In addition to the nine members provided for above, former Presidents of the Republic shall be ex officio life members of the Constitutional Council.

The President shall be appointed by the President of the Republic. He shall have a casting vote in the event of a tie.

Article 57

The office of member of the Constitutional Council shall be incompatible with that of minister or Member of Parliament. Other incompatibilities shall be determined by an institutional Act.

Article 58

The Constitutional Council shall ensure the proper conduct of the election of the President of the Republic.

It shall examine complaints and shall declare the results of the vote.

Article 59

The Constitutional Council shall rule on the proper conduct of the election of deputies and senators in disputed cases.

Article 60

The Constitutional Council shall ensure the proper conduct of referendum proceedings as provided for in articles 11 and 89 and in Title XV and shall declare the results of the referendum.

Article 61

Institutional Acts, before their promulgation, and the rules of procedure of the parliamentary assemblies, before their entry into force, must be referred to the Constitutional Council, which shall rule on their conformity with the Constitution.

To the same end, Acts of Parliament may be referred to the Constitutional Council, before their promulgation, by the President of the Republic, the Prime Minister, the President of the National Assembly, the President of the Senate, or sixty deputies or sixty senators.

In the cases provided for in the two preceding paragraphs, the Constitutional Council must rule within one month. However, at the request of the Government, if the matter is urgent, this period shall be reduced to eight days.

In these same cases, reference to the Constitutional Council shall suspend the time limit for promulgation.

Article 62

A provision declared unconstitutional shall be neither promulgated nor implemented.

No appeal shall lie from the decisions of the Constitutional Council. They shall be binding on public authorities and on all administrative authorities and all courts.

Article 63

An institutional Act shall determine the rules of organization and operation of the Constitutional Council, the procedure to be followed before it and, in particular, the time limits allowed for referring disputes to it.

TITLE VIII - on judicial authority

Article 64

The President of the Republic shall be the guarantor of the independence of the judicial authority.

He shall be assisted by the High Council of the Judiciary.

An institutional Act shall determine the regulations governing the members of the judiciary. Judges shall be irremovable.

Article 65

The High Council of the Judiciary shall be presided over by the President of the Republic. The Minister of Justice shall be its vice-president ex officio. He may deputize for the President of the Republic.

The High Council of the Judiciary shall consist of two sections, one with jurisdiction for judges, the other for public prosecutors.

The section with jurisdiction for judges shall comprise, in addition to the President of the Republic and the Minister of Justice, five judges and one public prosecutor, one conseiller d'État appointed by the Conseil d'État, and three prominent citizens who are not members either of Parliament or of the judiciary, appointed respectively by the President of the Republic, the President of the National Assembly and the President of the Senate.

The section with jurisdiction for public prosecutors shall comprise, in addition to the President of the Republic and the Minister of Justice, five public prosecutors and one judge, and the conseiller d'État and the three prominent citizens referred to in the preceding paragraph.

The section of the High Council of the Judiciary with jurisdiction for judges shall make nominations for the appointment of judges in the Court of Cassation, the first presidents of the courts of appeal and the presidents of the tribunaux de grande instance. Other judges shall be appointed with its assent.

It shall act as the disciplinary council for judges. When acting in that capacity, it shall be presided over by the first president of the Court of Cassation. The section of the High Council of the Judiciary with jurisdiction for public prosecutors shall give its opinion on the appointment of public prosecutors, with the exception of posts to be filled in the Council of Ministers.

It shall give its opinion on disciplinary penalties with regard to public prosecutors. When acting in that capacity, it shall be presided over by the chief public prosecutor at the Court of Cassation.

An institutional Act shall determine the manner in which this article is to be implemented.

Article 66

No one shall be arbitrarily detained.

The judicial authority, guardian of individual liberty, shall ensure the observance of this principle as provided by statute.

Article 66-1

No one shall be sentenced to death.

TITLE IX - the High Court

Article 67

The President of the Republic shall incur no liability by reason of acts carried out in this official capacity, subject to the provisions of Articles 53-2 and 68 hereof.

Throughout his term of office, the President shall not be required to testify and shall not be the object of any criminal or civil proceedings, nor of any preferring of charges or investigatory measures. All limitation periods shall be suspended for the duration of said term of office.

All actions and proceedings thus stayed may be reactivated or brought against the President no sooner than one month after the end of his term of office.

Article 68

The President of the Republic shall not be removed from office during the term thereof on any grounds other than a breach of his duties patently incompatible with his continuing in office. Such removal from office shall be proclaimed by Parliament sitting as the High Court.

The proposal to convene the High Court adopted by one of the two Houses of Parliament shall be immediately transmitted to the other House which shall make its decision known within fifteen days of the receipt thereof.

The High Court shall be presided by the President of the National Assembly. It shall give its ruling as to the removal from office of the President, by secret ballot, within one month. Its ruling shall take effect immediately.

Rulings given hereunder shall require a majority of two thirds of the members of the House involved or of the High Court. No proxy voting shall be allowed. Only votes in favour of the removal from office or the convening of the High Court shall be counted.

An Institutional Act shall determine the conditions for the application hereof.

TITLE X - on the criminal liability of members of the government

Article 68-1

Members of the Government shall be criminally liable for acts performed in the exercise of their duties and classified as serious crimes or other major offences at the time they were committed.

They shall be tried by the Court of Justice of the Republic.

The Court of Justice of the Republic shall be bound by such definition of serious crimes and other major offences and such determination of penalties as are laid down by statute.

Article 68-2

The Court of Justice of the Republic shall consist of fifteen members: twelve Members of Parliament, elected in equal number from among their ranks by the National Assembly and the Senate after each general or partial renewal by election of these assemblies, and three judges of the Court of Cassation, one of whom shall preside over the Court of Justice of the Republic.

Any person claiming to be a victim of a serious crime or other major offence committed by a Member of the Government in the exercise of his duties may lodge a complaint with a petitions committee.

This committee shall order the case to be either closed or forwarded to the chief public prosecutor at the Court of Cassation for referral to the Court of Justice of the Republic.

The chief public prosecutor at the Court of Cassation may also make a reference ex officio to the Court of Justice of the Republic with the assent of the petitions committee. An institutional Act shall determine the manner in which this article is to be implemented.

Article 68-3

The provisions of this title shall apply to acts committed before its entry into force.

TITLE XI - the Economic and Social Council

Article 69

The Economic and Social Council, on a reference from the Government, shall give its opinion on such Government bills, draft ordinances or decrees, and Members' bills as have been submitted to it.

A member of the Economic and Social Council may be designated by the Council to present, to the parliamentary assemblies, the opinion of the Council on such bills or drafts as have been submitted to it.

Article 70

The Economic and Social Council may likewise be consulted by the Government on any economic or social issue. Any plan or programme bill of an economic or social character shall be submitted to it for its opinion.

Article 71

The composition of the Economic and Social Council and its rules of procedure shall be determined by an institutional Act.

TITLE XII - on territorial units

Article 72

The territorial units of the Republic shall be the communes, the departments, the regions, the special-status areas and the overseas territories to which article 74 applies. Any other territorial unit shall be established by statute, in appropriate cases in place of one or more units provided for by this paragraph.

Territorial units may make decisions in all matters that are within powers that can best be exercised at their level.

In the manner provided by statute, these units shall be self-governing through elected councils and have power to make regulations.

In the manner provided by institutional Act, where the essential conditions for the exercise of public liberties or of a right secured by the Constitution are not affected, territorial units or associations thereof may, where provision is made by statute or regulation, as the case may be, derogate on an experimental basis for limited purposes and duration from provisions laid down by statute or regulation governing the exercise of their powers.

No territorial unit may exercise authority over another. However, where the exercise of a power requires the combined action of several territorial units, one of those units or one of their associations may be authorised by statute to organise their joint action.

In the territorial units of the Republic, the State representative, representing each of the Members of the Government, shall be responsible for national interests, administrative supervision and the observance of the law.

Article 72-1

The conditions in which voters in each territorial unit may use their right of petition to ask for a matter within the powers of the unit to be entered on the agenda of its decision-making assembly shall be determined by statute.

In the conditions determined by institutional Act, draft decisions or acts within the powers of a territorial unit may, on its initiative, be presented for a decision to be taken by the voters in that unit by referendum.

Where there is a proposal to establish a special-status territorial unit or to modify its organisation, a decision may be taken by statute to consult the voters registered in the relevant units. Voters may also be consulted on changes to the boundaries of territorial units under the conditions determined by statute.

Article 72-2

Territorial units shall enjoy resources of which they may dispose freely on the conditions determined by statute.

They may receive all or part of the proceeds of taxes of all kinds. They may be authorised by statute to determine the basis of assessment and the rates, within the limits set by such statutes.

The tax revenue and other own resources of territorial units shall, for each category of territorial unit, represent a decisive share of their resources. The conditions for the implementation of this rule shall be determined by institutional Act.

Whenever powers are transferred between central government and the territorial units, resources equivalent to those which were devoted to the exercise of those powers shall be transferred also. Wherever the effect of powers newly created or extended is to increase the expenditure to be borne by territorial units, resources determined by statute shall be allocated.

Equalisation mechanisms to promote equality between territorial units shall be provided for by statute.

Article 72-3

The Republic shall recognise the overseas populations within the French people in a common ideal of freedom, equality and fraternity.

Guadeloupe, Guyane, Martinique, Réunion, Mayotte, Saint-Pierre-et-Miquelon, the Wallis and Futuna Islands and French Polynesia shall be governed by article 73 for the overseas departments and regions and for the territorial units established by virtue of the final paragraph of article 73, and by article 74 for the other units.

The status of New Caledonia shall be governed by Title XIII.

The legislative system and special organisation of the French Southern and Antarctic Territories shall be determined by statute.

Article 72-4

There may be no change for all or part of one of the units to which the second paragraph of article 72-3 applies, from one to another of the statuses provided for by articles 73 and 74, without the prior consent of voters in the relevant unit or part of a unit being sought in the manner provided for by the paragraph below. Such change of status shall be made by institutional Act.

The President of the Republic may, on a proposal from the Government when Parliament is in session or on a joint motion of the two assemblies, published in either case in the Journal officiel, decide to consult voters in an overseas territorial unit on a question relating to its organisation, its powers or its legislative system. Where the referendum concerns a change as provided for by the foregoing paragraph and is held in response to a proposal by the Government, the Government shall make a statement before each assembly which shall be followed by a debate.

Article 73

In the overseas departments and regions, statutes and regulations shall be automatically applicable. They may be adapted in the light of the specific characteristics and constraints of those units.

Those adaptations may be decided on by the units in areas in which their powers are exercised if the relevant units have been empowered to that end by statute.

By way of derogation from the first paragraph and in order to take account of their specific features, units to which this article applies may be empowered by statute to determine themselves the rules applicable in their territory in a limited number of matters that fail to be determined by statute.

These rules may not concern nationality, civic rights, the guarantees of public liberties, the status and capacity of persons, the organisation of justice, criminal law, criminal procedure, foreign policy, defence, public security and public order, currency, credit and exchange, or electoral law. This enumeration may be clarified and amplified by an institutional Act.

The two foregoing paragraphs shall not apply in the department and region of Réunion.

The powers to be conferred pursuant to the second and third paragraphs shall be decided on at the request of the relevant territorial unit in the conditions and subject to the reservations provided for by an institutional Act. They may not be conferred where the essential conditions for the exercise of public liberties or of a right secured by the Constitution are affected.

A territorial unit taking the place of an overseas department and region or a single decision-making assembly for the two units may not be established by statute unless the consent of the voters registered there has first been sought as provided by the second paragraph of article 72-4.

Article 74

The overseas territorial units to which this article applies shall have a status reflecting their respective local interests within the Republic.

This status shall be determined by an institutional Act adopted after the opinion of the decision-making assembly has been received and specifying:

- the conditions in which statutes and regulations shall apply there;

- the powers of the territorial unit; subject to those already exercised by it, the transfer of central government powers may not relate to the matters listed in the fourth paragraph of article 73, as specified and amplified by the institutional Act therein referred to;

- the rules governing the organisation and operation of the institutions of the territorial unit and the electoral system for its decision-making assembly;

- the conditions in which its institutions are consulted on Government or Members' bills and draft ordinances or decrees containing provisions relating specifically to the unit and to the ratification or approval of international commitments entered into in matters within its powers.

The institutional Act may also, for such territorial units as enjoy autonomy, determine the conditions in which:

- the Council of State shall exercise specific judicial review of certain categories of acts adopted by the decision-making assembly in matters which are within its powers in the areas reserved for statute;

- the decision-making assembly may amend a statute promulgated after the entry into force of the territorial unit's new status, where the Constitutional Council, acting notably on a referral from the authorities of the territorial unit, has confirmed that the statute governs matters that are within the powers of the relevant unit;

- measures justified by local needs may be taken by the territorial unit in favour of its population as regards access to employment, the right of establishment for the exercise of a professional activity or the protection of the land;

- the unit may, subject to review by the central Government, participate in exercise of the powers that it retains, in full respect for the guaranties given throughout national territory for the exercise of public liberties.

The other rules governing the specific organisation of the territorial units to which this article applies shall be determined and amended by statute after consultation with their decision-making assembly.

Article 74-1

In the territorial units to which article 74 applies and in New Caledonia, the Government may, in matters which remain within its power, extend by ordinance, with the requisite adaptations, the legislative provisions applying in metropolitan France, provided the statute has not expressly excluded the use of this procedure in the specific matters.

Such ordinances shall be issued in the Council of Ministers after receiving the opinion of the relevant decision-making assemblies and the Council of State. They shall enter into force upon publication. They shall lapse if they are not ratified by Parliament within eighteen months following their publication.

Article 75

Citizens of the Republic who do not have ordinary civil status, the only one referred to in article 34, shall retain their personal status so long as they have not renounced it.

TITLE XIII - transitional provisions relating to New Caledonia

Article 76

The population of New Caledonia is called upon to vote by 31 December 1998 on the provisions of the agreement signed at Nouméa on 5 May 1998, which was published in the Journal officiel of the French Republic on 27 May 1998.

Persons satisfying the requirements laid down in article 2 of Act No. 88-1028 of 9 November 1988 shall be eligible to take part in the vote.

The measures required to organize the ballot shall be taken by decree adopted after consultation with the Conseil d'État and discussion in the Council of Ministers.

Article 77

After approval of the agreement by the vote provided for in article 76, the institutional Act passed after consultation with the deliberative assembly of New Caledonia shall determine, in order to ensure the development of New Caledonia in accordance with the guidelines set out in that agreement and as required for its implementation:

- the powers of the State which are to be transferred definitively to the institutions of New Caledonia, at what time and in what manner such transfers are to be made, and how the costs incurred thereby are to be apportioned;

- the rules for the organization and operation of the institutions of New Caledonia, notably the circumstances in which certain kinds of instruments passed by the deliberative assembly of New Caledonia may be referred to the Constitutional Council for review before publication;

- the rules concerning citizenship, the electoral system, employment, and personal status as laid down by customary law;

- the circumstances and the time limit within which the population concerned in New Caledonia is to vote on the attainment of full sovereignty.

- Any other measures required to give effect to the agreement referred to in article 76 shall be determined by statute.

For the purpose of defining the body of electors called upon to elect members of the deliberative assemblies of New Caledonia and the provinces, the list referred to in the Agreement mentioned in Article 76 hereof and Sections 188 and 189 of Institutional Act n° 99-209 of March 19th 1999 pertaining to New Caledonia is the list drawn up for the ballot provided for in article 76 herein above which includes those persons not eligible to vote.

Articles 78 to 87 (Repealed)

TITLE XIV - on association agreements

Article 88

The Republic may conclude agreements with States that wish to associate themselves with it in order to develop their civilizations.

TITLE XV - on the European Communities and the European Union

Article 88-1

The Republic shall participate in the European Communities and in the European Union constituted by States that have freely chosen, by virtue of the treaties that established them, to exercise some of their powers in common.

It shall participate in the European Union under the conditions provided for by the Treaty establishing a Constitution for Europe signed on 29 October 2004.

Article 88-2

Subject to reciprocity and in accordance with the terms of the Treaty on European Union signed on 7 February 1992, France agrees to the transfer of powers necessary for the establishment of European economic and monetary union.

Subject to the same reservation and in accordance with the terms of the Treaty establishing the European Community, as amended by the Treaty signed on 2 October 1997, the transfer of powers necessary for the determination of rules concerning freedom of movement for persons and related areas may be agreed.

Statutes shall determine the rules relating to the European arrest warrant pursuant to acts adopted under the Treaty on European Union.

Article 88-3

Subject to reciprocity and in accordance with the terms of the Treaty on European Union signed on 7 February 1992, the right to vote and stand as a candidate in municipal elections shall be granted only to citizens of the Union residing in France. Such citizens shall neither exercise the office of mayor or deputy mayor nor participate in the designation of Senate electors or in the election of senators. An institutional Act passed in identical terms by the two assemblies shall determine the manner of implementation of this article.

Article 88-4

The Government shall lay before the National Assembly and the Senate draft proposals for legislation of the European Union together with drafts of or proposals for acts of the European Communities or the European Union containing provisions which are matters for statute as soon as they have been transmitted to the Council of the European Union. It may also lay before them other drafts of or proposals for acts or any document issuing from a European Union institution.

In the manner laid down by the rules of procedure of each assembly, resolutions may be passed, even if Parliament is not in session, on the drafts, proposals or documents referred to in the preceding paragraph.

Article 88-5

Any legislative proposal authorising the ratification of a Treaty pertaining to the accession of a State to the European Union and to the European Communities shall be submitted to referendum by the President of the Republic.

[Section 3 of the Constitutional Act n° 2005-204 of March 1st 2005 provides that "as from the coming into effect of the Treaty establishing a Constitution for Europe, Title XV of the Constitution shall be worded as follows"]

TITLE XV - on the European Union

Article 88-1

The Republic shall, in the conditions laid down by the Treaty establishing a Constitution for Europe signed on 29 October 2004, participate in the European Union constituted by States that have freely chosen to exercise some of their powers in common.

Article 88-2

Statutes shall determine the rules relating to the European arrest warrant pursuant to acts adopted by the Institutions of the European Union.

Article 88-3

The right to vote and stand as a candidate in municipal elections may be granted to citizens of the Union residing in France. Such citizens shall neither exercise the office of mayor or deputy mayor nor participate in the designation of Senate electors or in the election of senators. An institutional Act passed in identical terms by the two assemblies shall determine the manner of implementation of this article.

Article 88-4

The Government shall lay before the National Assembly and the Senate, drafts of or proposals for Acts of the European Union containing provisions which are of a statutory nature as soon as they have been transmitted to the Council of the European Union. It may also lay before them other drafts of or proposals for Acts or any instrument issuing from a European Union Institution.

In the manner laid down by the rules of procedure of each assembly, resolutions may be passed, even if Parliament is not in session, on the drafts, proposals or instruments referred to in the preceding paragraph.

Article 88-5

The National Assembly or the Senate may issue a reasoned opinion as to the conformity of a draft proposal for a European Act with the principle of subsidiarity. Said opinion shall be addressed by the President of the Assembly involved, to the Presidents of the European Parliament, the Council of the European Union and the European Commission. The Government shall be informed of said opinion.

Each Assembly may institute proceedings before the Court of Justice of the European Communities against a European Act for noncompliance with the principle of subsidiarity. Such proceedings shall be referred to the Court of Justice of the European Communities by the Government.

For the purpose of the foregoing, resolutions may be passed, even if Parliament is not in session, in the manner fixed by the rules of the National Assembly or the Senate for the tabling and discussion thereof.

Article 88-6

Parliament may, after a motion is passed in identical terms by the National Assembly and the Senate, oppose any modification of the rules governing the passing of Acts of the European Union under the simplified revision procedure as set forth in the Treaty establishing a Constitution for Europe.

Article 88-7

Any legislative proposal authorising the ratification of a Treaty pertaining to the accession of a State to the European Union shall be submitted to referendum by the President of the Republic.

TITLE XVI - on the amendment of the Constitution

Article 89

The President of the Republic, on a proposal by the Prime Minister, and Members of Parliament alike shall have the right to initiate amendment of the Constitution.

A Government or a Member's bill to amend the Constitution shall be passed by the two assemblies in identical terms. The amendment shall have effect after approval by referendum.

However, a Government bill to amend the Constitution shall not be submitted to referendum where the President of the Republic decides to submit it to Parliament convened in Congress; the Government bill to amend the Constitution shall then be approved only if it is adopted by a three-fifths majority of the votes cast. The Bureau of the Congress shall be that of the National Assembly.

No amendment procedure shall be commenced or continued where the integrity of the territory is jeopardized.

The republican form of government shall not be the object of an amendment.

TITLE XVII - *(Repealed)*

CHARTER FOR THE ENVIRONMENT

The French People
Considering that
Natural resources and equilibriums have conditioned the emergence of mankind;
The future and very existence of mankind are inextricably linked with its natural environment;
The environment is the common heritage of all mankind;
Mankind exerts ever-increasing influence over the conditions for life and its own evolution;
Biological diversity, the fulfilment of the person and the progress of human societies are affected by certain types of consumption or production and by excessive exploitation of natural resources;
Care must be taken to safeguard the environment along with the other fundamental interests of the Nation;
In order to ensure sustainable development, choices designed to meet the needs of the present generation should not jeopardise the ability of future generations and other peoples to meet their own needs,
Hereby proclaim:

Art. 1 - Everyone has the right to live in a balanced environment which shows due respect for health.

Art. 2 - Everyone is under a duty to participate in preserving and enhancing the environment.

Art. 3 - Everyone shall, in the conditions provided for by law, foresee and avoid the occurrence of any damage which he or she may cause to the environment or, failing that, limit the consequences of such damage.

Art. 4 - Everyone shall be required, in the conditions provided for by law, to contribute to the making good of any damage he or she may have caused to the environment.

Art. 5 - When the occurrence of any damage, albeit unpredictable in the current state of scientific knowledge, may seriously and irreversibly harm the environment, public authorities shall, with due respect for the principle of precaution and the areas within their jurisdiction, ensure the implementation of procedures for risk assessment and the adoption of temporary measures commensurate with the risk involved in order to preclude the occurrence of such damage.

Art. 6 - Public policies shall promote sustainable development. To this end they shall reconcile the protection and enhancement of the environment with economic development and social progress.

Art. 7 - Everyone has the right, in the conditions and to the extent provided for by law, to have access to information pertaining to the environment in the possession of public bodies and to participate in the public decision-taking process likely to affect the environment.

Art. 8 - Education and training with regard to the environment shall contribute to the exercising of the rights and duties set out in this Charter.

Art. 9 - Research and innovation shall contribute to the preservation and development of the environment.

Art.10 - This Charter shall inspire France's actions at both European and international levels.

Further Reading

Below is a list of books and articles to enhance your understanding of French politics. They are presented alphabetically, because there is no way to tie most of them to a single chapter or several adjacent ones.

Ardagh, John. *France in the New Century*. New York: Penguin, 2000.

Bell, David. *François Mitterrand*. Cambridge UK: Polity Press, 2005.

Birnbaum, Pierre. *The Idea of France*. New York: Hill and Wang, 1998.

Charlot, Jean. *The Gaullist Phenomenon*. London: George Allen and Unwin, 1971.

Chesnoff, Raymond. *The Arrogance of the French*. New York: Sentinel, 2005.

Cobban, Alfred. *A Short History of France,* vol 3. New York: Penguin, 1990.

Cogan, Charles. *French Negotiating Behavior.* Washington, D.C.: United States Institute of Peace, 2003.

Cohen, Steven. *Modern Capitalist Planning: The French Model.* Berkeley: University of California Press, 2007.

Converse, Philip, and Roy Pierce. *Representation in France*. Cambridge: Harvard University Press, 1986.

Elgie, Robert. *French Politics*. London: Routledge, 2000.

Flynn, Gergory. *Remaking the Hexagon*. Boulder, Colo.: Westview, 1995.

Hayward, Jack. *De Gaulle to Mitterrand: Presidential Power in France.* London: Hurst, 1992.

Hoffmann, Stanley. *Decline or Renewal? France Since the 1930s*. New York: Viking, 1974.

Kuisel, Richard. *Seducing the French*. Berkeley: University of California Press, 1994.

Lewis-Beck, Michael. *How France Votes.* Washington, D.C.: CQ Press, 2000.

Marcus, Jonathan. *The National Front and French Politics.* London: McMillan, 1995.

Mendras, Henri, and Alastair Cole. *Social Change in France.* New York: Cambridge University Press, 1989.

Paxson, Richard. *Vichy France.* New York. W. W. Norton, 1977.

Sa'adah, Annie. *Contemporary France.* Boulder, Colo.: Rowman and Littlefield, 2004.

Sarkozy, Nicolas. *Testimony.* New York: Pantheon, 2007.

Schama, Simon. *Citizens: A Chronicle of the French Revolution.* New York: Knopf, 1989.

Schmidt, Vivienne. *Democratizing France.* New York: Cambridge University Press, 1990.

Smith, Timothy. *France in Crisis.* New York: Cambridge University Press, 2004.

Stovall, Tyler. *France Since the Second World War.* London: Pearson, 2004.

Suleiman, Ezra. *Politics, Power, and Bureaucracy.* Princeton: Princeton University Press, 1974.

Thompson, David. *Democracy in France.* Oxford: Oxford University Press, 1964.

Tiersky, Ronald. *France in the New Europe.* Belmont, Calif.: Wadsworth, 2004.

Williams, Philip. *Crisis and Compromise.* Hamden, Conn.: Archon Books, 1964.

Web Resources

A t a recent conference, a young French scholar noted that in France it is possible to have a very successful career as a political scientist concentrating on French politics, and not speak English. Unfortunately for some in the Anglophone world, as far as the Web is concerned, this can mean that non-French speakers researching French politics may have a tough time finding material in English. Below are some general and focused sites on France. Most, but not all, have English versions.

News, Politics, and Political History

The first challenge is to get news on France. While the major American and other English-language newspapers cover France, they miss a lot. This site includes **daily news** from France (including lots on real estate in Provence):

www.french-news.com. French News.

There are dozens of good sites on **French political history.** This is the best gateway. It includes plenty of links that will take you further in your research.

europeanhistory.about.com/od/france/France.htm. About.com's page on European history with external links.

There are also a few sites that offer **general information and links to politics in France.** These four are as good as any and are designed to serve academics and policy wonks.

www.wsu.edu/~frg/ The French Politics Group's Web site, a division of the American Political Science Association.

www.h-france.net/ The Society for French Historical Studies' discussion list and Web site.

www.ttc.org/. The Tocqueville Connection, a resource for French news and analysis.

Most **French polling agencies** have good Web sites. Here is the one with the best resources in English.

www.csa-fr.com/accueil.asp?lang=en.

For **general political resources,** consider these two Web sites:

www.politicalresources.net/france3.htm.

www.adminet.com/index_fr.html.

Most **French government agencies** have Web sites with at least partial mirrors in English. These five can get you started.

www.premier-ministre.gouv.fr/en/. Portal for the prime minister's office.

www.assemblee-nationale.fr/english/index.asp. The English-language Web site for the national assembly.

www.senat.fr/lng/en/index.html. Official site for the Senate.

www.elysee.fr. La Presidence de la Republique, Web site for the presidential office.

http://www.ena.fr/en/accueil.php. Web site for L'Ecole National d'Administration. (ENA).

All of the political parties have Web sites. Here are those for the four biggest ones. I don't know when or if English language versions will follow.

www.parti-socialiste.fr/ France's Socialist Party (French only).

www.u-m-p.org/site/index.php Union pour un Mouvement Populaire, France's center-right party. (French only).

www.frontnational.com/ National Front (French only).

www.pcf.fr France's Communist Party (French only).

Glossary

Key Concepts

Agents of political socialization. Actors and institutions through which children and young people learn about political life.

Alienation. A feeling of anger, hostility, or estrangement from politics.

Anticlericals. People who believe that the state should not support church activities.

Autogestion. A self-managed form of socialism that relies on the market and workers' control of industry.

Baccalauréat exam. Taken at the end of high school (*lycée*), it determines if a student can enroll in a university.

Bloc vote. Procedure included in the 1958 constitution that allows the government to force the National Assembly to vote on a bill in its entirety without any amendments.

Bureaucratic phenomenon. A term used to describe the importance of highly centralized and bureaucratically rigid organizations in all areas of French life.

Catch-all parties. Parties that rely on slogans, the media, and telegenic leaders rather than ideology and activists.

Centralization. The concentration of almost all political power in the national government.

Charismatic leader. A leader whose popularity and power lies in the strength of his or her personality.

Coalition. A group of political parties that come together to form a parliamentary majority and form a government.

Cohabitation. This occurs when the presidency is controlled by one party or coalition while the opposition has the majority in the National Assembly.

Communist Party. Traditionally the most left-wing party with close ties to the Soviet Union. In serious trouble since the end of the Cold War.

Constitutional Consultative Commission. A body created to review the 1958 constitution in its draft forms.

Corporatism. A term used to describe cooperative policymaking, typically involving the government and business and labor leaders.

Crisis and compromise. A phrase used to describe how a loss of confidence (crisis) led to a compromise in the formation of the next government in the Third and Fourth Republics.

Decentralization. Giving subnational authorities more power, important in France since 1981.

Decision makers. All people, inside of government and outside of it, who shape public policy.

Democracy. A form of government in which people rule either directly or through elected representatives.

Direct election of the president. Since 1965, French presidents have been chosen through direct elections, rather than by votes in an electoral college.

Dirigisme. The French practice of using the state to help "guide" the evolution of its capitalist economy.

Distribution. A type of public policy that shifts resources from one group to another.

Ecole polytechnique. One of the two leading *grandes écoles* that is a source for future leaders in the public and private sector.

Ecoles maternelles. State-funded preschools open to all children from two to five years of age.

ENA. The National School of Administration trains France's bureaucratic elite, who later take on leadership positions in politics and the private sector.

Environment. A term used to describe those elements outside of a political system that have an impact on it.

European Union. The international organization made up of twenty-seven member states that has tremendous impact on domestic policy in all of those countries.

Events of May 1968. The largest protest movement in the history of the Fifth Republic; the most impressive movement of the New Left in the 1960s and 1970s.

Family allocations. Funds given to parents to help defray the cost of raising children.

Feedback. The processes through which people learn about politics today, which helps them shape their actions tomorrow.

Fifth Republic. The current regime in France, founded by Charles de Gaulle and his colleagues in 1958.

Force de frappe. France's nuclear arsenal.

Fourth Republic. The political regime in place from 1946 to 1958.

Gaullists. Generic term for all the political parties that have supported either General de Gaulle or his legacy.

General Planning Commission. An advisory body created in 1946 by the president of the interim post–World War II French government to design a plan to rebuild the French economy and modernize French social and economic institutions. Through this group, Jean Monnet developed the plans leading to the European Coal and Steel Community (ECSC), the first step toward a unified European common market.

Globalization. The processes through which the world's governments, economies, and societies are becoming increasingly interrelated and inter-dependent.

Grandes écoles. Selective schools that train most of France's elite.

Grandeur. A term used by de Gaulle and others to describe France's putative place in the world as a major power.

Heroic leaders. Unusually popular and powerful leaders brought to power for short periods during the Third and Fourth Republics to address crises.

Incompatibility clause. The provision of the French constitution that forbids cabinet members from retaining their seats in parliament.

Industrial Revolution. Describes the transition from a primarily agricultural economy to one based more on manufacturing.

Inputs. In systems theory, what groups and individuals do to try to shape public policy.

Interest groups. Private, voluntary organizations that try to promote the "interests" of particular occupational, ideological, regional, and other groups.

Iron triangle. The close relationship linking current and former civil servants, politicians, and business executives.

Legitimacy. People's sense that a regime and system are acceptable, even if the current leaders are not.

Market failures. Events that occur when markets cannot produce economically optimal results, and some group or groups are harmed.

Means testing. Restrictions on eligibility for social service funds based on a potential recipient's income and wealth.

Nation. The entity created through the psychological identification of people with the country they live in.

National Assembly. The lower house of the French parliament, which can cast a vote of censure against the government.

Nationalized firms. Formerly private firms taken into state ownership.

Output. The public policy of any political system.

Pantouflage. Colloquial term for the practice of leaving the top levels of the civil service for political or business careers.

Parity law. A recent law and constitutional amendment that guarantees an equal number of male and female candidates in most elections.

Pillars. A word used to describe the three areas in which the European Union operates in regard to public policy.

Political culture. The values and assumptions that shape people's basic political understanding and commitment.

Political participation. The ways individuals and the groups they form are engaged in political life.

Political parties. Organizations that compete for votes in elections in an attempt to form a government.

Postindustrial society. Today's society in a country like France in which information technology, office work, and the like dominate the economy.

Provisional government. The temporary regime created and headed by de Gaulle after France's liberation in 1944.

Public policy. The laws and other documents emerging from the decision-making process.

Qualified Majority Voting. In the European Union, the way most decisions are made today; determined on the basis of votes assigned to each country according to its size.

Regime. The constitutional order and other basic rules of the game that survive from one administration to the next.

Regulatory (policies). Public policies that determine what citizens can and cannot do.

Single-member district two-ballot system. France's unusual electoral system in which two rounds of voting normally turn a divided electorate into a majority.

Sovereignty. The political science concept that states are free to chart their own domestic policy without outside interference.

State. All the institutions and people who make and implement public policy; it includes the government but often much more as well.

Symbolic (policies). Policies that use visual and other symbols to enhance compliance and legitimacy.

Systems theory. A way of looking at politics that views the interaction of all actors over time.

Union for a Permanent Majority. Current name of the Gaullist Party, used since 2002.

Vote of censure. A vote by the National Assembly that can force the government from office; also a vote of confidence in the United Kingdom.

Welfare state. The package of economic and other policies that provides a safety net for people in need.

Key People, Entities, and Events

Algeria. Former French colony in North Africa. Revolts there led to the collapse of the Fourth Republic.

Article 11. Constitutional provision authorizing reference.

Article 16. Constitutional provision authorizing emergency rule.

Article 23. Incompatibility clause that denies members of parliament the right to retain their seats in parliament while serving in government.

Berlin Wall. Barrier between East and West Germany that was knocked down on November 9, 1989.

Bonaparte, Louis-Napoléon. President and later emperor from 1848 until 1871.

Bonaparte, Napoléon. Emperor of revolutionary France until defeated in 1815.

Chamber of Deputies. The lower house of parliament in the Third and Fourth Republics.

Chirac, Jacques. Long-term leader on the French Right and president from 1995 to 2007.

Cold War. The period of tension between the United States and the Soviet Union, stretching from 1945 until 1991.

Colons. White settlers in Algeria, most of whom, but not all, were of French origin.

Council of the European Union. The ultimate decision-making body in the EU. Made up of prime ministers and other representatives of member states.

Debré, Michel. Architect of the Fifth Republic's constitution and its first prime minister.

Declaration of the Rights of Man. The first constitutional document to affirm the human rights of all people, created in 1793.

de Gaulle, Charles. Leader of the French resistance during World War II, head of the provisional government, and creator of the Fifth Republic.

Delors, Jacques. Prominent Socialist politician who became president of the European Commission in 1985.

de Villepin, Dominique. Former foreign and prime minister who is most noted for his role at the United Nations just before the invasion of Iraq in 2003.

Dien Bien Phu. Site of the decisive battle in the Indochinese war that led France to withdraw from the region in 1954.

Dreyfus Affair. The trial and persecution of a Jewish French army captain that almost destroyed the Third Republic in the 1890s and early 1900s.

European Coal and Steel Community. Original international organization that gave rise to the European Union of today.

European Commission. Day-to-day leaders of the European Union. The most important force trying to deepen its powers.

European Court of Justice. Central constitutional court of the European Union.

European Economic Community. The original name of what is now the European Union.

European Parliament. Elected assembly that is one of the weaker links among institutions of the European Union.

European Union. The semi-state currently composed of twenty-seven European countries.

Foccart, Jacques. Long-standing adviser charged with African affairs.

Fourth Republic. French regime, 1946–1958.

François Fillon. Named prime minister by Nicolas Sarkozy after the 2007 elections.

French Section of the Workers' International. Official name of the Socialist Party before 1971.

Giscard d'Estaing, Valéry. Third president of the Fifth Republic.

Giscardiens. Influential but small group of centrist politicians whose initial inspiration was the work of former president Valéry Giscard d'Estaing.

Gorbachev, Mikhail Sergeyevich. President of the Soviet Union when it collapsed.

Greens. Environmental party that has had fleeting influence since the 1980s.

High Commission on the French Language. Determines which words can officially be used in the French language.

Independent Republicans. One of the labels used for the parties that grew out of support for Giscard.

Indochina. Site of the first war that would lead to the collapse of the Fourth Republic.

Jospin, Lionel. Former Socialist prime minister and a failed presidential candidate in 1995 and 2002.

Kohl, Helmut. German chancellor largely responsible for Germany's pragmatic response to the collapse of communism.

Le Pen, Jean-Marie. Founder and leader of the National Front.

Louis XIV. The "sun king" who is often seen as the "father" of the centralized French state.

Mendés-France, Pierre. Prominent politician during the Fourth Republic; an early critic of de Gaulle's regime.

Mitterrand, François. First and, so far, only Socialist to serve as president of the Fifth Republic.

Monnet, Jean. A key architect of both French planning and the European Union.

Mouvement républicain populaire. The Christian Democratic Party under the Fourth Republic.

National Center for Independents and Peasants. Fourth Republic centrist party that was almost always in government.

National Front. Far right party that has done well at the polls for the last twenty years.

National Liberation Front. Arab-based freedom fighters in Algeria during the 1950s.

National Planning Commission. Key agency that helped rebuild France after World War II and part of the iron triangle in the early years of the Fifth Republic.

North Atlantic Treaty Organization. Alliance of countries close to the United States that was formed at the height of the Cold War and now includes most European countries.

Organization of Petroleum Exporting Countries oil embargo. Oil cartel, whose embargo brought on a recession in 1973–1974.

Pompidou, Georges. Second president of the Fifth Republic.

Provisional government. The ad hoc government in place from 1944 until the Fourth Republic went into effect.

Radicals. Center left party that was central to the survival of the Third and Fourth Republics.

Rally of the French People. Official name of the Gaullist Party during most of the time Chirac led it.

Royal, Ségolène. Failed Socialist candidate for the presidency in 2007, but the first woman to be a serious candidate.

Sarkozy, Nicolas. Elected president in 2007.

Senate. Relatively powerless upper house of parliament.

Single European Act. Removed all remaining barriers to trade among European nations.

Socialist Party. Social democratic party that dominates the Left.

Third Republic. Regime in place from 1875 until 1940.

Treaty of Maastricht. Created the European Union and paved the way for adoption of the euro.

Treaty of Rome. Initial treaty creating the European Economic Community.

Two by four negotiations. Discussions leading to German unification that included the two Germanys and the four powers that occupied the country after World War II.

Union for a Popular Movement. The current name of the Gaullist Party since 2002.

Union for French Democracy. The formal name of Giscard's party for most of the last third of the twentieth century.

Vichy regime. Government that collaborated with the Germans during World War II.

Index

Figures , maps, and tables are denoted by "f," "m," and "t."